ID0706923

PRECISION

A New Approach to Communication

by
Michael McMaster & John Grinder

Library of Congress 80–84313
ISBN 0–9605414–0–3

Precision Models
9701 Wilshire Boulevard, Suite 712
Beverly Hills, California 90212

"... he must stay alert to these and countless other options. A desk is a dangerous place from which to watch the world."

The Honourable Schoolboy
John Le Carré

Foreword

One test of good theory is that it should provide obvious and immeditate implications for action. As a practitioner and researcher in the field of human behavior for twenty-five years, I have been deeply concerned with translating management development theory into practical and useful action: suggesting behaviors that managers can learn quickly and employ immediately to improve their effectiveness with the people they lead.

In this volume John Grinder and Michael McMaster have provided such useful theory; they have explained how and when to apply it. Their theory and the style in which they present it are congruent.

The value of this book is that it provides all of us with an approach to improving our communication and, thereby, our ability to influence others successfully. As the authors point out so aptly in the text, the closer our words are to experience, the more likely we are to be understood. Creating high quality verbal and non-verbal representations of the ideas we want to communicate has been recognized as a fine and valuable art for centuries. In this volume, we have a theory that makes this art an easily learnable skill, with the potential to improve dramatically the effectiveness of organizational and personal relationships.

Paul Hersey, Ph.D.
Center for Leadership Studies
Escondido, California

Preface

It is our purpose in writing this book to provide the manager with a personal technology for the development and use of information appropriate to successful business communications. We stand next in a rather distinguished line of authors who have appropriately identified the ability to handle information as the single most powerful determinant of success for managers in business. We too lament the fact that there has been no specific training, no practical procedures to explicate successful information processing for managers. And with diffidence to our predecessors we intend to change that situation—we offer the Precision Model as a practical, explicit technology for information processing.

For information flow in a business organization to be both effective and efficient, it must meet two conditions—specifically, it must include:

(1) need to know information and
(2) need not to know information.

Our professional experience has led us to the judgement that the information network in the typical business contains all or nearly all of the need to know information. Typically, however, it is scattered throughout a morass of irrelevant or need not to know information.

The Precision Model offers an explicit set of communication patterns called Frames designed to allow the using manager to exercise control over the relevancy of information being developed while promoting participation. The Outcome Frame, for example, allows the manager to explicitly communicate what the boundary conditions of a transaction are. Once the boundary conditions are identified, they may be used in a rather obvious fashion to insure the information being developed is relevant—that it lies within the boundary conditions explicitly presented.

Our consulting experience also has led us to note that large sums of money, time, human and physical resources are all too often squandered in the misdirection and confusion resulting from the inability of managers to be explicit enough to effectively instruct and direct their organization. The directions issued by a manager may seem crystal clear to him or her. Whether such directives are effective for reaching the economic goals which motivate them may be entirely another issue—more specifically, those directives need to connect with the perceptions and understandings of the individuals who will actually carry those directives out.

The Precision Model offers an explicit set of communication patterns called Pointers which automatically lead to the development of higher quality information; that is, more specific, thus more connected with the perceptions of the rest of the business organization.

This book differs from other treatments of the subject of managerial success in information processing in that it is explicit. Step-by-step procedures are offered throughout which when followed by the reader will yield the results desired. Located at the front of this hard cover book is a short pamphlet extract of some of the major points covered by the Precision Model. In it we have touched lightly on portions of the model. The reader who is in a hurry may desire to examine this abbreviated version first. The hard cover book itself is a more detailed, extended, logically developed representation of the Precision Model complete with procedures which the serious reader may use to train him or herself in the model. We have discovered in our training seminars that many business people find it useful to be offered the Precision Model in both an explicit direct form as well as in metaphor or story form. Thus, we have included metaphors—should any particular reader find them less than useful, nothing will be lost by moving directly to the text. We wish you success and invite you to join us in any of the Precision Model seminars being offered in the U.S. or Canada.

John Grinder
Michael McMaster

Precision—An Overview

The raw material of management is information. The preponderance of this information is coded in language. The personal success of men and women in business and the survival and growth of their companies depend in large part on the effectiveness and efficiency with which information is handled within those organizations. The criteria for determining whether the information flow within a business organization is effective and efficient are quite simple—the information flow must meet two conditions:

1. the need to know
2. the need not to know

Each member of a business organization has some particular set of functions. In order to know how and when specifically to carry out each of those particular functions that person needs to know certain information. Within that organization the information flowing to any particular individual must include the information he or she requires to execute their functions—the information they need to know. Rarely does one find in business organizations that the various individuals do not have available, in some form, the need to know information. What one does find is that the need to know information essential for an appropriate, timely execution of the business functions is buried within an enormous quantity of need not to know information which is simultaneously presented to the members of that business organization. It may be difficult to find a needle in a haystack but it is even more difficult to find specific straws in a haystack. And this is precisely the situation faced by present day managers attempting to operate successfully in the era of the information explosion. The net result is that the particular individuals are uncertain about which information they should attend to and act upon—which information they need to know. They become cautious, their behavior hesitant and their personal effectiveness and efficiency and that of their business organizations is significantly reduced.

This book—Precision—is primarily designed to address in practical terms the need of managers to control verbal information flow within their areas of accountibility—to provide then with explicit, learnable, step-by-step techniques which lead to effective communication and personal and professional success in business. Communication which supports an effective and efficient transfer of verbal information is in large part a process of matching one set of experiences, a model of the world, with another. If you read these words and cannot relate them to your own experience, no communication will take place. If you tell an employee that she should work cooperatively for a common goal and she thinks only of being exploited, it is likely that neither you nor she will get satisfactory results. The models of experience allowed no shared meaning and no base for working toward the same end.

Language allows us to share experience by a commonly understood set of signals. Or is it commonly understood? The more things or actions in experience that a word could refer to, the less likely it is to be understood in the way the speaker intends. Common business words—such as productivity, motivation, company policy, return, profits—are of low quality. Quality is a measure of the word's relationship to direct sensory experience. The highest quality is what can actually be seen, heard or felt. The highest quality words describe things or actions in the world which could not be confused with others—such as machine #42 in plant #65, machinist Joe Walker, conveyor belt #6 moving at 4 miles per hour. Many management mistakes are the result of acting on a belief in a common understanding of words which, in fact, doesn't exist. To prevent actions taken on this type of inadequate communication, two verbal level skills are needed. The first is the ability to ask explicit questions to get precisely the information needed in an explicit manner. The second is a requirement to determine the level of quality needed in each particular situation or context.

The Precision Model is an explicit set of responses to particular types of words to elicit exactly the information desired and respect both the need to know *and* the need not to know of a manager. Each question or response asks for precisely that piece of experience (higher quality information) which the manager needs to make sense of a statement in reference to his own model or understanding. A statement such as "sales are dropping and we need training for all the representatives" would have the following appropriate responses within the model:

Which sales specifically?

How specifically are they dropping?

Dropping? Compared to what?

What will happen if we don't give more training?

Which training in particular?

All the representatives?

Within the context established by the reporting relationship, prior knowledge and relative importance of the issue, these questions will lead directly towards explicit representations needed before decisions or actions can be taken. It is precisely at this point that the model we have designed and are presenting distinguishes itself from other guides for effective communication. Models for successful communication prior to Precision have invariably been constructed on the principle of the check list. That is, men and women who are experienced and successful in the world of business have explicated the set of questions which they have noticed seems to be repetative and effective in the specific phase of business they have mastered. There are two significant shortcomings of such models:

(1) the questions in the checklist model will be appropriate to a rather limited number of situations, all within the specific phase of business from which it was developed. In actuality, managers typically are required to handle effectively a much larger number of business situations than any of these models are designed for. In other words, the business world is variable where the checklist model is fixed and rigid.

(2) the questions in the checklist model are the questions which were effectively used by the author of that model within the context of their particular business organizations and with their own particu-

lar style of non-verbal communication. The author's non-verbal style of communication is never explicated in these models. Thus, the effectiveness of the checklist model for any particular manager will be largely an issue of whether their non-verbal style and the non-verbal style of the author (unknown) of the checklist coincide.

The Precision Model represents a radical departure from previous models in that (1) the questions are based entirely on the form of the language and (2) the model is entirely feedback determined. The questions the manager asks to secure the next chunk of need to know information is determined entirely by the form of the information; not the content. This insures that the model will be equally applicable to communication about any phase of business activity. It can easily be used effectively by a manager in an area where he or she is not technically qualified. Notice in addition that the model is feedback determined—the question the manager asks next is determined soley by the form of the information just received. Thus the integrity and personal style of the staff and employees the manager communicates with is respected while the task of passing only need to know information is accomplished effectively and efficiently. This model does not force human beings into pre-set categories or pigeon holes as checklist models with their fixed questions invariably do.

The second requirement in an appropriate verbal model for business is the ability to establish and maintain a framework or context for what is appropriate. Business is *the* human outcome oriented activity. It is an activity continually seeking to change an existing state of affairs to a different, more desired state. It changes raw material into useful goods, time and effort into services—and continually seeks better ways to do it.

The Precision Model has an organizing structure which matches the outcome oriented nature of business. A set of Frames was developed based on a guiding model of knowing the present state, defining the desired state (the situation to be achieved) and developing strategies to move in the desired direction. The responses above are part of these strategies. The frames or contexts are established for economy of movement and to set appropriate boundary conditions on information relevant to the task. They provide focus or an explicit way of sorting the appropriate out of the myriad options potentially available. They may, for example, gather resources for a common starting point or expand boundaries which are too restrictive for a particular outcome. They may access resources which even the holder was not aware he or she had.

The first of these Frames is the Outcome Frame. The Outcome Frame is a description of the state the manager desires to achieve at the end of a particular communication. It specifies which comments or contributions, which experiences or resources, are appropriate in the context of that particular communication or meeting. The outcome will be specified in a manner precise enough for the manager, and others if shared overtly, to recognize when it is achieved and whether any particular communication is leading forward into realization or not.

The Outcome Frame applies from the overall goal right down to a specific question asked. Each part of a communication has a purpose and will either contribute to or inhibit reaching the desired outcome. Each step of a process, say for a meeting to solve a problem, will have its own Outcome Frame.

The overall outcome for a meeting may be "to find 3 potential ways to increase sales". Ideas related to increasing sales will be accepted, ideas related to cutting costs or other problems will not. The next level of outcome will be for the first phase, "to define in high quality language the desired state". Comments about the present state, who is to blame for the current lack of sales, etc. will all be ruled out by this control of the process. At the lowest level the outcome for a response to the question, "which people specifically" is an answer in the class of "those in department B' or some other refinement and not non-responses such as "they never do what they're told over there".

Each piece of communication needs a test, the Outcome Frame, to determine its relevancy. Any not within the Outcome Frame should be challenged. If it is relevant, the information and its connection is a valuable contribution. If not, it needs to be rejected or a great deal of time and good will may be jeopardized. Hidden agenda, reacting to the wrong situation and getting lost in side tracks are all problems which commonly occur without explicit use of the Outcome Frame.

The presentation includes procedures of elegance for obtaining fast, efficient results with the basic tools provided in the language model. The details and specific step-by-step procedures of the Precision Model are presented within the context of a model for problem solving in our book Precision. We have also applied it to models for planning and for performance. We refer you to that book or to our management workshops to increase your ability to succeed in such situations.

Beyond Words

This volume of the Precision Model addresses itself primarily to information coded in language. This is consistent with the conscious perceptions of the business community. It is, however, our experience that the non-verbal component of communication is easily the most influential factor in face-to-face communication. In creating the Precision Model by studying the communication patterns of extremely successful managers, we were consistently impressed by the strong influence exerted by the personal power of the individual involved. A large component of personal power is the ability to appreciate behavioral signals such as voice tone, tempo of speech, body postures, breathing pattern, eye movements, voice timbre quality in others and to use these non-verbal channels of communication oneself to actively influence the behavior of others. These skills create a communication context which supports the systematic and elegant use of the verbal portion of the Precision Model. These skills move the individual from adequacy to artistry. In a future volume of Precision as well as in our Precision training seminars we explicate this component of personal power. These are behavioral skills grounded in sensory perception and eminently learnable and not interpretations in the sense of "body languages". They are specific communication responses to body movement and posture, eye movements and types of representations which require only sensory awareness. No guessing at content is required—in fact, we ask you to avoid such activity.

We offer an example of these skills for the reader's consideration. We call this area representational systems. We obtain information through our senses. That is, we see, hear, feel things or events. We also represent or store these experiences in similar ways. We have the ability to recall pictures, sounds and feelings just as they happened or as we create them. Planning is the ability to create representations of future possibilities from past experiences by combining them in different ways. Our minds record all of our experience in all of these ways.

Most people develop favored ways of representing the world and their experience. Some are primarily conscious of visual memory and representation, some of sounds and talking, and others of feelings. These are the essentially private maps or model of the world which each of us creates. These are the source of the words, the language forms which are the focus of this first volume of Precision. These representations are one step closer to the actual experiences we have. These representational systems may be thought of as the way that people think. The storage, sorting and retrieval of information is done in some sequence of these forms. To choose between two alternatives, the manager creates images of the first; talks to himself about it; refines the images; finally checks his feelings about it. He does the same with the second alternative. Finally, he compares the feelings he had for 1 and 2 and makes a choice. The structure of our thoughts is the representations of our experience.

Knowing how a person is thinking—that is, what representational system or sequence of systems they are using—is a powerful piece of information. Communication can be tailored to have maximum impact. For ease of understanding, fewer mistakes and greater motivation, communication matched to the favored represential system of the recipient is most effective.

Each representational system or mode of thinking has a unique set of external signals which accompanies it. The easiest ones to identify are eye movements and predicates used. Others include vocal patterns, breathing patterns and skin color changes. Predicates for visual representation include such words as *see, look, picture, imagine, clear, bright;* for auditory representations such words as *hear, listen, sound, tell, harmony, tone;* for kinesthetic (feeling) representations such words as *feel, touch, smooth, handle, grasp, rough.* You might recall hearing a manager back from humanistic training involved in the following exchange:

Subordinate: I can really get a clear picture of how that will work.
Manager: Feels good to you?
Subordinate: Well, uh, I can really see it'll be effective.
Manager: Yeah! It's something you can really get a handle on.

Subordinate: Well, anyway, it looks good to me.

If this mismatch of representational systems (compare the predicates) is extended much longer, the subordinate will come to doubt his original enthusiastic endorsement and communication will grind to a halt as rapport between the two people deteriorates.

Eye movements are also reliable indicators of the representational system being employed by the person communicating. Specifically, as you look at a person and see eye movements which match below the representation is at the end of each arrow.

Visual constructions (things the person has not seen before)

Visual memory (things the person has seen before)

Auditory representation

Auditory representation

Kinesthetic representation

Auditory representation

For the right handed population.

The eye movements are an amazingly robust indicator of mode of thinking or representation, even cross culturally.

Systematic unconscious use of the information offered by representational system indicators—predicates and eye movements—is one of the most pervasive characteristics of top managers and executives. Such information has wide applicability and its systematic use gives the user the ability to:

— rapidly establish and maintain rapport
— gain access to high quality information and resources
— insure directives and instructions are thoroughly understood
— motivate others
— make group presentations appealing to all group members

Such choices move the manager from competency to artistry.

This first volume of Precision offers learnable step-by-step procedures for effective verbal communication. This book is intended as a guide for behavior—the exercises and procedures must be converted into behavioral patterns if the reader is to reap the benefit of the technology presented.

Precision

A long time ago in the Canton province of China, there was a famous and very wealthy merchant who had, it was said, an amazing ability to choose just the right person for the job in his organization. Indeed, it was said that it was just this skill which had made the merchant so successful and rich.

It came about that this merchant was seeking a young man to serve as the coordinator and director of his vast fleet of ships. The job entailed tremendous responsibilities as well as great rewards. A large number of men applied for the position—some were skilled in accounting, some in the maritime arts, some had worked in nearly every phase of commerce. The wily old merchant knew how to go about selecting the right man for this complex task of coordinating and directing his fleet. As each candidate who had applied entered the merchant's offices, he was sworn to secrecy by the merchant—so that no matter what the result of the interview the man had to agree to keep the details of what occurred there secret. The candidate was then instructed that he had to complete a certain task. The merchant next led the candidate to the rear of his office where the wall was covered by a fine tapestry. Pulling the tapestry aside, the merchant pointed to a door of bronze, richly inlaid with silver from which hung a huge chain and padlock. Addressing the candidate, the merchant stated that his personal treasure house lay behind that door and that the task was for the candidate to gain entry to this storehouse of vast wealth. Further, the merchant continued, the only point of entry to be attempted was through the bronze door, and that the candidate could expect to find behind the door additional obstacles. The merchant then led the man to the center of the large office where, resting on a small table, was a large Chinese box. Pointing to the box, the merchant simply stated that within this box the candidate might find objects which would assist him in his task. With an air of finality, the merchant warned the candidate that there was a time limit for the task which he would not reveal until either the candidate had gained entry to the treasure house or the time had expired. So saying, the merchant turned and strode to his desk which was placed at the opposite end of the room and apparently occupied himself with some papers.

To the merchant's disappointment, candidate after candidate followed one of two courses. Some of the candidates would ransack the entire assemblage of Chinese boxes—opening the entire collection until all of the various objects contained within—candle, matches, incense sticks, . . .—were secured, at which point the candidate would gather up the objects and carry them to the door. Selecting from the pile of objects all of the keys which were of a size and shape which suggested that they might fit the padlock which hung on the chain on the bronze door, the candidate would frantically attempt to open the padlock to no avail as none of the keys would fit the lock. At this point the merchant would approach the candidate and announce in a clear, resonant voice that the time limit for the task had been exceeded. If the candidate maintained his composure at this announcement, the merchant would invite him to apply for a position as a trader for his organization.

The second course of action chosen by the candidates was that as soon as the merchant had occupied himself at his desk, the candidate would open the first of the Chinese boxes, and then the second and so forth until they had discovered the first of the keys which was of a size and shape that suggested that it might fit the padlock hung on the chain on the bronze door. Once the candidate had secured the first of the keys, he would move quickly to the bronze door where to his disappointment he would discover that the key failed to fit the padlock. He would then return to the Chinese boxes and open further boxes until he found a second key of the appropriate size and shape. After this procedure had been repeated several times, the merchant would approach and announce that the time limit had expired. Again, if the candidate retained his poise in the face of this announcement, the merchant would invite him to apply for a position in the organization—only this time, he would mention the position of accountant.

The merchant was about to despair when the next candidate arrived. This candidate had a different air about him. While remaining attentive and courteous in the presence of the famous merchant, he seemed to take in his surroundings with a sense of confidence. The merchant repeated his instructions and retired to his desk to await further developments. The young candidate paused for several minutes as if repeating the instructions offered by the merchant. He then turned to the Chinese boxes, picked up the table and boxes and carried them to the immediate vicinity of the bronze door. Arriving there, he then turned his attention to the door itself. He examined the fit of the door in the recess in the wall. He examined with great care the chain and padlock until with a soft laugh, he planted himself firmly and placing both hands on the bronze door, he pushed hard. To his delight, the door swung open, revealing a beautifully worked wrought iron door. Examining this new obstacle, he determined that it was indeed secured by a lock built into the door itself. Turning to the Chinese boxes, the candidate began to open the boxes which revealed in turn, a candle, matches, and the next, a key. Securing the key the candidate turned back to the door and again to his pleasure, the door yielded. As the door opened inward, it revealed a darkened chamber in which all the candidate could distinguish was a pair of yellow eyes which peered out of the darkness with seeming malevolence. Pulling the wrought iron door closed with a quick, sure movement, the candidate hurried back into the room where the merchant stood watching with intense interest. The candidate hurried to a corner of the room where he had earlier noted the presence of a long slender knife. He seized the weapon and hastened back to the wrought iron door. Pushing the door open cautiously, he thrust the lighted candle into the chamber by the light of which he could see a large cobra sitting inside a cage, the door of which was standing open. Lunging forward, he used the knife to flip the door of the cage closed and secured it quickly. Striding around the cage, he drew back a large piece of finely worked silk and his eyes fell upon treasures beyond his wildest dreams. Hearing the soft tread of a sandal behind him, the candidate turned and looked into the eyes of the merchant. Extending the knife toward the merchant handle first, the candidate thanked the merchant for the temporary use of the knife, explaining that he would need it no longer since he had already accomplished everything with it that he needed to accomplish. The merchant, needless to say, had found his man, and their association was marked by supreme success.

Table of Contents

Chapter 1

THE CONTEXT

How can the manager improve his performance in analyzing problems? The key to the answer lies in the fundamental fact that the raw material of management is information. This is all that any manager has to work with—information about the world around him, about his organization and its plans, about the performance of that segment of the organization where he is responsible for carrying out those plans, about people and things and conditions. He has to know what information he has about any problem, what information he doesn't have and how he can get it, and how he can use all the information he has to the best advantage in getting the problem solved. He must be as perceptive in recognizing, before the fact, what information will be relevant and important and what will not as he is in recognizing, with the benefit of hindsight, the obvious relevance and importance of certain information.

Kepner and Tregoe,
The Rational Manager, p. 39

The highest quality information is behavioral. The actual performance of an individual or organization offers the attentive observer/listener the richest source of information regarding that individual's or that organization's present capability.

Some of the human beings who are involved in the world of business work directly with raw or partially processed material to shape and mold such material into products or services which are offered in the marketplace—we call these people laborers. Some of the human beings who are involved in the world of business interact directly with sophisticated machines, to produce products or services available to the public—we call these people technicians. The remainder of us who are involved in the world of business process information. This information is offered to us in diverse forms— reports, conferences, movements of restlessness, telephone calls, predictions, smiles, planning meetings, looks of attentiveness, interruptions, technical brochures, . . . In the midst of the daily flurry of words and paper, it is useful to keep in mind that no matter in what form the information is presented, the single most powerful determinant of our personal success and the success of our organization is the effectiveness with which we process that information.

The carpenter who shapes raw and semi-processed materials into a cabinet or a stairway does so with the aid of specialized tools—the saw to cut, the plane to trim, the hammer to nail. Each of these implements offers the carpenter a way to interact with the raw or semi-processed material to transform it into the finished product effectively and with some degree of precision.

The crane operator uses the tremendous mechanical advantages offered by the motor which drives the crane to accomplish work which would take the unaided worker a great deal longer. He operates on raw or semi-processed material through the medium of the crane just as the carpenter uses his hammer and saw.

The console operator directing the operations of a computer at an automated processing plant has before her a keyboard, light indicators, an array of buttons and switches, . . . These devices offer her the points of interaction with the computer which she chooses from in order to direct the complex machine which in turn will dictate the operation of less complex machines which accomplish the actual work.

What, then, of the rest of us? Where are the tools of our trade? What device offers us the advantage of specialized interaction with the material we handle? Which is the tool to cut and trim the information we are presented with? Which device offers us the tremendous mechanical advantages of the crane? Where are the keyboards, light indicators and array of buttons and switches that we may choose from?

The carpenter who is building a cabinet knows immediately as he begins to assemble the pieces of wood he has measured and cut whether they fit together. He has his direct sensory experience of assembling the cabinet—what he sees, hears and feels—to allow him to make accurate judgments of whether he is accomplishing his task or not.

In the cab of the crane, the operator has a set of dials and gauges as well as his direct experience of observing the effect of the complex interplay of his hands and feet on the levers and pedals on the task he is attempting to accomplish. He has little difficulty determining whether the bucket is rising or falling as the result of his manipulations. There is a direct experiential base to his judgments and decisions in this matter.

The console operator monitors the various console indicators to insure that they are reporting operating conditions which show the machines controlled by the computer are functioning properly. When a light indicator on the keyboard signals that some portion of the operation requires the console operator's attention, the operator relies on her knowledge of the console operating procedures to select the appropriate response. Again, once she has selected and made her response, there is little or no ambiguity as to whether it is effective —the light indicator will go off, the keyboard will immediately indicate to the operator whether operating conditions have returned to their appropriate levels. She sees the result directly.

The information processor reads the reports, talks on the telephone, attends meetings, issues instructions, decides on a specific plan of action, selects a person for promotion, questions his staff. What in that seemingly endless flow of information distinguishes the indicators, the signals which demand the information handler's attention and require his assertive action from the information which he may usefully and safely ignore? Where in this complex stream of activity is that special class of information called "feedback" which allows the information handler to determine whether the reports were accurate, the talks on the telephone productive, the time in meetings well spent, the instructions understood, the decisions wise, the selection optimal, the questions penetrating and precise enough?

The carpenter reaches for his level to verify what looks and feels like a horizontal plane; the crane operator listens to the hum of the powerful motor as he edges the lever gently forward guiding the bucket toward the material to be picked up; the console operator watches the light indicator as she enters the new instruction through the keyboard.

What does the information processor reach for, what does he listen to, what does he watch to know that he has identified the appropriate signals and that he is performing successfully?

A REFINEMENT

The logic behind the strategy of control outlined above is so subtly persuasive that it is difficult to argue against it: Every manager is responsible for results within that portion of the organization which is under his supervision. He is held accountable by those above him. Obviously he cannot fulfill this responsibility unless (1) he knows what is going on within the unit, and (2) he is able to do something about things that go wrong.

McGregor,
The Human Side of Enterprise, p. 151

Sorting the human beings involved in the world of business into categories such as laborer, technician, and information processor solely on the basis of information yields an interesting—even provocative—picture of the business world around us, but as with most language categories, a closer examination shows a more complex situation.

As we stated earlier, the highest quality information is behavioral. If you wish to know the present capability of an individual or organization, the most complete and trustworthy information will be available through direct observation of that individual's or organization's present performance.

The carpenter assembling the cabinet has the highest quality information possible available to him. He has direct sensory grounded feedback to guide him.

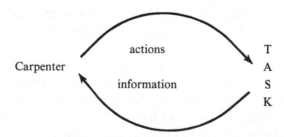

The carpenter is following a familiar path—he knows how to build a cabinet, and at each point in the process he is offered directly, at the sensory level, information as to how he is progressing. As he drives a nail, he can see whether he is striking the nail squarely. Note that the same information is offered to him by the sound the hammer makes as it strikes the nail as well as by the feeling of the hammer striking the nail transmitted by vibration through the hammer to his hand. The time lag between the movement of the carpenter's hand grasping the hammer and swinging it toward the nail, and the information about how effective that movement was is minimal.

The crane operator guiding the bucket toward the pile of material to be picked up uses both direct experience of the task at hand as well as arbitrary signal codes to know whether he is being effective. The operator's ability to judge visually the distance between the leading edge of the bucket and the pile of material is again the highest quality information possible—direct sensory grounded (in this case—visual) information as to his effectiveness. At the same time the crane operator is monitoring the various gauges and dials in the cab of the crane. The gauges which signal him as to the temperature of the motor or the amount of fuel in the tank are examples of arbitrary signal codes arranged by the designer of the crane to provide a symbolic representation of the actual state of affairs of engine temperature and fuel level. These gauges are arbitrary in the sense that the form the information is displayed in for the operator is entirely independent of the original information and could be varied while maintaining the effectiveness of the signal offered. For example, the information regarding the temperature of the motor could equally effectively be displayed in any of the following forms:

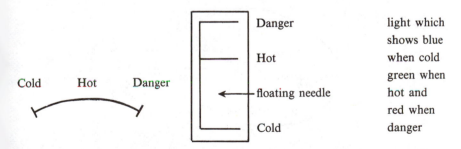

The levers and pedals the operator uses to operate the crane are themselves an interesting blend of natural and arbitrary information display codes. By pushing on the right braking pedal, the operator causes the crane to swing to the right front—the same movement that the child makes on a sled by dragging his right foot when he wishes to turn to the right. The movement of the levers forward and back is a reduced reflection of the up and down movements of the bucket.

For those portions of his performance where the crane operator is dependent on information arriving through an engineered input channel, he is performing with less than the highest quality information. The information is no longer the direct perception of the task itself; rather it is information about that experience filtered through an arbitrary signal system. For those portions of his task where he has direct sensory access to the effect of his actions on the task itself, he operates as does the carpenter.

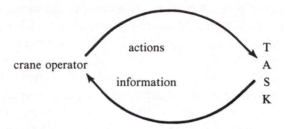

For those portions where he must depend on arbitrary signal codes in the engineered input channel, he is one step removed from a direct sensory grounded source of information about his progress with the task and the effects of his actions on the task itself.

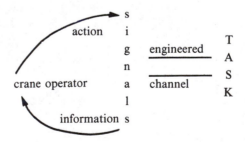

The console operator is even further removed from the actual experience which is the justification for the business activity. By the time the information about the operation of the automated processing plant which is the end result of the business activity arrives at the computer it has been coded and re-coded in arbitrary signal codes to the extent that it is rare to find a computer console operator who can even guess at the experiential significance of the information being processed by the computer.

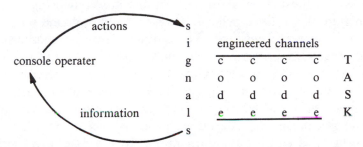

The console operator is many steps removed from the direct sensory grounded source of information of what effects her activities have on the task itself.

The console operator is provided information about the actual functioning of the plant through engineered input channels only. Here, however, there is an additional separation of the human from the plant operation—not only is the information flowing from the actual operation of the plant filtered through an engineered input channel, but the set of appropriate responses to be made by the human operator to the signals received at the console is fixed. The information flowing from the human operator is also filtered as it moves back through the console to control the functioning of the plant machinery. In the design and development of the automated plant machinery, the computer and the linkage between them, the choices not only regarding what the human operator should pay attention to (the engineered input channels) but also the set of responses that the human is allowed to make (engineered output channel) have been made.

In this situation the quality of both the information moving from the point of production to the human operator and of the information moving from the human operator to the machines operating at the point of production, although appropriate to the context, is less than the highest quality. The operator's responsibility is limited to a finite set of engineered inputs—the arbitrary signal codes she must learn to identify—and a finite set of engineered responses—the class of procedures which specify which console response she is required to make.

The particular classification for business activities we have been developing here based on communication principles such as the type and quality of information the person is required to handle is, no doubt, novel to the reader. Whatever attractiveness it may or may not have for the reader, there is a simple but convincing way to demonstrate that it has a behavioral reality, and profound repercussions in the world of business. We point to one of the most basic of all the organizing principles of business activity—that of accountability. More specifically, we refer to the relationship between how close to or distant from the point of the economic activity the human being involved is and whether he is accountable for that activity.

In the case of the carpenter, there is no distance involved and the responsibility is entirely the carpenter's. In the case of the crane operator, the situation is more complex. If in running the crane during a job, the operator makes an error of judgment visually about the relative position of the leading edge of the bucket and a wall the material to be picked up is located next to, and the bucket swings into the wall damaging it severely, the crane operator will be held accountable. If, however, the operator can demonstrate that a lever jammed or a pedal malfunctioned (an engineered output channel) as the incident occurred, then he is relieved of the responsibility—the incident becomes an accident. If the crane motor heats up to the danger point and catches fire, the operator will be held responsible for the damage if it can be shown that the temperature gauge (an engineered input channel) was functioning properly and he simply failed to detect and respond appropriately to the gauge. If the gauge—the arbitrary signal code for engine temperature—is defective then the crane operator is absolved of all blame in the incident. Similarly, if the computer console operator can demonstrate that she responded appropriately (engineered output) to the signals (engineered input) offered her at the console, she is entirely blameless even if the plant explodes during her shift. Her responsibility stops at the bank of signals and discrete responses available to her on the console.

An examination of the cases offered reveals a powerful and basic organizing principle of business:

Accountability follows information flow

An individual in the world of business can be held accountable for only those portions of the sequence of business activities for which he or she has either direct sensory grounded information or is provided engineered channels of information flow. In the case where the individual is provided with engineered channels of information flow, his or her accountability is limited to the timely detection of information presented in the form of the arbitrary signal codes (engineered input) and the selection of an appropriate response from the set of responses available (engineered output).

There is one extremely important exception to the accountability following information flow rule—the information processors themselves—the managers, the executives, the directors. Managers are held accountable for results which they have no direct experience of nor been provided engineered channels of information for. Consider the question again:

What does the information processor reach for; what does he listen to; what does he watch to know whether he has identified the appropriate signals and that he is performing successfully?

The ultimate answer is the performance of the business organization —the financial statements—the annual report.

The information processor is held accountable for the final outcome of the entire business venture. His or her personal success is invariably tied up with the success of the full chain of activities reaching from the manager's office to the point of production or services. The final measure of the effectiveness of those words and paper is profits. If return on invested capital is up, then the information processor did, in fact, identify the appropriate signals and did perform successfully.

After the flurry of words and paper has subsided, there is the proverbial bottom line.

The ultimate feedback to the information processor is the survival and growth of the business organization he runs.

The implications of this characterization of the manager's position as an exception to the accountability follows information flow rule are enormous. The rule states that an individual can be held accountable for only those portions of the business activity for which he or she either has direct sensory grounded information or is provided engineered channels of information flow. The information processors surely fail to have direct sensory grounded information regarding the activity at the points between them and the point of production or service. Some information processors make it a practice to visit different parts of the production/service process. We applaud such practices. These same information processors will be the first to confess that their position precludes using the practice as the primary source of information.

It is equally obvious that the information processor is provided with no engineered channels of information: an engineered information channel being one through which only information that respects both the need to know and the need not to know flows. We gratefully acknowledge Curt Symonds as the source for the happy phrase "need not to know", although we use it in a somewhat different manner. Such engineered channels are referred to as "clean." The manager's typical information channels—face-to-face meetings, periodic written reports . . . fail both of these requirements primarily since these channels use one of the dirtiest or noisiest codes—language—as their base. Unless some device such as the Precision Model is available for engineering or controlling the quality of the information being carried by the language code, these channels of information flow will continue to be inadequate and the source of costly errors.

Thus the information processor is held accountable for a complex sequence of business activities stretching from his or her office to the point of production without the conditions of information flow for accountability being met. Further, the information system they use to determine what is occurring and to exercise control over the complex activities taking place within the business they are accountable for is of uncertain quality. Yet the success of the information processor will in large part be a function of the effectiveness with which he or she handles information.

What does the information processor reach for: what does he listen to; what does he watch for to know whether he has identified the appropriate signals and that he is performing successfully?

The easy answer—the financial statements, the annual report—is nearly useless. It is the final feedback for an information processor. However, the delay involved renders it useless as a guide to the day-to-day operation of the business.

The information concerning the business activities of the organization which flows up and down the information processor's lines of accountability is the life blood of the organization. The effectiveness with which the information processor employs this information is the single most powerful determinant of success. A prerequisite for the effective handling of information is that the information be of controlled quality. No matter how skilled the information processor is, if the information he or she is using their skills with is of uncertain quality, so will the results of their actions based on it tend to be of uncertain quality. The vast bulk of this information is coded in a special arbitrary code called language.

In both its written and spoken form, language carries the information which decides the economic fate of the members of the business organization through which it flows whether worker, technician, or information processor; and especially information processor.

Any systematic way of controlling the quality of the language information the information processor works with will increase that individual's success and the success of his organization. This book presents a model of an explicit and learnable set of techniques which, when systematically applied in the day-to-day business activities of the manager, the executive, the director will yield the most appropriate quality language information possible—the Precision Model.

INFORMATION AND REPRESENTATION

In the 15th and 16th centuries, Dutch, Portuguese, Spanish and English mariners ventured forth on voyages of discovery. Many of these voyages were financed by the governments of those countries and had as their primary objective the discovery of maritime routes which led to parts of the world where unusual (for occidentals) products, herbs, spices, perfumes, . . . were available for trade. The ruling members of those nations understood clearly that charted, mapped, reliable routes to heretofore undiscovered civilizations or routes to previously contacted civilizations which were more reliable, shorter or safer than previously discovered ones would give the finders of such routes domination in trade with their competitors. Each of the various competing nations entered the contest with different attitudes, personnel and ships. Some of the ships sacrificed stability for speed,—others, robustness for load capacity. In this intensely competitive era, the most widely recognized and closely guarded of objects which gave its possessor the critical advantage in this contest was the rutter—a personal log religiously kept by the pilot/navigator on these voyages of discovery.

As James Clavell expressed it in his magnificent historical novel *Shogun:*

> "A rutter was a small book containing the detailed observations of a pilot who had been there before. It recorded magnetic compass courses between ports and capes, headlands and channels. It noted the sounding and depths and color of the water and the nature of the seabed. It set down the how we got there and how we got back; how many days on a special tack, the pattern of the wind, when it blew and from where; the time of storms and the time of fair winds; where to careen the ship and where to water; where there were friends and where foes; shoals, reefs, tides, havens; at best, everything necessary for a safe voyage.
>
> The English, Dutch, and French had rutters for their own waters, but the waters of the rest of the world had been sailed only by captains from Portugal and Spain, and these two countries considered all rutters secret. Rutters that revealed the seaways to the New World or unravelled the mysteries of the Pass of Magellan and the Cape of Good Hope—both Portuguese discoveries—and thence the seaways to Asia were guarded as national treasures by the Portuguese and Spanish, and sought after with equal ferocity by their Dutch and English enemies."

James Clavell
Shogun, 1978 p. 11

The rutter, then, was a chronicle of a voyage—a series of sensory grounded descriptions which could be used as a guide to travel safely and efficiently to a destination and back again.

The basis of our personal success is the knowledge we possess regarding appropriate and effective actions we may take in the situations we find ourselves in. The individual who finds himself in a canoe on a raging river will succeed in extricating himself from that situation if he has adequate knowledge regarding the possible effective courses of action appropriate to him in that situation and takes such action. This knowledge in turn is the result of experience accumulated by that person in the course of his lifetime. Our experience is the sum total of all the stimulation we have been exposed to which we have detected through our sensory channels. Exposure to stimulation at the sensory level is, of course, no guarantee of knowledge. All of us can remember a person in our experience who seems nearly impervious to experience—no matter how frequently or intensely he is subjected to certain experiences, he seems to glean little or nothing from it and persists in inappropriate or naive behavior. Thus knowledge requires a second step—one which follows exposure to sensory stimulation. This second step is the construction of internal representations or maps. In the world of business these internal representations or maps are usually called ideas, thoughts, hunches, plans. The principles of construction of these internal representations have, until recently (see second volume in this series as well as Neuro Linguistic Programming, Volume I) been considered beyond the grasp and perception of systematic study. Hence, the subject of effective representation in the world of business has been focused almost exclusively on external or shared representations—the flip chart, the graph, the five year plan. Even here, the solid, clear gains which have been made regarding the principles of effective shared representation have been minimal; the men and women who are noted for their success in this area operate intuitively, without an explicit understanding of their personal effectiveness. To our way of thinking, this limited success in making explicit and precise the principles of effective shared representations is a natural outcome of the fact that the principles of construction of internal maps are unavailable. The effectiveness of external shared representations is judged intuitively by humans on the basis of how well they match and organize their internal representations. Thus without an explicit understanding of the construction principles of internal maps, the very limited success achieved in making precise the principles of external representation construction is fully understandable.

Each of us has at our disposal several systems which we can use to create effective detailed internal representations of our experience —thereby making ourselves the beneficiary of our own experience. Most commonly, in North American culture, these systems are visualization—the ability to make detailed, vivid internal images; auditory digital—the ability to use language internally to plan, analyze, ...; and kinesthetics—the ability to sense through physical sensation how we feel about a situation, plan, possibility. Within North American culture in the world of business, the first two of these representational systems are overtly the most highly valued. The visualization system and the auditory digital system differ in several important respects. Of special interest to us here is the fact that the internal visual images created by a business person are not directly communicable to another person while the auditory digital system—language —can be directly communicated. Indeed, the experience of having an exciting and detailed insight into a problem or of having a new perspective on a lucrative business venture and then being faced with the task of translating that picture into a form that can be communicated to others for implementation is altogether too well known to planners, decision makers, executives and managers to require documentation. In fact, in most cases the business person in question falls back on the auditory digital representation system to communicate that original insight—that is, he talks to his associates. Thus the nature of internal visual representations is rather personal while the auditory digital system has the flexibility to be used either internally or externally. Hence, of the various internal systems used by business people, the most immediately accessible is language.

In addition to being the only one of the major representational systems culturally available which serves for both internal personal use as well as external shared use, language has several other features of value in business. Suppose that you have been assigned the task of presenting information to the board of directors about inventory levels. There are several choices you have—first, you could transport the directors to the warehouse, conduct guided tours, and point out the various inventory items; secondly, you might have laborers carry the inventory through the board room, pointing out the various inventory items; thirdly, you might make your representation in language to the board of directors. The example is deliberately ridiculous to point up the fact that language has a particularly powerful feature as a representational system. Specifically, it has the ability to refer to things, events, activities, etc., which are not physically present. The savings in time and energy are obvious. Thus the symbolic nature of language is, in the example, an important asset. This same feature, an asset in the example given, can inadvertently become a liability. Thousands of volumes of philosophy (and the trees from which the paper came) have been utterly wasted by some philosophers who have been seduced into arguing about whether if we can say something, must it then exist. Within the business world, billions of dollars have been wasted on this same difficulty. When I talk about the Washington Monument, the reader/listener understands the specific real world object I am pointing to with my words. When, however, I talk about customer relations or human resources I would be quite surprised if any two readers/listeners could agree on what my words were pointing to. The meaning of a segment of language —a word, a phrase, a sentence, . . .—is the sum total of the individual reader/listener's experience of the thing or activity the word represents. Since each of us have but a single stabilized, uniform experience corresponding to the Washington Monument, those words are efficacious in eliciting the same experience in the reader/listener.

The words 'customer relations' or 'human resources', however, refer to such a diverse collection of activities, widely divergent in the experience of the reader/listener, that there will be as many experiences elicited by those words as there are readers/listeners. Accepting the illusion that we understand what a person is saying when they use such low quality words is the basis for untold numbers of costly errors in the world of business. Much of this book is devoted to offering the reader procedures by which they can exercise control over the quality of information represented in the language/representation system—thereby having the ability to avoid the costly errors which result from the illusion that low quality language was understood.

If you and I were sitting in a circle of people on the prairie, and if I were then to place a painted drum or an eagle feather in the middle of this circle, each of us would perceive these objects differently. Our vision of them would vary according to our individual positions in the circle, each of which would be unique.

Our personal perceptions of these objects would also depend upon much more than just the different positions from which we looked upon them. For example, one or more of us might suffer from color blindness, or from weak eyesight. Either of these two physical differences would influence our perceptions of the objects.

There are levels upon levels of perspectives we must consider when we try to understand our individual perceptions of things, or when we try to relate our own perceptions to those of our brothers and sisters. Every single one of our previous experiences in life will affect in some way the mental perspective from which we see the world around us.

Because of this, a particular object or event may appear fearful to you at the same time that it gives pleasure to me, or appears completely uninteresting to a third person. All things that we perceive stimulate our individual imaginations in different ways, which in turn causes us to create our own unique interpretations of them. Love, hate, fear, confusion, happiness, envy, and all the other emotions we feel, act upon us to paint our perceptions of things in different colors.

If the thing I were to place within our circle should be an abstraction, such as an idea, a feeling, or a philosophy, our perceptions of it would then be even more complicated than if the object had been a tangible thing. And further, the number of different perceptions of it would become greater and greater as more and more people were added to our circle. The perception of any object, either tangible or abstract, is ultimately made a thousand times more complicated whenever it is viewed within the circle of an entire people as a whole. The understanding of this truth is the first lesson of the Medicine Wheel, and it is a vital part of Sun Dance Teaching.

Hyeneyohsts Storm
Seven Arrows, p. 13

An experienced manager will be effective to the extent his personal representation, his rutter, is richer than others. The technology presented in this book is the means to create and refine your own rutter and gain access to the resources provided by the rutters of others.

The ability to develop information, organize that information into some useful representation and take effective action on the basis of that information is one of the most highly valued skills in the complex world of business today. Among the men and women of the business world who perform these tasks in a satisfactory manner, there are individuals who excel. Such individuals are presented with the same initial information as the rest of us, yet they seem to do something extra with it. Somehow they always seem to come up with an action which is a little more precisely to the point; an action which doesn't seem to occur to the rest of us; an action which has some degree of novelty or surprise to it while exhibiting the clean effectiveness that we all have come to strive for. These same individuals, in a situation where the initial plan or action they have set out upon runs into some unanticipated obstacle, always seem to have another choice—another take on the activity—another pathway which leads where we want to go. Where do these a little more precise, a little bit novel yet cleanly effective choices come from? How is it that these individuals always have that extra pathway to our objective?

Each of us is bombarded during our waking hours with large

amounts of information. The portions of the information available to us that we actually pay attention to is rather small and is determined largely by what we have come to understand is useful for us to know about. Naturally, what is useful for us to know about is in turn a function of what we are doing, what task or activity we are involved in at the point in our day when the information becomes available. Each of us carries within us representations of the experiences and events we typically encounter in our daily lives—internal maps of the various situations, tasks and activities that we are competent to involve ourselves with.

The secretary who arranges the material her boss will need for a business conference knows from her experience that certain items will be required. She also knows the order in which she can arrange the material to make it fit best with the way her boss typically runs his conference. As she sets about preparing the material, she will talk to herself, reminding herself of the specific material to be included; she might visualize the last time she successfully prepared the material for the conference using those images as a guide for her present activity. Having organized the material, she will sit back, scan the material, its appearance, the order it is in, and ask herself whether she has finished, whether there is anything left to be done. In all these activities she is using internally stored maps, representations, guides formed by her experience in having done this or similar tasks successfully in the past to know how in this particular case to accomplish the task that she is involved in successfully. The previous experience is available to her through the internally stored maps. The more complete, detailed and organized these internal maps, the higher the probability that somewhere within these representations created by her past experience is an example of the optimal solution for the task she is presently engaged in. The vaguer, the less explicit and well organized her internal maps, the less likely she will perform effectively in this task. If she is a shared secretary who works for a number of people, she will be sought after and appreciated just in case she has the flexibility to create and keep separate the idiosyncrasies of the various people for whom she acts as secretary. If she can recognize and store in her internal representations, the preferences of the various people for whom she performs tasks, she will have the ability to tailor her secretarial services for each of the individual members of her office, much to their satisfaction and appreciation. If she is unable or unwilling to detect and store in her internal maps these differences, her response to each of the members of the office will be uniform and in the perceptions of the office members less satisfactory, and much less appreciated by them.

The difference between these two cases is the richness and detail of the internally stored map. The secretary who performs adequately has a single map or guide for her behavior in preparing material for a conference—thus, her preparations will be the same for all such occasions. The secretary with the ability to tailor her services to the individual preferences of the members of the office also has a single map for the activity of preparing material for a conference—however, her map, if we were able to examine it directly, would be a much expanded version of the map the other secretary uses. In it we would find many more distinctions—distinctions like the preferred order of material, the detail with which the agenda should be prepared, the placement of tables, graphs and statistics, . . . for each of the office members she works for.

One useful way of discussing this difference is to point out that the secretary with the more extended, detailed and organized map literally has choices where the other secretary has none. We may now offer a preliminary answer to the questions we raised earlier—Where do these a little more precise, a little bit novel yet cleanly effective choices come from? How is it that these individuals always have that extra pathway to our objective? The answer, of course, is the only place such a little more precise, a little bit novel yet cleanly effective choices and extra pathways could come from—the rich, detailed internal maps of the specific individuals who performed with excellence.

Business is not the only domain where differences in the richness and detail of internal maps dictates a person's effectiveness and success. Take, for example, the skilled athlete—a tournament class golfer. The primary difference between this man or woman and those of us who manage a round or so on weekends and, if things are running right, sometimes a round during the week, is the detail and richness of the internal maps we use as a guide for our behavior while playing golf. Indeed, those individuals who have achieved excellence in some sport—those individuals who have just such extended and detailed internal maps to guide their behavior—are called professionals. Those of us with relatively impoverished maps—ones with significantly fewer distinctions, less detail and which cover a more limited area of the sport—have to make do with the designation of amateur.

The point is obvious—the more precise, detailed and extended the internally stored maps that an individual operating in the complex world of business has, the wider the range of choices he or she will have available in responding to those complex situations. The wider the range of choices represented in the internal map, the more effectively the information processor will be able to tailor the actions which he or she takes in responding to the situations which arise in the business world with excellence.

For purposes of exposition, the involved process by which a member of the business community comes to have such extended, detailed and effective maps can be represented as having three phases.

1. information elicitation

2. information representation

3. information application

These phases are, of course, intimately interwoven in practice—the representation of information will yield a rich detailed internal map only if the information which is elicited is of sufficiently high quality. The application of the information to some specific transaction in business will be effective only if the internal map has an adequately rich and detailed representation for the specific kind of transaction the information is being applied to.

This series—High Quality Information Processing in Business—treats the three phases of high quality information processing in three volumes, one for each of the phases. Thus, this volume—Precision—addresses itself to the presentation of an explicit model which gives the user the ability to develop high quality, contextually appropriate information during the elicitation phase of high quality information processing. The Precision Model is a technology which allows the user full control over the quality of the information carried by the language code. An overall understanding of the code which carries the vast bulk of this information is thus in order.

LANGUAGE AS A REPRESENTATIONAL SYSTEM FOR INFORMATION

As we noted in the opening section, language is a special symbolic code. This statement deserves some elaboration. Language is a code —by this, we mean to point out that language is symbolic. The words

—an IBM typewriter—are not an IBM typewriter. This is precisely parallel to the situation regarding the temperature gauge in the cab of the crane or the indicators on the computer console—the gauges and indicators themselves are not the thing they are signaling about. The temperature gauge is not itself hot when the gauge is reporting information that the engine is hot. The console indicator is not itself wet when it signals that one of the vats of liquid is overflowing. Language is likewise a symbol system in which a set of objects—words, phrases, sentences, paragraphs—are used in certain specified orders to refer to things and activities which are going on at the level of real experience. As in the case of the temperature gauge in the cab of the crane, the particular form the information can be represented in is variable. The fact that the information regarding the temperature of the engine is presented in a vertical scale with the low temperature located at the bottom of the vertical line and the high temperature located at the top is wholly arbitrary as we pointed out earlier.

Language is special in that encoding the things and activities at the level of real experience—creating the language representations which refer to the world of experience—the encoder has a great deal of freedom of choice in the selection of the specific words and phrases. An example will serve well here. Suppose that we were given the task of describing the activity of a carpenter finishing the last piece of labor required to complete the construction of a cabinet. Any of the following descriptions would suffice:

> The carpenter, sweat dripping from his brow, hammer gripped tightly in his hand, leans forward, swinging the hammer in a two foot arc which terminates in a solid strike on the last nail in the upper right hand corner of the cabinet, driving it home with a polished and practiced movement.

> The carpenter finished the cabinet by driving home the last nail with a practiced motion.

> The carpenter finished the cabinet.

> The cabinet is finished.

> The job is complete.

> Everything is ready.

Any of the above descriptions are accurate representations of the situation concerning the carpenter and the cabinet. Thus any of them would satisfy the task. However, as the reader is no doubt aware, the quality of information each of the descriptions offers is profoundly different. In fact there is a gradient of quality which runs through the sequence of descriptions—the first description being of the highest quality, the last of the lowest quality.

Notice, for example, that the number of real world experiences that each of the descriptions could accurately refer to expands as the description become more attenuated—as the distance between the original scene of the carpenter working and the language representation increases. The first description—the most vivid and richest of the lot—could actually apply to only a limited number of real world events. The next in line—lower in quality—could refer accurately to more real world events, and so forth until by the time we arrive at the description:

Everything is ready.

the number of real world events that the sentence could accurately refer to is astronomical. The description in question could even refer to the fact that the reader has just completed reading this sentence.

Language allows a series of descriptions or encodings of real world experiences to be created by a language user—all of which are accurate representations of the original raw experience but which differ from one another in quality.

The greater the number of real world situations which the description is an accurate representation of, the lower the quality of the information represented in the language description. Conversely, the fewer the real world situations which the language description could accurately represent, the higher the quality of information.

INFORMATION AND THE INFORMATION PROCESSOR

We return now to the issue raised earlier—namely, the relationship between accountability and information. Specifically, the formulation we offered earlier of one of the most basic organizing principles in the world of business:

Accountability follows information flow

And, more specifically to the exception to that rule—the information processor. The general manager, for example, is held accountable for the entire chain of business activities which stretch from his desk to the point of production or services which is the justification for that chain of activities. Yet, as we pointed out, he has neither direct sensory experience of the vast bulk of those events, nor does he have engineered information flow channels which allow him to read, through some simple set of dials, gauges and indicators, the status of these various activities.

The ideal solution to this dilemma would be to provide the information processor with a device which accomplished for information coded in language the same thing that the blow-up process associated with aerial photography does for information coded in photos. There is a procedure in photography which provides a good substitute, an engineered channel, for direct visual inspection. Duplicated for verbal information it would be extremely effective. It would provide the techniques for creating the engineered channel presently missing.

Suppose that you were the general manager for a huge paper manufacturer, and that your organization was vertically integrated, stretching from the harvesting of timber to the marketing of the resulting products. Suppose further that you had decided to visit several of the harvesting sites which were scattered at great distances from one another. Because of a shortage of time, you were unable to schedule in a stop at one of the sites but by an accident of the itinerary noted that you would be flying nearly over the site on your return to the home office. You instruct the pilot to fly over the site using the aerial photography cameras. Later, of course, at your leisure in your office you might examine the photos. It is quite likely from an examination of the medium level blow-ups you could arrive at a reasonably accurate assessment of the level of activity on the site. You could determine whether all of the burning towers, rigs and other equipment were being used or, indeed, whether some were idle. You could determine the amount of actual harvesting which had occurred since the opening of the site. There would be enough information for you to reassure yourself that the operation was generally in good shape. In other words, that level of blow-up—that refined a representation—would satisfy the basic questions in the assessment. In fact, for you to request more refined blow-ups with higher quality detail would be inappropriate—the process of blowing the photos up is a costly one involving technicians and expensive equipment. In addition, it might, in fact, make it more difficult for you to arrive at an overall assessment of the situation on the site—you might become so involved in the details that the larger picture becomes difficult to appreciate. Suppose further that a report arrives at your desk that there is a problem that has come up at that particular site. One excellent choice would be for you, knowing what the problem is reported to be, to figure out what you could see on the site that would give you precisely the information you need to fully understand the situation there—perhaps, even to identify an effective solution. At that point, it would be entirely appropriate for you to order a set of high quality blow-ups of exactly those portions of the site where the information will be apparent. Or, alternatively, suppose that you were personally convinced that, while the operation on that site was a profitable one consistent with the margins the other sites were showing, the operation on that site could be upgraded to a significantly higher level of productivity. Again, knowing the outcome you desired to achieve, you could figure out what specific changes you would institute in order to bring about this significantly higher level of productivity. Having decided on a number of possible pathways any one of which might lead to the desired outcome, it would then be appropriate for you to order higher quality blow-ups of those portions of the operation which contained the information that you needed to complete your planning. The technology of aerial photography and of the blow-up process allows the user to select the level of refinement of visual information. This decision about the level of refinement of the information will be dictated by the specific context of the issue or problem that the information processor requires information for.

As we indicated, the ideal solution would be to provide the information processor with a device which did for information coded in language what the technology of aerial photography and the blow-up process do for information stored in a visual representation. Such a device could accept as input a starting point of extremely low quality information and offer as output any level of refinement desired by the user. The device would operate on an input as low quality as the one following:

Everything is ready.

and from such a starting point elicit any grade of information required by the context set by the task the information processor is involved in.

Everything is ready.

> Q: what specifically is ready?
> A: the job—the job is ready.
> Q: which job specifically is ready?
> A: the cabinet is ready.
> Q: how specifically is the cabinet ready?
> A: the cabinet is finished.
> Q: who finished the cabinet?
> A: the carpenter finished the cabinet.
> Q: how specifically did the carpenter finish the cabinet?
> A: the carpenter finished the cabinet by driving home the last nail.
> Q: how specifically did the carpenter drive home the last nail?
> A: the carpenter finished the cabinet driving . . .

The reader no doubt recognized that the questioning technique is eliciting precisely increasingly high quality information which leads back, drawing closer and closer to the original experience that the initial low quality information alluded to. The parallelism to the aerial photography will be apparent to the reader. The questioning technique employed in the question/answer exchange is, of course, a sample of the set of questions drawn from the Precision Model which is the subject of this book.

If the Precision Model question techniques were fully employed in the exchange, the questioner would come up with information which matches the information presented in the original high quality description. Rarely, of course, would a manager, executive or director of a business organization require the quality of information contained in the original high quality description. Such a large amount of detail would be inappropriate in most situations. Herein lies the advantage—the full Precision Model allows the user to select precisely the quality of information required for the user to accomplish the task confronting him or her. The Precision Model device known as Frames maintains a context which determines what is appropriate.

The information processor's area of accountability extends from his or her office to the point of production or service. What such an information processor needs is the choice of travelling informationally to any point along that chain of activities to elicit precisely the information he or she requires to exercise the influence necessary.

Each of you, no doubt, has encountered the manager who consistently demands so much detail from his subordinates that they are completely demoralized and feel that their services and skills are not being utilized. At the opposite end of the continuum, the reader can remember a manager who consistently mistakes abdication for delegation. No two situations which the manager is confronted with are exactly the same. In one, it may be appropriate to elicit a great deal of detail while in another, a simple go/no go signal from those reporting is precisely what is required. The quality of information must be tailored on a situation to situation basis to respect both the need to know and the need not to know.

The Precision Model offers exactly that control over the quality of information which flows along the lines of accountability of concern to the information processor.

We may now offer a more useful answer to the question we raised at the beginning of this book:

> What does the information processor reach for, what does he listen to, what does he watch to know that he has identified the appropriate signals and that he is performing successfully?

The answer we offer is a set of language engineering tools which develop for the user precise information. By precise information we intend the following:

> Information coded in language will be said to be precise if the information is of the highest quality appropriate to the context in which it is used.

Thus, as this definition implies, the Precision Model must deliver two kinds of tools—a set of Frames which identify and establish the context or boundary conditions within which information is being elicited, and a set of Precision Model questions which develop the high quality information within that context.

THE INFORMATION PROCESSOR'S TASK

In the remainder of this book we will use the word *manager* to refer to that group of individuals in the world of business whose primary task is information processing—the manager, the executive, the director. This is for convenience only—we find the title *information processor* both accurate and awkward. We mention here briefly certain issues which, while they may be obvious to the reader are important enough that they deserve, in the authors' opinion, constant reiteration.

First, in the context of the day to day tasks of the manager, the effectiveness of his actions is strongly connected with the quality of the information which is used to assess as well as influence the operation that he is accountable for. The computer field has developed an idiom which we find wholly appropriate here:

garbage in, garbage out

This rule applies to the inbound information as well as the outbound information. The information elicited by the manager to assess the situation in the operation must be of the appropriate level of quality to allow effective action. However, it is as critical that the information in the form of directives and instructions also be of an appropriate level of quality. The fact that the present state information used by the manager is of the appropriate quality will be of little comfort when it is subsequently discovered that the quality of information in the directives and instructions was of too low a quality to adequately influence and guide the members of the organization in carrying out the potentially effective actions. As suggested later in the context of particular issues, the manager might well consider having members of the organization who consistently report to him trained in the Precision Model to insure the outbound information is of adequate high quality.

Secondly, the typical situation which the modern manager finds himself in is one of increasing technological complexity. It is rare these days to find a manager who happens to be technically competent with respect to the entire set of activities which he is accountable for. Thus the modern manager must rely more and more on information processing skills which will allow him to deal effectively and efficiently with information which he is not technically qualified to understand. Such a demand cries out for an explicit set of procedures for information processing—the point of this book.

Kepner and Tregoe describe the situation elegantly.

Perhaps the most significant implication of the concepts and procedures described in this book is that they anticipate the kind of manager that will be needed in the future. As the authors have pointed out, the continuing increases in technology inevitably mean that managers will know less and less about the skills and knowledge of those they are managing, and will have to depend more and more on their ability to manage the operating techniques of those reporting to them. And in order to manage the way a subordinate handles problems and decisions, a manager has to know how to ask just the right questions.

Kepner and Tregoe
The Rational Manager p. 6

But suppose a manager develops the skill of asking the kind of questions that will tap relevant information about problems? Suppose, for instance, he learns how to probe to determine whether the suspected cause of a problem is likely or not? Or whether the problem he has selected is really important? With such skill it is clear that he would need relatively less experience and specialized knowledge in order to manage the way his subordinates solved problems. In fact, the manager today has no choice. With management growing progressively more complex, and experience more obsolete more rapidly, the manager *must* rely more and more on skillful, rational questioning, and less and less on experience.

Kepner and Tregoe,
The Rational Manager, pp. 23

Further, note that in those cases where a manager happens to be technically competent with respect to the activities which he is accountable for, it would be disastrous for him to employ that technical competency directly to his area of accountability in any consistent manner. If he were to consistently, for example, solve technical problems which came up, he would be behaving as a technician, not a manager. We are not proposing that technically qualified managers who know of a solution to some technical problem hide such information from their subordinates. Rather we are referring to the mistake some managers inadvertently make—that of continuing in a behavior which was appropriate and successful when they occupied the position of a technician when, in fact, they now have a different position and function—that of manager. This situation is common enough that the business community has identified it and awarded it a title— the Peter Principle—from the book by Lawrence Peter. The technically qualified manager who persists in technical problem solving is not managing. Further, as many authors have documented, the net effect of a manager who does technical problem solving at the expense of managing is a disastrous lowering of the morale in his subordinates —especially, the technicians whose functions are being inadvertently usurped by the would-be manager. This demoralization is an understandable response to a situation where a technician's resources and training are not being employed. The would-be manager can easily become trapped in a vicious cycle once this pattern is established. The technicians' demoralization proceeds to the point where the quality of their work drops, thereby creating further technical problems which demand an increasing amount of the would-be manager's time and resources. Therefore, the manager spends even less time and energy managing and more fire fighting, and the cycle continues. The Precision Model offers a welcome exit from such vicious loops.

THE PERSONAL CONTEXT OF THE MANAGER

This book deals exclusively with information coded in language. As we have insisted from the opening sentence of this book, the highest quality information is behavioral—the actual performance of the individual or organization. The point of the Precision Model is to give the manager tools which will allow as high a quality of language information as is appropriate for the context in which he is operating. During each language interchange with another member of the business organization, there is passed a large amount of this highest quality information. We are here referring to the non-verbal component of communication which inevitably accompanies but is not limited to, the occasions on which there is a language exchange among the members of a business organization. The authors have taken a position in other books and workshops that the non-verbal component of any communication interchange will, over the long run, be the most influential, the most dominant of the two classes of communication—verbal (language) and non-verbal.

Thus, no matter how well organized the verbal transactions of the manager, unless the underlying, accompanying non-verbal behavior —the voice tone, the tempo of speech, the gestures, the body postures, . . .—support the information being offered or requested, the result will be less than optimal. The issues here are those of rapport —the skill of finding and developing working interpersonal relationships which recognize that certain business tasks must be accomplished and accomplished in a way which respects the integrity of the people involved—and congruency—the skill of matching the non-verbal and verbal behavior so that they reinforce and support one another. The appreciation and use of non-verbal communication is a vital and fascinating topic; unfortunately outside the domain of this volume.

Business is *the* human outcome oriented activity. The bottom line is the economic survival and growth of the business organization as well as the personal development and advancement of the human beings in that organization. The executive or manager who sacrifices specific business outcomes for positive interpersonal relationships in the business context is doing the people with whom he has those positive interpersonal relationships, as well as the business organization, a disservice. It is of little consolation to those people that they had fine interpersonal relationships with the managers and executives of a business organization when that organization folds because of a failure to meet specific business outcomes. Over the last decade a number of theories which originated in humanistic psychology have been imported into portions of the world of business. While there have been gains resulting from the importation of some of these theories, the most obvious consequence has been a reduction in efficiency. The issue here is one of control. The manager is held accountable for the complete chain of economic activities which stretches from his or her office down to the point of production or service. In order to be effective, the manager must exercise control over those activities to the extent required to insure that the goals of that organization are met. For us, the term control implies the ability both to know what is occurring along that chain of activities which the manager is accountable for and the ability to access the resources of the personnel operating in that chain and direct those resources to insure success. The word *control* itself is an example of low quality language representation. One may accurately say:

The carpenter controlled the hammer, swinging it through a two foot arc to drive home the last nail.

In this case the control over the hammer that the carpenter exercises is very close—his control determines completely the movement and position of the hammer. One may equally accurately say:

The foreman controlled the carpenter's activities.

In this case, a much looser relationship is indicated. If, for example, the foreman were to attempt to control the carpenter's activities in the close way that the carpenter controls the movement and position of the hammer, he should be dismissed. Rather, the foreman controls the activity of the carpenter by setting tasks or outcomes for him which are within his competence and through feedback—inspection and instruction—to ensure that the carpenter is producing the required products in the required time frame. By virtue of his or her position, the manager needs to exercise control over the economic activities of the personnel in his sphere of accountability. The first order of business is information both inbound—reports about the present state of the economic activity—and outbound—instructions and directives to continue in the present state or to move to some new target state. The effective manager insists on a close relationship between the inbound and the outbound information in the sense of using the inbound information to set goals in conjunction with his personnel which are within the competence of those personnel. A high quality set of instructions and directives conveying information regarding a new business plan will be ineffective unless they are based on a high quality representation about the present state of the organization. Conversely, the manager who insists on high quality information from those reporting to him about the present situation but fails to demand of himself and his staff the same high quality information flow outbound for implementation will likewise be ineffective.

Thus the manager needs tools to exercise control over the quality of information in his domain of accountability. The bulk of this work is aimed precisely at providing the manager with tools to engineer those information flow channels. Time and again, in seminars and workshops, managers have indicated to the authors that they find the processes of both eliciting information, and insuring that the instructions and directives they issue are understood, both painful and distasteful. This common situation is expressed in the following quote:

(The manager) often has neither the time nor the talent required to challenge the validity of the reports he receives, and in many cases might even consider it somewhat imprudent to do so.

Curtis W. Symonds,
A Design for Business Intelligence, p. 6

Nearly all of the cases fall into one of the two categories—first, situations where the manager requires some information concerning an activity in his domain of accountability and he ends up wading through an enormous amount of largely irrelevant information to secure the information he needs; second, situations where the manager is reluctant to probe for the information required as he is fearful of intruding on the initiative of his subordinates. The first is an example of what we refer to as a failure to respect the need not to know—the manager is not exercising adequate control over the information he needs in the sense of excluding information irrelevant for his purposes. The second is an example of failure to secure information that he needs to know and should have access to by virtue of his position—the fact that he is accountable for the economic activities for which he needs the information. Managers who have presented this situation to us report a hesitation to exercise adequate control over the information being offered by personnel reporting to them primarily because of a fear that such control would result in the deterioration of interpersonal relationships with the person, a reduction in rapport, even a destruction of the environment necessary for making the creative individual resources of the person available. These managers often explain that their hesitation stems from some set of learning experiences where the consultant or instructor used a humanistically oriented psychological base. Our experience leads us to believe that this is a particularly unhappy application of such theories resulting in a net reduction in efficiency. We take the position here that rapport, positive interpersonal relations, creating an environment where the creative resources of the personnel of a business organization are available is an essential part of the art of management; further that there is no necessary antagonism between efficiency and the humanistic goals stated above. Indeed, in the authors' experience, a necessary component of the foundation of excellent business rapport is the competence of the manager—especially the manager's ability to be effective in indicating with precision the information which he requires (the need to know) as well as the information which he does not wish to have at that particular time (the need not to know). One of the most powerful skills a manager can have is his ability to communicate explicitly to those personnel reporting to him what information he needs at any time. Such a skill offers the subordinates an orientation, a specific understanding of what exactly their job entails. An explicit set of requirements which define the job a person is employed to meet allows that person to know how to proceed in order to succeed. Where the requirements remain vague and unspecified, the employees are typically unable to mobilize their creative resources in an effective manner, and there is a resulting deterioration in the rapport and interpersonal relations. Business is *the* human outcome oriented activity. The effective manager sets explicit outcomes for his personnel and offers specific feedback to let them know whether they are satisfying those goals. The Precision Model is a specific way of approaching such behavior. It allows, for example, the manager to designate high quality outcomes for each phase of the business transaction which provides an explicit standard of relevance. Thus the issue of the need to know and the need not to know is made perfectly explicit, thereby removing it from the realm of the interpersonal and of personal power struggles. We have been gratified with the tremendous increases in efficiency in meetings, problem solving, planning sessions, decision making, . . . which result from the application of the Precision Model by managers trained in the system. We have been equally delighted to note the concommitant improvement in rapport, interpersonal relations and the environment promoting access to the creative resources of the personnel which result from their discovery, through the consistent behavior of their managers, of what is required from them.

THE OVERALL MODEL

The primary and most pervasive organizing principle in this volume is what we call the Present State/Desired State model. The term Present State refers to the situation which the individual or organization finds itself in—what is presently going on—while the term Desired State refers to a target situation which the individual or organization identifies as more highly valued than the present situation—what the goal or desirable outcome is.

Here we are referring to the fact that each business transaction is an attempt by the organization to track itself from some present level of effectiveness to some other situation which is characterized by an increase in effectiveness—a change for the better. This very general conceptual schema applies with equal force to goals of any size—a meeting, a five year plan, the elicitation of information, getting a cup of coffee. The mechanics of the application of this principle will be treated extensively in the remainder of the book.

While the Precision Model is appropriately and powerfully applicable to the entire range of business transactions, we are faced with the task of picking some specific set of examples to present in this volume. We have biased what follows toward the area of business transactions usually referred to as problem solving and decision making. The justification for this choice resides solely in the fact that our perception is that this area of business transactions consumes the greatest amount of time and energy on the part of the manager in the everyday execution of his or her responsibility. We include more abbreviated examples of the application of the Precision Model to the contexts of meetings, conflict management, and planning. Having selected the area of problem solving and decision making as the primary example of the application of the Precision Model, we are left with the task of organizing this complex area of business activity. We propose a four stage model:

| Defining the Difference | Path-finding | Surveying | Evaluating |

In creating this model for the purposes of exposition, we are indebted to the fine work of Kepner and Tregoe in their classic work *The Rational Manager.*

We hasten to add that the Precision Model itself is entirely independent of any particular organization of the complex activity called problem solving and decision making. Any method for organizing this complex area of business activity into specified stages with explicit outcomes is an appropriate environment for the implementation of the Precision Model.

Should the reader have a favored model which he uses to organize the complex human activity called business, we invite him to discard the proposals here in favor of his own organization and to note that the relocation of the Precision Model to another model has no effect on its effectiveness and power.

BACKTRACK

The highest quality information is behavioral. Our direct experience, or what we call sensory grounded information, is the highest possible quality. As we move away from this direct contact by our own senses, the information we receive becomes lower quality. Engineered channels for carrying information can provide adequate reliability upon which to base actions. The more that irrelevant material is permitted in the channel of communication, the lower the quality of that information, the less reliable it is for action.

Accountability in the process of producing goods and services is usually limited to those areas where there is direct sensory experience of relevant data or carefully engineered channels. Management, however, is a notable exception. Managers seldom have either direct sensory experience of the results of operations which are their responsibility nor are they provided with adequate information channels. Language is a means for sharing the representations of our experience. It is the most common one in business. We use language to understand the ideas of others and to gain understanding of their experience of business operations. An event does not become a disaster simply because one observer thinks it is. More information is needed before we can decide for ourselves. Similarly, because a service representative believes that a series of complaints is no cause for concern, a manager requires information before he can agree or disagree.

We are presenting an explicit technique which will obtain any desired amount of information. It provides a model which will get precise information. We define information to be adequately precise when it is of the highest quality appropriate to the situation.

We introduce the present state/desired state model which will recur throughout. This concept is used as an organizing principle in all communication. Its use permits the determination of adequate precision in any given context.

Chapter 2

DEFINING THE DIFFERENCE

It is true, as the saying goes, that a problem clearly stated is already half solved. It is also true that a problem cannot be efficiently solved unless it is *precisely* described. . . .

The kind of precise specification of a problem to be described in this chapter is, therefore, the most valuable single tool a manager can have for solving any kind of problem.

Kepner and Tregoe,
The Rational Manager, p. 73, 74

This chapter deals with the first phase of the overall model of business activity presented in the preceding chapter. The reader will recognize the following visual representation from the introduction:

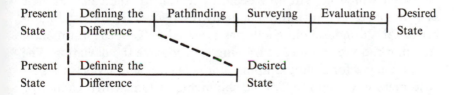

In 1965 Charles Kepner and Benjamin Tregoe published a book which was destined to become a classic in the field of business—*The Rational Manager.* The effectiveness of their work can be measured by the thousands of managers they have successfully trained in their methods as well as by the fact that the particular components that they identified in the model in their book continue to dominate discussions of problem solving and decision making even now, some fifteen years after their book was published. These components—for example, specifying the problem or analyzing for distinctions and changes—have proven their utility again and again. Thus it is only appropriate that we begin our presentation with a word of acknowledgement to the fine piece of work created by these two men that has so well stood the test of time.

Problems are generally recognized to exist when deviations from standards are recognized. For example, the manager of an auto assembly plant receives reports from his production manager that over the last quarter, actual production has fallen off 10% when compared with the budget which in turn was based on the production of the prior year's quarter. The standard of performance is the production achieved previously while the 10% reduction in production this quarter is easily identified as the deviation from that standard that the manager will now concern himself with.

The personnel manager brings the general manager of a textile factory figures which indicate that absenteeism on work days following weekends and holidays is up 13% in the last three month period. Again, the comparison is immediately available. The general manager understands that the standard of performance is the average number of workers absent on workdays following weekends and holidays during the previous three month (or longer) period, and that the deviation he will now initiate problem analysis with is the increase in that number.

The quality control manager notes that the number of quality rejected units has tripled on assembly line 6 on the night shift for three nights running. It requires no special skill to recognize the deviation which he will now begin to search for the cause of. The sales manager of a furniture company discovers that the total number of sales of household goods has dropped 33% in the last month. Again, it requires no special training to recognize the deviation. The sales manager for a photographic products company reports that his customers have returned whole shipments of film which cannot be developed clearly. The plant manager recognizes immediately that a previous satisfactory performance has become potentially disastrous and initiates appropriate action.

As the reader is no doubt well aware, reports of changes which are presented in percentage form have contained within them implicitly the standard of performance. The percentage increase or decrease in some figure is only intelligible when referred to some comparable performance period.

What the reader may or may not have noted is that there is a characteristic common to all the examples listed above—namely that in each case the deviation identified was a deviation from an *historically defined standard of performance*. That is to say, in each case the operation had at one point in the organization's recent history been functioning at a level of performance which was accepted as satisfactory. Thus, all the deviations were changes from this historically defined satisfactory standard of performance.

Our own experience has been that this characteristic is almost invariably present when the method of problem analysis is employed by skilled managers in their day-to-day operation. While most works on problem solving explicitly state that their notion of standard of performance should not be restricted to past performance or statistical averages, in practice the actual use of their models seems to be overwhelmingly oriented to historically defined standards of performance.

Given the day-to-day pressures experienced by managers in the actual performance of their functions, it is not surprising that the standard of performance which is unconsciously and systematically selected by managers in employing this powerful model is the historically defined standard or the actual track record of the organization. It is, however, unfortunate that the models in their implementation have this one-sided bias—this strong tendency to measure present functioning against previous functioning. It is possible to drive a car forward down a road using only the position of the car relative to the boundaries of the road as seen through the rear view mirror, however it severely limits the speed at which it is safe to travel and it offers little in the way of protection or warning regarding drastic changes in the direction of the road or obstacles which may be lying in the roadway.

Most problem solving models are initiated when there is a recognition on the part of the manager that something has gone wrong. The consequences of this are profound—specifically, it places the manager in a reactive position. Problem analysis has become a remedial approach to managing. Since the manager is in a reactive position, little or no time is left to attempt to achieve levels of excellence. The world of business is often perceived by the manager as a series of problems to be reacted to and solved—a sequence of deviations from previously existing satisfactory states of performance—a series of things to be fixed.

As mentioned above, while there is good evidence that Kepner & Tregoe and others intended their models not to be restricted simply to reactive, remedial situations but to serve as an effective guide for achieving maximum performance levels, it is easy to find within their works a bias in favor of past performance oriented standards. In other words, if a problem is defined as a deviation from a standard of performance and the cause of a problem is always a change that has taken place, then it follows that the cause of a problem is always a deviation or change from some standard of performance which existed prior to the change occurring.

We propose, then, a new terminology—one which we introduced in the preface—in order to leave no ambiguity about our intent with regard to the Precision Model presented here. We desire to make available to managers a model which is perfectly general in its application—a model which is as relevant for reactive problem solving as it is for planning—in order to achieve maximum performance levels. We shall use the terms, PRESENT STATE and DESIRED STATE to refer to the two areas where high quality information is essential for successful and efficient business functioning. The Present State is a description of the situation the organization finds itself in at the present time. The Desired State (sometimes called the Outcome State) is a description of the situation which the organization desires to achieve. A problem, then, can be easily defined:

A problem is defined as any difference between the Present State and the Desired State.

If   Present State $\neq$ Desired State

then a problem exists

This more general model now includes the common definition of a problem as a special case—specifically, when the Desired State is determined to be identical to a standard of performance which is historically available within the past performance of the organization. However, the new terms also immediately suggest that the definition of the Desired State need not be limited to historically defined standards of performance—sources for the definition of Desired States can be as diverse as performance of excellence achieved by competitors, performance of excellence achieved by organizations in other closely related product or service lines, planning based on the maximum capacity of the machinery and manpower available within the organization.

Examples of non-historically defined Desired States could include: The production manager states he cannot meet the budgeted unit production even though it represents only a 10% increase over the previous year, the machine capacity is rated considerably above the demand and those production levels had been achieved in peak months in the past. The standard of performance is an explicit, behavioral one which is based on optimum performance. The difference is clear and will cause the general manager to initiate analysis of the situation.

The computing center manager reports that he cannot get reports out as fast as agreed. The increase in business has slowed processing until, with additional applications, expected performance standards cannot be met. Although reports are still on time according to an older but inadequate standard, a problem analysis will be generated by comparison to a newly created standard.

An unsatisfactory condition which will initiate problem analysis may be due to standards which were required and expected to meet increases in demand or scope of operations. Growth, or even retrenchment, require standards which are not historical.

Hence, the model incorporates both the traditional area of problem analysis—the reactive situation to be remedied—as well as positive states of high quality performance defined by planning teams based on whatever inputs they might choose to consider.

THE MODEL FOR DEFINING THE DIFFERENCE

The Present State/Desired State model presented in the introduction is extremely comprehensive—it applies with full power to the entire business model as well as applying to each individual component of the overall business model.

The Present State for the segment Defining the Difference arises whenever a responsible party in an organization recognizes that there is a difference between a Desired State and the present functioning of that organization. The question of recognition of difference is itself a complex and fascinating topic which lies outside of the boundaries of this particular book. However, for our purposes here, it is irrelevant how the manager or responsible party comes to notice the difference. It may be the result of reading a report compiled by one of the employees complete with specific facts and figures. It may be the result of a complex largely unconscious thought process within the manager initiated by the observation of some of the employees at work. It may be the result of an explicit directive from the planning committee or board of directors insisting that certain production or sales goals be adopted and met in the next reporting period. It is unimportant for our purposes how specifically the recognition that there is a difference between the Desired State and the Present State arises. The important point is that once the recognition that there is a difference occurs the conditions for activating the model for Defining the Difference are met. Nor is it relevant how articulate or inarticulate the manager or responsible party is, or how thorough their initial understanding of the difference is, the Precision Model is designed specifically to elicit high quality information no matter what the conscious appreciation of the difference by the manager or responsible party is. It simply requires that the manager notice that there is a difference between what he wants (Desired State) and what he is getting (Present State). The simple realization that things could be different in some useful way is adequate to begin the process of Defining the Difference.

The outcome for this segment of the process—Defining the Difference—is achieved when the manager has a high quality description of the difference between that state of affairs which is the target—the overall Desired State—and the present state of the organization. When he has such a description, he has successfully Defined the Difference, and is ready to move onto the next segment—Pathfinding. The point of the Defining the Difference segment is to establish a high quality representation which identifies the end points of the entire process. A manager with an explicit, high quality representation of where he and his organization presently are and where they wish to arrive at is a manager who is well prepared to make that journey. Such information will provide a trajectory for the manager —knowing where he is and where he is going will tremendously increase the efficiency with which the manager can move. It allows him to make effective judgments about which classes of information he will need and equally importantly, which classes of information he will not need. His actions will, therefore, be characterized by an economy of movement.

PRESENT STATE

I had the occasion some years ago to travel to a remote part of East Africa where I was to meet a good friend whom I had not seen in years. My original travel arrangements involved my journeying first by commercial airlines to a major airport near one of the few urban areas in that part of the world, arriving early in the afternoon, and then by a small chartered plane to a jungle airstrip some few miles from my final destination—my friend's ranch home. Unfortunately, as is all too often the case these days, the commercial airliner was delayed some hours and I arrived late in the afternoon at the airport where I was to meet the small chartered aircraft. I was somewhat uneasy about my late arrival, having more than once in my traveling career experienced the bewilderment and disorientation which typically accompany missed connections in a part of the world where one is unfamiliar with the language and culture. I chose on this particular day to adopt the attitude that whatever consequences the missed connections had, I would treat them as part of my larger adventure. Having settled myself into a more advantageous frame of mind, I noted with much appreciation the canopy of the jungle over which we flew as well as the glimpses of wild life I could catch through the breaks in the green surface of the jungle below. I was nevertheless relieved when a tall, dignified and extremely competent looking man detached himself from the crowd of on-lookers at the arrival gate and approached me with an expectant look. Having satisfied ourselves as to our respective identities, he quickly guided me to his aircraft and only moments later we were winging our way on the next leg of my journey. We touched down at the small jungle airstrip several hours later, shortly before an astonishing African sunset. My pilot taxied his craft to the far end of the field where a Landrover was parked. As the small craft rolled to a stop a short distance from the parked vehicle, I was puzzled that my friend who presumably was waiting and who surely had heard the noise of our aircraft had yet to emerge from the car. This mystery was soon resolved as I discovered a hastily scrawled note from my friend that indicated that a rather tragic accident had occurred some distance from his home and he had been obliged to render medical assistance to some neighbors who had been involved. He expressed his sincere apologies that he was unable to meet me and stated that he would join me at his home sometime during the evening. Again apologizing for the inconvenience, he explained that he had had to take with him his entire crew to assist at the scene of the tragedy but that he had left the Landrover fully equipped including a detailed map and a compass which I could use to find my way to his home. The pilot approached and asked whether everything was in order. Remembering my earlier resolve to treat such situations as part of my adventure, I quickly explained the circumstances to him. Together we verified the presence of the compass and map. After several reassurances, he politely took his leave and I more heard than saw his departure. I now turned to the task at hand. Securing a flashlight from the glovebox I examined the map. It was a very good piece of work—detailed as to topography, the location of manmade objects, . . . Having had extensive experience with traveling by map and compass, I rather looked forward to the land navigation. My usual practice under such circumstances would be to locate on the map some land feature—a ridgeline, a sheer cliff, a river—which was located near my final destination and which was distinctive enough that I could identify it from a distance. Having accomplished this I then had a great deal of freedom of choice in selecting my precise route to that natural land feature. Having arrived at this object by whatever route struck my fancy, it would be easy to move to my final destination by closer navigation. However, since I was wholly unfamiliar with the territory and darkness had fallen, this practice offered nothing of value to me. I therefore quite naturally decided to employ a second method I had some skill and experience in—that of close navigation. In this second method one need only determine the point of origin and final destination and then first on the map and subsequently on the ground, guided by the map, select a route which connects the two points. An examination of the map revealed the location of my friend's home clearly marked from which led a number of passable roads. With a sudden realization that announced itself first by a contraction of my stomach muscles as if I had been struck a severe blow, I became aware that while I had a servicable vehicle capable of covering the ground, a compass, a detailed topo map of the region, and the personal skills required, I had no idea as to my present location—nowhere on the map could I find any mark which identified the airfield—my present loca-

tion. Of course, without such information I had little hope of reaching my destination.

In developing a high quality description of the present state, one of the major traps which a manager in the midst of his fast moving high pressure day must be wary of is the assumption that he knows what is going on within his organization. Further, and even less probable, is the assumption that the understanding which the manager has of what is happening within his organization is the same understanding which the individual members of staff have arrived at. It would be reassuring to think your staff is as alert and attentive to the information flow as you are. It would be reassuring to believe the alertness that did exist would be included in that flow in an appropriate manner. However, these are usually dangerous assumptions which lead to low quality information and consequently low quality performance at best. It is even more reassuring to think that your staff is able to draw conclusions from that information flow which match your own; and it is even more dangerous.

In the authors' experience discussions of present state functioning within an organization by members of that organization tend to be extremely low quality. References are made to a series of stock vocabulary items which are the particular buzz words of business and of that organization. We have heard descriptions of present state discussions from consultants which sometimes take on the appearance of a ritual during which members of the organizational tribe seated in their appropriate places utter their appropriate lines in the appropriate order.

During a recent executive training workshop conducted by one of the authors, a participant offered the following episode which had occurred within his organization as an example of the consequences of the failure on the part of a manager to insist on a high quality description of the present state. During a meeting called by the GM to review operations, the subject of present inventory levels came up.

GM: So you think that some of the inventory levels are too high?

Staff: Yes, we are operating right at our maximum capacity as far as storage space is concerned and the cost of constructing additional storage space for . . .

GM: (interrupting) Yeah, don't even bother to consider that one. I want to know how we can move some of that stuff.

Staff: Well, you know, we could pick out some of the inventory and create a campaign to move them—maybe even with a special price.

GM: What do you propose that we push?

Staff: The easiest way would be to single out the slow moving stuff and push there.

GM: Okay, stick with the slow moving inventory then. What about the special pricing you mentioned? . . . How much of a decrease do you think necessary to move that inventory?

Staff: Well, I can't be certain, of course, but I think that if I had the authorization to reduce prices, say, up to 10% of present price, I could design a campaign which would really move things.

GM: OK, you've got it—get cracking on this one.

The manager in our workshop who had been present at this meeting then related that the sales campaign with a special pricing was organized and launched in a relatively short period of time. After it had been underway for some months, the GM discovered to his horror that "the slow moving inventory" that he had authorized a price reduction and sales campaign for in order to reduce inventory was a very high margin item which had for years sold to a fixed market at a stable rate of sales. This item had been a major positive contributing component of overall margins because of its stability and high margins. A hurried review of the special price sales campaign to date revealed to everyone's chagrin that, indeed, there had been a rise in sales but that the sales were being made to the customers in the fixed market that the company had control over anyway. The result of this maneuver was painfully predictable over the next reporting period when sales on this item dropped an amount almost equivalent to the increase in sales during the special price campaign. Simply put, the company had sold a formerly high margin item at a reduced rate to its regular customers. While the inventory levels on this "slow moving inventory" dipped during the period of the special campaign, it rose again to the original levels in the period immediately following. Thus the company ended up simply reducing its margins by the maneuver.

Our understanding is that this unprofitable situation arose primarily because of the failure of the GM and staff to demand high quality information regarding the present state of the company's operation. Specifically, there was an assumption on the part of the GM and his staff that they knew what the staff member was referring to when he used the term "slow moving inventory." While it is impossible to know at this time what specific understanding the GM had of this term, his actions strongly suggest that he was thinking of some part of the inventory other than the high margin, stabilized item that the campaign was ultimately concerned with. In other words, had the GM demanded high quality information for the low quality phrase "slow moving inventory," he would have immediately recognized that he was dealing with a high margin, stabilized, limited market item which formed part of the foundation for overall positive margins. With such information, he would have immediately directed his staff toward other items which might have more appropriately been the subject of a special sales campaign which would have allowed him to decrease inventory and hold or raise margins at the same time. His failure to demand this high quality information resulted in a serious and costly error.

It is perhaps slightly paradoxical that the set of words most frequently used to describe portions of the business process are just the set of words which when challenged for high quality information during discussions of the present state yield the highest returns. The use of these general terms day after day exercises an almost hypnotic effect whereby the hearer comes to have the illusion that he understands what the speaker is referring to. Such illusions of shared maps and understandings of the world of business are rarely useful. Even (or especially) those members of a business organization who work side by side on a day to day basis, exposed to the same flow of information, will arrive at radically different perceptions and understandings of that information. We emphasize the need for tools which allow low grade information in communication to be converted into the high quality information necessary for precise planning and execution in business. Without a thoroughly explicit and sensory grounded shared understanding of the present functioning of your business organization, the most creative and intelligent of plans and operations will be rendered ineffective. It is a distinct disadvantage if you are interested in traveling somewhere to fail to identify the place you are leaving from.

DESIRED STATE

In business, the situation in which detailed discussions of desired states most frequently occur is in the area of planning. During a planning session the identification of what the business concern will attempt to achieve for some future period of time is the primary topic. The tools of the Precision Model will therefore prove a powerful asset in such a setting. As every planner knows, the higher the quality of information used to develop and elucidate business plans, the more probable the plan will meet with success. Hence, no special comments are necessary as a planner will recognize the value of the Present State/Desired State model.

It has been the authors' experience that most of the desired state planning that goes on in business occurs covertly—when we ask the members of a meeting whether planning occurred during a meeting not called for that specific purpose their response typically is negative. The discussion of desired states is all too often confined to the mentioning of a few highly valued phrases such as "higher profit margins," "increased productivity," "customer service," "public relations," or "higher quality." We agree that these phrases point in the general direction of the most important outcomes for a business organization—the desired states that effective business people will concern themselves with. However, unless these general phrases are used as a point of departure for the creation of precision statements which will allow the business people to recognize when they have achieved the desired state, mentioning them offers little other than the comfort of a ritual. Similarly, adding numbers is only one step in the right direction. It will be easier to agree on whether a goal has been reached or not by comparison of numbers. However, this is not a sufficient condition unless stated in appropriate chunks. That is, if only a final outcome is known, no action may be taken for adjustment until the final result is already known. Action is thereby limited to trying again next time—a less than optimal response. For example, "higher profit margins" is less adequate than "return on investment is to increase to 12%". Clearer still would be, "sales are to increase 8% and costs remain the same with no additions to capital." Finally, the method to be employed to increase sales would have to be stated in behavioral terms. The use of the Present State/Desired State model with the Precision techniques will allow the development of specific indicators which will appropriately signal the information processors that the Desired State has been reached.

The failure to develop specific, appropriate descriptions of the Desired State has a number of adverse consequences. The same businessman who accepts as adequate the formulation of Desired State as "increased productivity within the next three months" would seriously consider firing a secretary who told him he had a business appointment at 3:30 Friday somewhere in Los Angeles.

A participant in one of our workshops once objected to this analogy pointing out that the secretary could easily get to information which was more refined than *somewhere in Los Angeles* but that no such information was available in the case of the Desired State. While we are not convinced that a secretary would agree that such information regarding appointments is always easily available, we gently reminded the participant who had made the comment that the entire point of the Precision Model was to elicit such high quality information within Frames such as the Desired State. A precise formulation of the Desired State allows many people doing many different tasks to move toward a commonly identified destination. The more specific the destination, the more likely they will all arrive there at the appointed time. An explicit Desired State establishes a trajectory, a sense of direction and movement, which coordinates the efforts of different parts of an organization effectively. Failure to make a Desired State explicit typically leads to a situation where people know something is expected of them—thus they must act, they must move from their present position—however, without the appropriate maps and road signs their actions are random or even at times antagonistic to one another.

A second consequence of the failure to adequately define a Desired State is best given by an example brought to the attention of one of the authors during an Executive Training Workshop. This executive had been present at a meeting where discussions of solutions to the problem of decreased profits had occupied the bulk of the time. After the presentation of a number of possible solutions, it was decided that

given the particulars of this situation, the company could best rem-
edy the profits problem by increasing sales. The sales manager was
eager to take on the task, and requested some training for a number
of his reps and a graduated incentive program for all his sales reps.
He stated that he was convinced that with this training and the
incentive program, he could increase the sales by the amount that
would return margins to the appropriate levels. Thus, the Desired
State was characterized as rising margins which would result from
increased sales. The Desired State was not defined further. Six
months later the same sales manager sat in bewilderment studying
a set of figures which indicated that sales had risen only slightly. He
protested that the figures "just didn't match what I see going on."
He said that calls per sales rep was up, complaints were down and
that the verbal reports as well as the orders which passed through
him to production had given him the distinct impression that his
special efforts in increasing sales was working well. A check of the
figures verified their accuracy. Since the figures indicated the incentive program had not been effective in increasing sales, it was
dropped. As the meeting ended, it was obvious to all that the sales
manager was confused and demoralized by the results his special
efforts had failed to produce, and worried about the effect of inform-
ing his sales reps that the incentive program was being dropped. The
sense of frustration and demoralization spread through the sales
division following the cancellation of the incentive program. Thus,
everyone concerned was surprised and puzzled when an interim (3
month) report on sales showed an amazing jump in sales in the
period immediately succeeding the cancellation of the incentive program. The executive stated that he knew the sales manager personally and thought highly of his abilities. Hence, when the interim
report was issued, he determined to sort out what had occurred. The
mystery was solved when he demanded the order dates on the figures
that accounting had used to compute the sales for the two reporting
periods in question. What he discovered was that the information
that accounting had used to determine sales increase was the number
of units shipped to customers, which was the normal practice, rather
than the number of units ordered by customers during the period in
question. Thus when the figures were re-computed using the number
of orders placed by customers, the sales manager's intuitions regarding the success of his efforts were fully supported by the new figures.
The point, of course, is that if the Desired State had been determined

with higher quality at the beginning of the program, the appropriate measure or signal of having achieved that Desired State would have been identified—in this case, since there was a sizable lag time between order and shipment, the number of orders would easily have been identified as the appropriate measure, and the resulting confusion and demoralization would have been avoided. In addition, the company would have avoided the falling margins which occurred as the result of decreased sales in the period following the cancellation of the incentive program (which showed up in the number of units shipped six months later). Such expensive mistakes can be easily avoided by the use of the Precision Model in eliciting adequately high quality information which will allow the information processor to explicate the Desired State.

CASE STUDY I

We turn now to the presentation of a case in which the Precision Model is utilized to effectively and efficiently Define the Difference. The transactions are presented first, followed by commentary.

(after greetings have been exchanged, a few minutes into the meeting between the General Manager (GM) and the Divisional Manager (DM))

DM: . . . I've got a problem here I wanted to bring up.

GM: Go right ahead, Tom (pause) . . . you have a problem with what specifically?

DM: Well, it's just that my margins have been sliding some this last reporting period, and I'm concerned.

GM: How specifically have your margins been sliding?

DM: It's the same old story—my costs are up.

GM: Which costs in particular are up, Tom?

DM: Well, frankly, the costs are up because of head office over-charge.

GM: Head office overcharges on what in particular?

DM: Well, I've looked carefully at that—it boils down to the interest figures.

GM: The interest figures on what, Tom?

DM: On some of the inventory.

GM: On what specific part of the inventory?

DM: Well, primarily on all those motors.

GM: On *all* those motors?

DM: No, not really on all the motors.

GM: Well, then, on which motors in particular?

DM: On those newer type B motors.

GM: Let me make sure I've got this now—your margins are down because your costs are up. Specifically, the head office charges for interest on your inventory of type B motors have in-creased. (pause) . . . That's the picture I've got—does that match your understanding?

DM: Yes, I think that we've tracked the problem down.

GM: Now, Tom, before we jump into figuring out what to do about this situation, let's make sure we agree about where we're going. Set a target for yourself. What evidence could you use to know that you have solved this problem.

DM: That's easy—if my margins are up.

GM: Up to what, Tom?

DM: . . . I'm not sure that I understand what you're asking.

GM: You said if your margins are up—and I'm asking up how much—what are you shooting for?

DM: Oh, all right, well . . . I thought that we did really well in the reporting period before this last one. If I could get us back to that level of margins, I'd be satisfied.

GM: And the principle difference between the performance in the reporting period before the last and the last reporting period is what, Tom?

DM: Like I said, the interest charges on inventory—everything else showed up pretty much the same.

GM: OK, Tom. Your goal would be the following—you'll get your margins back up by reducing costs—specifically by decreasing the interest charges on your inventory of type B motors.

DM: Right! That's my target.

COMMENTARY

The situation portrayed in the transcript is one of the most common that managers face in their daily schedules, and one of the most important. One of the GM's managers has stated that he has a problem and implicitly by this statement requests the GM's skill and assistance in resolving this problem. The sensitivity and efficiency with which the GM responds to this request will be a major determinant of his success as the GM. Not only is the solution to this particular problem at issue in this meeting, but also the overall margins for the company as well as the relationship between the two men—a relationship which will effect all their future negotiations.

The authors recognize that, depending on the reader's personal style and situation, some of the dialogues will seem somewhat unrealistic. We assure you that these dialogues occur frequently and, even when the context is different, the same kinds of information blocks occur—the same precise questions are needed. We also recognize that some managers would refuse to deal with the issues involved and simply turn the problem back to the subordinate. We recommend that, in determining the desired outcome of a meeting, one of the first questions to ask yourself is, "Is there a basis or explicit purpose to the meeting proposed?"

In terms of the model being presented here, the information that there is a difference between the Present State and Desired State is stated baldly by the DM in his opening remark.

"I've got a problem here I wanted to bring up." The word *problem* always identifies a Present State/Desired State difference. Thus the condition for initiating the Defining the Difference model is met— namely, a responsible party (the DM) has recognized there is a difference between the present functioning of his division and the Desired State—specifically, that present margins are lower than desirable.

The GM tracks first from the initial low quality information to an adequately precise formulation of the Present State.

> . . . your margins are down because your costs are up. Specifically, the head office charges for interest on your inventory of type B motors have increased . . .

Having arrived at an adequately precise statement for the Present State, the GM now elicits the representation of the Desired State which turns out to be:

> . . . your margins back up by reducing costs—specifically by decreasing the interest charges on your inventory of type B motors . . .

Thus, at this point he has an adequately precise picture of the state of affairs in Tom's division, and what it is that Tom wants to achieve. The difference between the two states is given by each of the paired entries which defines the two states—note that the terms "up" and "down" are relative terms and that they are relative to the two states being considered—the reference "margins down" is to be understood as the margins are down relative to the margins of some comparable period—in this case "up" and "down" when compared to the corresponding item in the other reporting period.

Present State (last reporting period)	Difference	Desired State (reporting period prior to last one)
Margins	down compared to	Margins
Costs	up compared to	Costs
interest on inventory	up compared to	interest on inventory
inventory of type B motors	up compared to	inventory of type B motors

The question of consequence at this point is—how specifically did the GM accomplish these things. In a few minutes of conversation he has completed the first component of the overall model—he has Defined the Difference adequately to move to the second stage—Pathfinding. What techniques allowed him to accomplish this efficiently? The answer lies in his ability to control the quality of the information by the use of questioning.

POINTERS

The effectiveness of the GM's questioning resides in the fact that he systematically tracks from low quality information to successively higher quality representations. He accomplishes this by questioning which explicitly leads the DM to the area of information the GM wishes more refined information on. When offered a low quality representation which would, left unchallenged, block access to the information the manager requires to understand the Present State, the manager points precisely to what he needs to know. The results are an efficient and effective elicitation of increasingly high quality information. By using questions which point to precisely the information he needs, the manager also respects the need not to know condition of high quality information processing.

Each of his questions is dictated by the form of the statement that the DM has just offered—more specifically, as the DM begins to offer information, the GM examines the information to determine whether what he is being offered is specific enough for him to understand what the DM is referring to. Consider the following exchanges:

DM	GM
. . . I've got a *problem* . . .	. . . you have a *problem* with what specifically? . . .
. . . my *costs* are up . . .	. . . which *costs* in particular are up? . . .
. . . up because of *head office overcharges* . . .	. . . *head office overcharges* on what in particular? . . .
. . . boils down to *interest figures* . . .	. . . the *interest figures* on what, Tom? . . .
. . . on some of the *inventory* . . .	. . . on what specific part of the *inventory?* . . .
. . . not really on all the *motors* . . .	. . . then, on which *motors* in particular? . . .

FIRST POINTER—*NOUN BLOCKBUSTING*

One useful way to understand these exchanges is to consider the relationship between the statements made by the DM and the Questions which are the responses the GM makes to those statements. One characteristic of this relationship is that in each of the above cases the DM offers a very general low quality statement; the GM responds by requesting a more specific or higher quality representation in the same area that was pointed to by the DM's original statement. Each of the GM's Precision maneuvers introduces a refinement to the original broad area the DM is pointing to with his words.

We can represent the situation visually as follows:

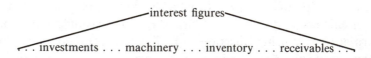

In words, then, when the DM states that it "boils down to interest figures", the GM pictures the area of the divisional operation which the DM could be referring to and realizes that he doesn't know what part of the area the DM could be talking about he intends to point to. As specified in the Precision Model, he selects the question which will elicit precisely that piece of information which will pick

out the area of the operation that the DM is referring to—the
question:

. . .interest figures on what, Tom?. . .

The DM now supplies precisely the piece of information which the
GM needs to refine his understanding of the situation in the division.
The transaction is precise and elicits only the information required
for the GM to appreciate the divisional situation—it meets both the
need to know and the need not to know conditions.

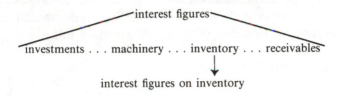

The same pattern can be found in all of the other examples presented.
For example:

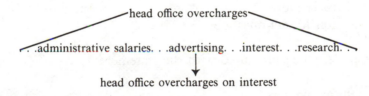

The systematic use of this pattern—called Noun Blockbusting in
the Precision Model—allows the GM to elicit from the DM exactly
the high quality information he needs to refine the low quality information initially presented. Each of the statements offered by the
DM can usefully be thought of as containing words—*problem,
costs, interest figures,* . . .—which cover such a large number of
activities that if accepted unchallenged, constitute a block to the
high quality information required. The noun Blockbuster pene-
trates the vague and low quality word block and elicits precisely
the information needed by the manager. The Blockbuster allows
the manager to track from the original extremely general and low
quality statement by the DM to a specific high quality representation of the Present State.

The GM's ability to use Blockbusters to efficiently track from a general low quality verbal statement to a high quality formulation can be usefully represented as having two steps:

1. a perceptual recognition program which allows him to know when he has been presented with a low quality statement

and

2. a response program to know which of the Precision Model questions is appropriate

Accordingly, we first present an explicit procedure which will allow the reader to likewise identify the low quality nouns to be challenged by the Blockbuster. When presented with a statement, the information processor picks out the nouns (the words which purport to refer to things). For each noun he proceeds as follows:

Noun Blockbuster

1. Write down the words which are nouns
2. Directly beneath write all the words which describe specific examples of the word placed above
3. If there is more than one word on the second line, form a Precision Model question.

For example, when presented with the statement:

My costs are up

Step one entails noticing the low quality noun *costs*

and

Step two requires writing below that word all the words which are examples of that word.

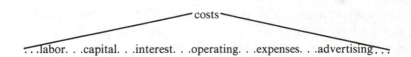

...labor. . .capital. . .interest. . .operating. . .expenses. . .advertising. . .

Step 3 involves a test condition—if there is more than one word, ask the Noun Blockbusting question. Since in the example there is more than one word, the information processor knows to proceed to the response program. With a small investment of time and practice, the manager can master this recognition program for Blockbusting.

The selection and asking of the appropriate Precision Model question—the Noun Blockbuster—is also a three step procedure:

1. Identify the noun word placed on the top line
2. Place that noun word in the language frame (the blank) "which _____ specifically?"
3. Ask the resulting question of the information source

Step 1 in carrying out this response program is complete when the manager identifies the word *costs* from the visual representation. Step 2 requires the placing of that word in the language frame "which _____ specifically?" thereby resulting in the question, "which costs specifically?". This Blockbuster question is then directed to the source of information.

An examination of the verbal behavior of the GM in the transcript will reveal that all of the question asked by the GM during the elicitation of Present State information fall into the Noun Blockbusting category presented above with two exceptions.

DM	GM
. . . just that my margins have been sliding this last . . .	. . . how specifically have your margins been sliding? . . .
. . . primarily on all those motors . . .	. . . on *all* those motors? . . .

SECOND POINTER—*ACTION BLOCKBUSTING*

The first of these examples is rather similar to the Blockbusting examples offered previously in that the phrase "margins have been sliding" points to a wide area of business activity. The number of ways in which margins could be sliding is quite large. The number of actual business actions which that phrase could accurately refer to is great. Thus the phrase is an example of low quality information much like the situation with nouns such as the ones we recently examined from the same transcript—nouns such as *costs, head office overcharges, motors, . . .* The primary difference between the previous pattern and this one is that this one involves Action Blockbusting—verbs—process words, relational words which are used to refer to complex activity. Note that the same visual representation serves well in the case of Action Blockbusting.

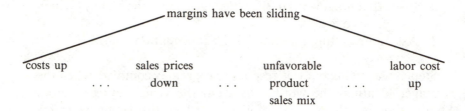

Further, as in the case of the noun pattern, the Action Blockbuster question picks out from the class of activities that the phrase could refer to exactly the activity the DM had in mind.

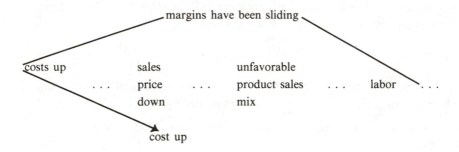

The principle difference between this pattern—Action Blockbusting—and the previous one—Noun Blockbusting—is that in this case the search for specificity is carried out in the domain of verbs. The set that the original phrase—"margins have been sliding"—could be referring to are activities or processes as opposed to things, people, objects in the world—the traditional difference between nouns and verbs.

Some additional examples will be useful to assist the reader in appreciating the pattern under discussion:

. . . improve customer relations . . .	. . . how specifically will you improve customer relations? . . .
. . . increase profits . . .	. . . how specifically will you increase profits?
. . . prepare a new sales campaign . . .	. . . how specifically will you prepare a new sales campaign?
. . . enhance the company image . . .	. . . how specifically will you enhance the company image? . . .

In each of the phrases presented the action words point to a wide range of human business activity which could be the intention of the speaker—however, the range is so wide that the information conveyed by the word representation is very low quality. Hence, the importance of having the ability to request with precision higher quality information by the pattern—Action Blockbuster. Visually, using the phrase *improve customer relations,* we have:

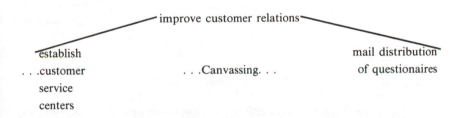

In words, the phrase *improve customer relations* includes a large number of possible activities such as those listed below it—that is, hearing or reading the phrase *improve customer relations* activates in the attentive receiver of that phrase a large number of possible activities which might lead to the outcome stated in the phrase. The quality of the information carried by the phrase can be easily upgraded by the use of the Action Blockbusting question. As in the case of Noun Blockbusting, the skill of selecting the precise question which will elicit the higher quality information is usefully presented as a two stage procedure—involving a perceptual recognition program followed by a responsive program. The perceptual recognition program consists of three steps:

Action Blockbuster

1. Write down the action words in question
2. Directly below it write down all of the action words which describe more specific actions which are examples of the action written above.
3. If there is more than one item plus accompanying words on the second line, ask the Precision Model question

Step 1 specifies the creation of an external visual representation similar to the one following:

. . . improve customer relations . . .

Step 2 involves placing below that action word all the action word phrases which are descriptions of activities which are examples of the action originally written:

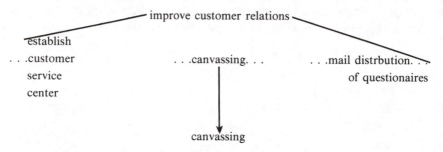

Step three is the test condition—if there is more than one item on the second line, ask the Action Blockbuster Precision Model question. The response program for selecting the appropriate Precision Model question has three steps as well:

1. find the action phrase placed on the top line
2. if the action phrase has words in front of the verb, place the phrase in the language frame "how specifically have _____?" if there are no words in front of the verb phrase place the phrase in the language frame "how specifically will you _____?"
3. ask the resulting question of the information source.

Again, applying the procedure to the example from the transcript, we have:

1. the phrase "improve customer relations"
2. place the phrase in the appropriate language frame—"improve customer relations, how, specifically?"
3. ask the question formed in step 2 of the person involved

There is one other important class of the verbs which the Action Blockbuster covers. These are sentences which superficially have the verb *to be* as their main verb. For example, sentences such as:

> . .margins *are* down . . .
> . .morale *is* not what it should be. .
> . .it *is* ridiculous to consider. .
> . .that the production quota *is* very messy. .

In these cases the verb to be is followed by single words *(down, ridiculous, messy)* or an entire phrase *(what it should be)*. Thus, the form of the sentence when recognized as having a low quality verb of this special class is:

> . . . word^1, verb to be, words^2 . . .

The question (the Blockbuster) to be used is the language frame:

> . . . how specifically, verb to be, word^1, word^2 . . .

Applying these forms to the phrases above, we have the unspecified verb questions:

. .margins are down . . .	. . . how specifically are margins down . . .
. . . morale is not what it should be . . .	. . . how specifically is morale not what it should be? . . .
. . . it is ridiculous to . . .	. . . how specifically is it ridiculous to . . . ?
. . . that the production quota is messy . . .	. . . how specifically is the production quota messy? . . .

In the world of business, numbers are used extensively for purposes of understanding certain portions of the operation. Because of the relative importance of numbers, we offer one additional question which is relevant in questioning low quality Action descriptions—the quantification question. If in the process of developing high quality information about the specifics of some activity by use of the Blockbuster question, it is useful to elicit numbers, then challenge the low quality verb with the quantification variant of the Blockbusting question:

. . . margins have been sliding . . .	. . . how much have margins been sliding? . . .
. . . program to increase profits . . .	. . . how much will the program increase profits? . . .
. . . the margins are up. .	. . . how much are the margins up? . . .

In general, it is an effective strategy to penetrate the verb rather closely using the regular Action Blockbuster question prior to resorting to the quantification variant of the Action Blockbuster question. The application of the two forms of the Blockbuster question—the regular followed by the quantification question—is typically optimal as the regular form introduces refinements and distinctions within the general area of activities covered by the low quality Action phrases first offered. Once the refinements and distinction required for an adequately precise representation of the area of activity under question have been elicited, the quantification variant of the Blockbuster question can be usefully applied.

THIRD POINTER—*UNIVERSAL BLOCKBUSTER*

The second of the exception examples involves the use of universal quantifiers.

DM	GM
. . . primarily on all those motors . . .	. . . on *all* those motors? . . .

Once again the visual representation we have been utilizing for the other Blockbusting patterns is effective in this case.

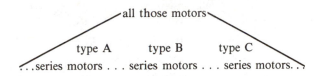

The phrase *all those motors* when uttered by the DM elicits two pieces of information in the understanding of the GM—first, it identifies a set of objects in the world—*the motors*—and secondly, it quantifies the class—the word *all.* Consider the verbal context in which the phrase *all those motors* occurs. The GM and the DM are tracking down the chain of events which has resulted in an unacceptable Present State (margins sliding). Collapsing several exchanges just prior to the use of the phrase in question, we have:

interest figures on <u>some of the inventory</u>

The GM, recognizing that the underlined phrase is low quality, requests more specificity and the following exchange occurs:

GM: on what specific part of the inventory?

DM: well, primarily on all of those motors

Adding this information to that already extracted from the transcript, we have:

interest figures on the inventory of all those motors

Thus, in this verbal context the phrase *all those motors* makes the claim that the class of motors—that is, *all* of the motors—is the culprit with respect to interest charges.

The GM, sensitive to the potential blocks to refined high quality information in the form of universal quantifiers, challenges the language representation offered by the DM. The DM's response confirms what might well be suspected whenever universal quantifi-

ers are encountered during the elicitation of high quality information
—namely, that the speaker is being less than precise in his thinking,
and that a more refined representation is available upon challenge.

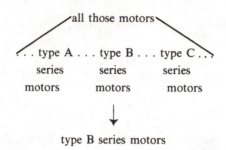

Here, as in the two Blockbusting patterns already presented, the skill
displayed by the GM in challenging the verbal representation is a two
part procedure:

Universal Blockbusting

1. a perceptual recognition program—in this case, the Precision
   Modeler hears the universal quantifier, recognizing it from the
   short list of universal quantifiers in English

all	none
every	never
each	no one
always	nothing
any	nobody

2. a response program which challenges the representation—in
   this case by echoing the phrase with stress on the universal
   quantifier and a rising (question) intonation at the end of the
   phrase

   . . . on *all* those motors? . . .

There is another common form which the universal quantifier
takes in English which is not included on the list just offered. Consider the following phrases:

. . . the maintenance on *the motors* on line #3 is high . . .

. . . talked to *the workers* in plant 5 . . .

. .contact *the customers* who have orders overdue to . . .

The reader may notice that the portion of the phrases in italics are understood as blocks to more refined information—that is, as if they had an explicit universal quantifier—that is, there is an equivalence relationship:

. . . on the motors on . . .	. . . on all of the motors on . . .
. . . to the workers in . . .	. . . to all of the workers in . . .
. . . contact the customers . . .	. . . contact all of the customers . . .

Generic names (motors, workers, . . .) or the names of whole classes or categories usually imply a universal quantifier. The reader therefore might consider learning to recognize such examples of covert universal quantifiers. The Precision Model question simply requires the insertion of the overt quantifier prior to the use of the echo. If the reader chooses not to learn this skill, small loss is sustained since any generic words which contain an implicit universal quantifier will fall under the category of the Precision Model Noun Blockbusting question:

. . . on the motors on . . .	. . . on which of the motors on . . . ?

The reader interested in mastering Universal Blockbusting questions may choose either the auditory based test just presented— recognizing the universal quantifier when he or she hears it as belonging to the list presented, or, if preferred, may choose the visually based test identical to the ones offered for the previous two Blockbusting patterns involving the display of the phrase with the noun and a second line of more specific nouns which are possible examples of the original noun listed above them. The response program would be identical to the one already stated—echo the original phrase with stress on the universal quantifier and a rising (question) intonation at the end of the phrase.

The overall movement of the information elicitation regarding the Present State as the GM uses Blockbusting patterns to track from a low quality representation to an adequately precise high quality representation can be represented visually as follows:

Tracking to high quality information—Present State

problem

. . . labor . . . machinery . . . personnel . . . production . . .

margins sliding

. . . sale price down . . . material cost up . . . production down . . .

costs up

. . . labor . . . capital . . . interest . . . advertising . . .

. . . advertising . . . research . . . interest . . .

head office overcharges

. . . advertising . . . research . . . interest . . .

interest

. . . investments . . . machinery . . . receivables . . .

inventory

. . . power units . . . motors . . . kits . . .

motors

. . type A . . . type B . . .

type A

Thus, as the visual representation makes clear the Precision Model Blockbusting questions move the discussion from low quality information to an adequately precise high quality representation of the Present State with effectiveness and economy of effort.

FRAMES

A review of the transcript shows that at the point where the GM has used the set of Precision Model pointers he has succeeded in eliciting an adequately precise representation of the Present State—that is, he understands what the current situation is in the division with respect to margins. The GM now uses one of the Frames provided by the Precision Model to verify a shared map or understanding and to establish a context for the next step in the discussion—specifically, he backtracks:

BACKTRACK FRAME

GM: Let me make sure I've got this now—your margins are down because your costs are up. Specifically, the head office charges for interest on your inventory of type B motors have increased.

Having satisfied himself that he has an adequate understanding of the Present State, the GM verbally walks back through the track that he established through his Precision questioning of the DM. This framing has two positive consequences—first, it states in a concise verbal format the track which the two men have just established. This orients the information processors specifically to the Present State description. Secondly, having summarized the track they have pursued, the GM pauses and insures that the DM agrees—that no important components of the discussion have been lost; no essential pieces of information have been dropped. The agreement he secures from the DM insures that they are operating together in a smooth and coordinated manner in the exchange.

GM: . .That's the picture I've got—does that match your understanding?

DM: Yes, I think that we've tracked the problem down.

The contextualizing pattern that the GM uses is referred to as the *Backtrack Frame:*

> The Backtrack Frame is appropriate when either the manager has reached what he or she considers an adequately precise understanding of some segment of the transaction or when a great deal of information has been elicited and in the opinion of the manager, there is danger of the participants losing track of the trajectory they are working on or the outcome they are working toward. The use of the Backtrack Frame is also indicated when new members join the group or meeting after some information has been elicited which they need to carry out their responsibilities. The Backtrack Frame is simply a verbal recapitulation of the information elicited in the immediately preceeding portion of the discussion (since the last Backtrack Frame). The purpose of the Backtrack Frame is to refresh the participants' memory or to establish in the new member's understanding the track the discussion has taken up to that point and to secure their agreement as to what the important information thus far brought to light is.

OUTCOME FRAME

Having insured that the DM is also satisfied with the description of the Present State, the GM presents the next contextualizing Frame —specifically, he identifies the next step to be taken to arrive at a precise formulation which will complete the first stage of the segment Defining the Difference:

GM: Now, Tom, before we jump into figuring out what to do about this situation, let's make sure we agree about where we're going. Set a target for yourself.

Trained in the Precision Model, the GM knows precisely where in the process he is—he has succeeded in eliciting adequately precise information regarding the Present State. This leaves only the development of an adequately precise statement of the Desired State to complete Defining the Difference. From the transcript, it is also obvious that he knows about the tendency many managers have to jump into the development of solutions without a firm grasp on the Desired State that they are attempting to achieve. The GM forestalls this possibility explicitly:

> GM: Now, Tom, before we jump into figuring out what to do about this situation . . .

The GM then identifies the outcome he wishes to pursue as the next step:

> GM: . . . make sure we agree about where we are going. Set a target for yourself.

The GM here is using the Frame known in the Precision Model as the *Outcome Frame:*

> The Outcome Frame is appropriate when either beginning the elicitation of high quality information which is designed to lead to some specified outcome or when, during some segment of developing high quality information leading to some specified outcome, the information processor determines that the participants have lost their direction. The Outcome Frame is simply a statement of what the point of the present step in the procedure or discussion is—a verbal reminder to the participants to orient themselves toward reaching the outcome established as the point of the present discussion. The purpose of the Outcome Frame is to orient or re-orient the participants of the discussion to reach the outcome and to specify explicitly what information is relevant to the present discussion in order to complete the next step of the process.

EVIDENCE QUESTION

The Outcome Frame is one of the most powerful organizing devices available to a skilled manager to enable him or her to demand and get in a principled way contextualized to the point information. The gain in efficiency through the use of this Frame is tremendous. One of the most frequent uses of the Outcome Frame is to remind participants of a group to orient specifically to the Desired State they are attempting to achieve. One specific way of accomplishing this is a question associated with the Outcome Frame called the *Evidence Question*—the exchange in the transcript:

> GM: . . . set a target for yourself. What evidence could you use to know that you've solved the problem?

The GM's first statement—*set a target for yourself*—is an example of the Outcome Frame. It is a specific instruction to the DM to orient to the next step of the process which is the development of high quality information defining the characteristics of the overall desired state. The second utterance—*what evidence could you . . .*—is an example of the Evidence Question so often used in conjunction with Outcome Frame. It requests of the information source that he or she make a mental leap to the state which is the target for their activity and describe the characteristics of that desired state—the question: . . . *what evidence could you . . .*—forces that leap and allows the information source to decide how they would know when they had solved the problem—high quality information which defines the characteristics of the desired state. The specific form of the Evidence Question is variable—any verbalization which elicits a description of the characteristics of the outcome state is adequate—we offer several variants:

> . . . what evidence could you use to know that . . .
> . . . how would you know that you had succeeded in . . .
> . . . what specifically would you see and hear that would let you know that . . .
> . . . what would convince you that you had arrived at a solution to . . .

We invite the reader to develop his or her own variant of this Evidence Question—some variant which is consistent with the style of their own verbal communication.

THE RELEVANCY CHALLENGE

There is a second maneuver associated with the Outcome Frame. This is called the Relevancy Challenge. All too often in the authors' experience, enormous amounts of time, energy and, therefore, money are expended in interminable meetings in which the discussion drifts from point to point with little or no direction, and with even less in the way of high quality results.

The Outcome Frame represents a giant step in the direction of creating a movement, a trajectory toward an explicitly identified goal or target state. The question remains, however, of how specifically to deal effectively with comments, questions and other contributions by participants, after the Outcome Frame has been established, which are off the verbal point—verbal offerings which have nothing to do with the point under discussion. The issue is an extremely important one as it has been the authors' observation that in most cases it is precisely these off the verbal point, out of context contributions which are the starting point for extended low quality and disconnected discussions of the type to be avoided. One off the point, out of context remark left unchallenged is usually a signal which unleashes a veritable avalanche of free associations—a technique more appropriate for a psychiatrist's couch than for a board room meeting. Historically, the movement seems to be been away from efficiency in terms of meetings. One of the contributing factors to this loss of efficiency is the incorporation in recent years of a number of "psychologically oriented" theories about how meetings "should" be run. As we stated in the introduction, we believe that it is unwise and, more specifically, unprofitable to mix information regarding the relationships of the individuals who make up the business organization and information regarding the actual conduct of the business. Both of these classes of information are valid concerns of managers in the world of business. In any case, as we indicated earlier, we suspect from our observations of and later discussions with managers running or, in many cases, not running meetings that the recent emphasis on these "psychologically oriented" theories has had the effect of inhibiting these men and women from exercising the guidance and control needed to elicit high quality information in an efficient manner. They fear leaving someone out or hurting the feelings of some of the participants or failing to create an environment where the creative resources of the personnel emerge. The Outcome Frame removes the question of relevancy in a meeting from the realm of interpersonal relationships and creates an explicit test thereby making it solely an informational issue. It offers the information processor in charge an outside standard which can be used in a principled way to make the elicitation of information effective and efficient and which simultaneously respects the integrity of the participants. The specific way in which the person in charge may enforce the Outcome Frame is quite simple. When managers detect a remark, comment, question, statement which they do not recognize as being relevant to the established Outcome Frame, they immediately and courteously enter the discussion at that point and make the Relevancy Challenge —that is, they request that the contributor who made the remark, question, . . . connect that offering with the outcome the group is working towards. Verbalizations such as the following are examples of how the *Relevancy Challenge* might be presented:

. . . would you please connect that question with the outcome we're presently working on? . . .

. . . I don't understand the relevance of that remark with respect to what we're doing here right now—please explain . . .

. . . your last statement throws me—how is that pertinent to what this part of the meeting is about?

Most frequently, it is unnecessary to ask the contributor for a justification—it is usually sufficient for the manager to state that he does not believe that the offering is relevant to the outcome being worked on. If the contributor still insists on making the point, the manager would use the full Relevancy Challenge (the questions, for example, listed above). If after the Relevancy Challenge is made, the contributor can explain the relevancy of the contribution, then the manager welcomes the contribution and the discussion continues. If the contributor cannot demonstrate the relevancy of the contribution, then the discussion returns to the point just prior to that contribution. The point here is that the issue is decided entirely independent of personalities or of interpersonal issues—rather it is decided with respect to an agreed upon Outcome Frame, an outside standard which all participants have equal access to.

Many of the out of context remarks and questions which the Relevancy Challenge takes care of are interesting contributions which properly belong in the discussion of some related outcome— the manager may choose to lighten the challenge by instructing the contributor to save that contribution until some later point where it will be both relevant and welcome. In organizations where the CEO or GM has been trained in the use of the Precision Model Outcome Frame and the Relevancy Challenge, the efficiency of meetings is upgraded many times over previous standard, and the participants of such meetings begin to look forward to meetings as they become efficient, have direction and lead to high quality outcomes. Thus, the meetings become an occasion for them to actually get important aspects of the overall business activity accomplished. The portions of transcript which occur in following segments contain a series of examples of the potential uses of the Relevancy Challenge in conjunction with established Outcome Frames—we recommend them to the reader's careful study.

To the instruction to select a target, the DM responds by selecting an historically defined standard of performance as the target or Desired State. The GM here exercises some discretion—he accepts a previously occurring state as an adequate target without insisting either on a specific exploration of that historical state or without insisting on the DM considering any additional alternatives—both also effective maneuvers at that point in the exchange.

Since the GM has accepted the historically defined state as a target state, and the DM has expressed his satisfaction with this choice, he may move directly to the difference between the two states with the question:

GM: and the principle difference between the performance in the reporting period before the last (now identified also as the target state) and the last reporting period is what, Tom?

This maneuver—called the *Difference Question*—is appropriate whenever information regarding both a Present State and a Desired State has been elicited. At that point the manager may ask directly for the difference. This will be treated more fully following the second case study.

The segment Defining the Difference now terminates effectively with a Backtrack Frame by the GM. This particular backtrack which is the completion of the first segment, the Desired State of Defining the Difference, is the initiation point—the Present State—of the second segment—Finding Pathways.

VARIANTS ON CASE STUDY I

VARIANT I

In the next few pages we present for the purposes of comparison several short transcripts. These transcripts are different from the one we have just analyzed in that the Precision Model is available to neither of the participants in the exchange. The same opening is used and the content—that portion of it which the two men manage to get to—is the same. The characters in the scenario are the same as in the last transcript. While the transcript which you are about to read never actually occurred, we are convinced that the experienced information processor reading the exchange will all too readily recognize the various elements in the communication between the two men. It may remind you of some manager you have been acquainted with: Or possibly, even yourself on one of your "off" days. One of the advantages of a perfectly explicit model such as the Precision Model is that you need never have another "off" day.

. . . (after small talk or middle of the meeting) . . .

DM: I've got a problem here I wanted to bring up

GM: Go right ahead, Tom . . . What's the problem?

DM: Well, it's my margins—they've slid some this last reporting period.

GM: Yeah, I know, and you're right. When your margins slide, you've got a problem.

DM: Yeah, well, I hope that you keep in mind that this is the first reporting period since I've taken over as division manager that my division profit margins have dropped.

GM: I'm well aware of that, Tom. And as we both know, your margins are the bottom line. They are your primary responsibility as division manager. Now what's the problem?

DM: Well, I've looked carefully at the situation and I really believe that the problem is head office overcharges.

GM: What the hell is that supposed to mean—*over*charges, head office *over*charges? Are you trying to tell me that we charge your division higher prices for advertising or material or something? Look, I can show the figures for the charges against the other divisions and you can compare them with the charges against your division and you'll see that we play no favorites up here.

DM: Wait, George, I didn't mean that you play favorites or that you charge my division more than other divisions.

GM: Well, if you believe that we're charging your division the same as the others then what's this talk about head office overcharges? It seems to me that you'd better look a little closer at your own operation.

DM: OK, I understand. I'll take a closer look. Maybe I can tighten up production a bit . . . and have a talk with my sales manager.

GM: That's right! Get those sales reps of yours moving, Tom. If they know you're watching and interested in their performance they'll pick it up some. What's your sales manager's name, Tom? I remember him as being really good.

DM: Larry Gindaster, and he is really good, a real hustler.

GM: Yes, old Larry. By the way, you're really fortunate to have old Larry. In fact, I recommend strongly that you call Larry in and explain the situation to him—you know, build a fire under him. Once he understands the situation your division is in, he'll get his people out there—I remember Larry as being a real team man. You get my meaning, Tom?

DM: I think so, George. I'll get together with Larry this coming week.

GM: The sooner the better, Tom. You have got to get your margins up—that's your job. I'll be watching those figures . . . and, Tom, if you need any more help on this, remember, my office door is open to you as division manager any time you want to use it.

DM: Ahh, sure, George, I've got the picture.

COMMENTARY

The most telling comment to be made with respect to the transcript is that the meeting between the two men terminated without the "problem" the DM initiated the conversation with ever being defined. It is highly unlikely that any effective action will result from this exchange on the part of either man. In fact, the odds are high that a similar meeting will occur between these two men with precisely the same "problem" in exactly six months. The communication patterns between the two men can only be judged by their ultimate effectiveness relative to the survival and growth of the organization. Therefore, necessarily, there can be no "right" way to approach the problem the DM has. Business is *the* human outcome oriented activity—therefore, any patterns which consistently result in the success states as defined by the business community are to be valued. It is the thesis of this book and the point of the Precision Model presented here that there is a strong positive relationship between successful control of the quality of the information used in business transactions and the success of those transactions—the more appropriate the quality of the information which forms the basis of action in business the more probable the success of those actions. The value of the Precision Model rests directly on the fact that it is a completely explicit model—therefore guaranteed learnable—which allows the user to develop with precision the quality of information required for the success of the specific transaction he is presently confronted with. With this understanding we turn to a discussion of specifics of how this transcript differs from the previous one.

The reader will note that the quality of information presented in the transcript is uniformly low. For example, at no point is the general block or area referred to by the phrase *head office overcharges* penetrated. The original "problem" is refined minimally—

the sole gain in informational quality as the result of the various exchanges is the movement from the general area referred to as "problem" to the general area referred to as "head office charges." The information regarding the Present State is inadequate to define the difference between the present state and some entirely implicit desired state. The mechanics of this failure to elicit adequately high quality information are instructive. For example, consider the following exchange:

DM	GM
. . . believe that the problem is head office overcharges. .	. . . what the hell is that supposed to mean—*over*charges, head office *over*charges? Are you trying to tell me that . . .

Whatever else one might legitimately say regarding this exchange, it is obvious that the DM has made a poor choice of words as far as the GM is concerned. Contrast this exchange with the one which occurred in the original transcript at roughly the same point:

DM	GM
. .up because of head office overcharges . . .	. . . head office overcharges on what in particular? . . .

The GM's response in this case is designed to elicit a higher grade of information—he is using the Precision Model to come to an understanding of the divisional situation. The GM's response in the abortive transcript has nothing to do with information. If anything, a more appropriate characterization would be that the GM is behaving as if he had to justify head office practices. Most relevantly, in any case, the GM's response blocks any further exploration of the general area referred to by the phrase *head office overcharges*— thereby preventing an upgrading of the information initially offered. In the context of the DM, the GM's response itself would be challenged, and thereby removed, by a Relevancy Challenge as inappropriate to the outcome of eliciting high quality information defining the Present State.

The second feature of this abortive transcript which distinguishes it from the original is the movement both men made to the segment of the overall model phase we refer to as Pathfinding prior to having any clear notion of the Present State. The leap to solution without any high quality information regarding the present state typically occurs in undisciplined information processors or those who have no systematic way of approaching information handling. The leap in this case seems to be spurred by a remark by GM:

GM	DM
. .better look a little closer at your own operation . . .	. . . I'll take a closer look. Maybe I can tighten production a bit, . . . and have a talk with my sales manager . . .

It is unlikely that the stock maneuvers proposed by the DM in response to the GM's comment to "look . . . closer at your own operation" will have much effect as they at best would be applied without any adequate representation of the present situation and how specifically it is different from some more desirable state.

Again, it is worth mentioning in passing that the authors have no disagreement with the informational content of the remark by the GM. The difficulty arises as the result of the timing of the remark (thus inappropriate in the context of attempting to reach an understanding of the Present State—the Relevancy Challenge).

VARIANT II

We shall assume for the purposes of continuing that the DM survives the outburst by the GM to his use of the term *head office overcharges* and we pick up the exchange just at the GM has finished justifying his head office charges and is instructing the DM to look to his own operation.

GM: . . . seems to me that you'd better look a little closer at your own operation.

DM: Yes sir, I understand. As a matter of fact, I spent some serious time studying the difference between my division's performance last reporting period and the performance during the period prior to that one. One of the big things that's killing us with respect to the margins is the amount of interest we've been allocated this last period.

GM: Is that a fact? What do you intend to do about bringing that figure down?

DM: Well, a minute ago when I brought up the issue about head office charges, I had the thought that perhaps you and I could look more closely at the figures. I would like to try to convince you that the interest figures are too high and perhaps you could take the question up with . . .

GM: (interrupting) Tom, I'll be blunt with you about this interest question. The head office has almost no freedom of action in this case. The interest charges imposed on you are determined by the going interest rates we are presented with. Remember you and I agreed last year that even though the interest was going to hurt for a while, those new machines would cover the difference because of their higher production capacity, and lower maintenance. Are you using those newer machines at capacity, Tom? That might be where your real problem lies.

DM: Huh, Oh no, no, sorry, George, I wasn't talking about the interest charges on the new machines. The radically increased charges are the interest charges on the inventory, not on the new model machines—they're paying for themselves and then some.

GM: Interest allocated to your inventory, oh, I understand.

DM: Yeah, that's what's really killing us. Would you like to take a look at some of those figures with me? I can show you exactly where the differences are.

GM: Sure, Tom I'm willing to look at your figures but I'll tell you right now that the practice of charging interest to your division on inventory was established a long time ago and with good reasons. It's really basic economics, Tom. The inventories your division carries, over the authorized levels of course, represents a capital investment, and if it's sitting in the warehouse doing nothing, we're losing money—so you get the interest charges. Do you follow me, Tom?

DM: Yes, but I believe that we ought to . . .

GM: Sorry, but let me finish. In addition to the question of capital, if we didn't have interest as a way of controlling the level of inventory, who knows what would happen in the divisions? We could have huge excesses, stockpiling is not a profitable way for us to conduct our business. Surely, you can see my point?

DM: OK, I understand what you are saying but I still feel that the key to solving this is the high interest charges on the inventory and I think . . .

GM: Let me interrupt with one other fact that's important for you to understand clearly. We're wasting our time sitting here talking about the issue of interest charges on inventory. That is company policy—has been since before I took over as GM. We'd just be spinning our wheels to go over this ground again.

DM: Well, all right but I still feel like we're not getting a fair shake on the interest on inventory thing here.

GM: Well, I really don't see any point in continuing this discussion—company policy is company policy. (pause) . . . Look, Tom, I can appreciate your position. You've got to get your margins back up and so you look around for the easiest and quickest way to accomplish that and that's right—that's what you're supposed to do as DM. And the thing that you notice is that your head office interest charges are higher than last time. So you come to me for help. Let me tell you something. A lot of times the thing that looks like the easiest and most immediate solution from the divisional point of view, turns out to be impossible if you look at it from the company head office point of view. So it's understandable that you would seize on inventory interest charges by the head office as the solution. But it's not, Tom. Company policy is company policy. Look inside your own operation more thoroughly and I have confidence that you'll find a good solution. OK?

DM: All right, George, it'll be rough but I'll get right on it.

COMMENTARY

Again, the exchange between the two men must ultimately be judged on the basis of the outcome that exchange achieves. And, again, while the quality of information finally elicited in this transcript is higher than in the first variant, it is not adequately precise to allow the men to define the difference between the present operating conditions in the division and some as yet unidentified desired state—thus, failing to provide an adequate basis for effective action. The simple fact is, that since the "problem" is never adequately defined, no solutions will later be developed and the meeting aborts without the resources of either of the two skilled men having been applied to the "problem." It is ironical that at one point in the transcript the DM states:

DM: OK, I understand what you are saying but I still feel that the key to solving this is the high interest charges . . .

Unfortunately, without the Precision Model questioning, the remark is never pursued. Once again, it is useful to remind the reader that the authors are not arguing with most of the statements and explanations offered by the GM. There can be little quarrel with statements such as:

GM: . . . huge excesses, stock piling is not a profitable way for us to conduct our business . . .

However, we simply point out that this explanatory behavior on the part of the GM does not in fact lead to a high quality definition of the *problem* in the division. In Precision Model terms, the GM has failed to establish an Outcome Frame which would focus and direct the skills of the two toward the issue at hand—developing high quality information adequate to an understanding of the present problem. Since no contextual frame has been explicitly established, there is no principled way for the participants to determine whether any particular statement is appropriate in the context—no systematic way of directing the exchange toward a successful outcome by the use of the Relevancy Challenge.

As in the previous variant, the absence of Precision Model Blockbusting questioning leaves blocked and unexplored areas which are referred to but never penetrated. At four separate points in the exchange, the GM overtly refuses to consider further the area of interest allocated to inventory. Finally, he terminates further attempts at discussion by the DM by stating:

> GM: We're wasting our time . . . just be spinning our wheels to go over this ground again . . . really don't see any point in continuing this discussion . . .

After this series the DM reluctantly gives up his attempts to discuss the inventory interest issue; unfortunately without ever having penetrated the ground that the GM characterized them as just spinning their wheels over. The communications maneuver used by the GM to align himself with the DM after the topic of inventory interest charges is finally dropped may have been effective in restoring some of the rapport between the two men:

> GM: . . . Look, Tom, I can appreciate your position. You've got to get your margins back up and so you look around for the easiest and quickest way to accomplish that and that's right —that's what you're supposed to do as DM . . .

Our point is that such a maneuver would have been entirely unnecessary had the GM used Precision Model questioning to elicit the high quality information potential available from the DM. Further, independent of the issue of rapport, the difference is never defined— the specific business outcome is never achieved.

There is one semi-amusing exchange which illustrates a common result of the failure to refine information systematically:

GM: . . . Remember you and I agreed last year that even though the interest was going to hurt for a while, those new machines would cover the difference because of their higher production capacity and lower maintenance. Are you using those new machines at capacity, Tom? That might be where your real problem lies.

DM: Huh, oh no, no, sorry, George, I wasn't talking about the interest charges on the new machines. The radically increased charges are the interest charges on the inventory, not on the new model machines—they're paying for themselves and then some.

What has occurred here is that when the DM first mentions interest figures, the GM jumps to the conclusion that the DM is talking about interest figures on some new machinery. Visually, this jump can be represented as:

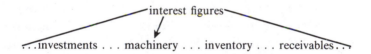

In words, the GM understands the phrase *interest figures* as used by the DM to refer more specifically to *interest figures on machinery*. This conclusion is wholly unwarranted and in this particular case, inaccurate. Again, we have no quarrel with such leaps as long as the information processor recognizes that it introduces the possibility of error. The Precision Model Blockbusting questions offers an alternative to such guessing.

CASE STUDY II

We present now a second transcript—in this one the responsible agent who first notices a Present State situation which is less than optimal is the Sales Manager (SM), Richard. He calls and informs the GM that his figures show that they are losing about 10 sales a month. After asking the SM a few preliminary questions, the GM decides to call a meeting—present at this meeting is the SM, the Production Manager (PM), Joe, the Controller (C), and the GM himself.

Having been exposed to some of the Precision Model techniques the reader is better able to appreciate the effectiveness and economy of movement with which the GM sets frames to establish a trajectory for the meeting and the precision with which he rapidly elicits high quality information which allows the group to efficiently Define the Difference between the Present State and a Desired State.

In the transcript the reader will notice the use of the Outcome Frame occurs much more frequently than it did in Case Study I. This is a natural outcome of the fact that the meeting is a multi-person meeting—that is, the GM has the task of eliciting information from three different information sources. As anyone who has ever gone through the experience of learning how to juggle can attest, there is a profound difference in the skill required to juggle with two objects and the skill required to juggle with three or more objects. Each of the men that the GM has called to the meeting has represented within his own understanding high quality information which will be of great assistance in developing a shared map or representation of the difference between the present situation within the organization and what they desired to achieve. The GM has the task as the information processor to elicit high quality information relevant to the issue under scrutiny in an order which will allow the development of that shared map or understanding. In a situation where an information processor has to construct such a map from multiple sources of information, he will make extensive use of Frames to direct the attention of the participants to precisely the class of high quality information needed to complete the portion of the shared map he is working on. Without such Frames and the sense of direction they explicitly provide, there is the danger that the multi-person meeting will deteriorate into a series of disconnected monologues by the participants in which they focus their attention on supplying their private understandings of the problem, their favorite solutions or pointing to some other portion of the operation as the source of the problem. In addition to being lengthy, tedious and demoralizing, such meetings rarely produce enough high quality information to form a basis for the development of an intelligent and effective plan of action. Thus the emphasis on Frames to create a context for directed discussion.

GM: Richard has complained that he's losing orders and even customers because we aren't getting our orders shipped on time. His salesmen are getting a lot of complaints, too. We're here to determine the cause of the problem and determine what we might do about it. Right now I'd like to stick to finding out precisely what our present situation is and what we want it to be. Richard, what is the problem, specifically?

R: Shipments are going out of here three weeks late.

GM: All shipments?

R: All the special orders. Actually some are taking even longer. Some of our regular orders are going out late, too.

GM: Which orders are you losing?

R: We lose about 10 units a month of the special units that go out more than 2 weeks late.

GM: Late? Late compared to what?

R: We quote one month for delivery, which we used to meet, and it's taking three weeks longer than that. Our competitors deliver three weeks from the order date!

GM: What's the difference between the time when we used to meet our schedule and our present situation that might account for the the difference in shipping?

R: Well, we produced and shipped 60 special units a month last year and we're selling 70 special units a month this year.

GM: Did we produce 60 special units a month *every* month?

R: I don't know.

The GM initiates the meeting by offering the participants the information that he already has—*losing orders and even customers . . . getting complaints . . . because we aren't getting our orders shipped on time.* He then specifies the first frame—*. . . right now . . . stick to finding out precisely what our present situation is and what we want it to be.* This Frame—The Outcome Frame—specifies the target for the first step of the meeting. This assists the individual participants in knowing what pieces of information are appropriate to the context they are operating in and provides a trajectory for the group as a unit. The reader will recognize that the verbal statement by the GM . . . finding out precisely what our present situation is and what we want it to be . . .—is the Present State/Desired State for the first segment of the model Defining the Difference. The GM then turns to the source of information—the SM—who first brought the issue to his attention and instructs him to begin. The next few exchanges are examples of the Precision Model Blockbusting questioning already introduced. Using the visual representations we developed previously:

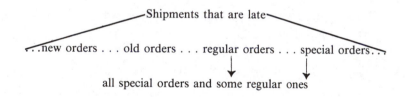

FOURTH POINTER—*THE COMPARATOR*

The GM, having challenged the general term *shipments* learns that the shipments in question are *all special orders and some regular ones.* Now, making use of the fact that the orders that he is primarily interested in are the ones that the SM has reported they are losing, he pointed to a further refinement of the last answer:

> . . . all special orders and some regular ones . . .

by asking which of the late orders (the answer to the last question) are the ones which they are losing.

. .all special orders and some regular ones . . .

Pointer—Noun Blockbuster (which orders . . .?)

. . . special units that go out more than 2 weeks late . . .

The GM now employs a Precision Model question called the *Comparator*. (We thank Chris Dunkley for this term.) Consider the exchange:

SM	GM
. .that go out more than 2 weeks late. .	. . . late? late compared to what?

The answer he receives is finally our *schedule* (the one promised to the customers) and the performance of our *competitors*.

   Here are some additional examples to allow the reader to get a feel for the pattern:

. . . that our margins are up . . .	. .up compared with what? . .
. . . labor force is more stabilized . . .	. . . more stabilized than what? . . .
. . . productivity is down three units . . .	. . . down three units compared with what? . . .
. . . because the price of raw materials is 30% higher . . .	. . . 30% higher than what? . . .

In each of the cases some information is being offered which involves a change—this can be determined by a sensitivity to the relational words used—*up . . . more* as in *more stabilized . . . down* as in *down three units . . . higher* as in *30% higher*. These words imply a comparison with some other situation without stating explicitly what the other situation is. A full appreciation of the information being offered requires that the hearer/reader of such statements be provided with the situation that the statement is implicitly being compared to. To upgrade the information, the situation being used as the basis for the comparison must be made explicit. As in the earlier patterns, we offer this Precision Model question in two parts—the perceptual recognition program and a following response program.

The Comparator

1.   Examine the statement, writing down any relational words contained therein.
2.   For each relational word written down, write to the left and right of the relational word the two situations being compared or related.
3.   If there is no word written on one side of the relational word, ask the Precision Model question.

The easiest way to begin to develop your sensitivity to the presence of relational words is to familiarize yourself with the special language markers used in English to identify these covert comparisons and to acquaint yourself with the list of relational words we have collected which are some of the most common encountered in business communication. There are two special language markers used in English to identify the comparative form:

the ending *er* as in:
  high*er*
  fast*er*
  clean*er*

the word *more/less* as in:
more productive/*less* demand
more competitive/*less* responsible
more thorough/*less* material

Any statement container either of these language markers is subject to the Precision Model question for the comparator. We offer in addition a short list of some of the more common relational words encountered in business communications:

any percentage or ratio figure as in *30%* or
  a *four fold increase* or
  2½ times the previous rate
up as in *profits up*
down as in *expenses down*
over as in *we're over on production*

under as in *we're under on sales*
slow as in *a slow day*
fast as in *a fast sale*
late as in *a late shipment*
early as in *an early estimate*
ahead as in *we're ahead on sales*
behind as in *we're behind on line #3*

The response program for the Comparator Pointer is quite simple:

1. Identify the relational word originally written down
2. Place the relational word in the frame "_____ compared with what?" unless the relational word is *more* or *less,* in which case place the term *more* or *less* plus the word which follows that word in the original statement in the frame "_____ compared with what?"
3. Direct this question to the information source.

For example, when presented with the phrase *margins are up,* the procedure yields the Precision Model question *up compared with what?*

THE DIFFERENCE PROCEDURE

Most commonly the manager will discover the comparative occurring when there is an implicit reference being made by the speaker/-writer to some standard of performance or Desired State, typically one which the organization has achieved in the past. The danger of inefficient communication increases greatly when implicit reference to comparable situations is made without the implicit reference being challenged and refined into explicit, high quality information concerning that situation. Through the previous blockbusting, the GM has available the following information:

1. he knows the organization is losing orders
2. the orders being lost are the special orders which are delayed more the two weeks over schedule
3. there was a period when the shipping was on schedule

This last information fits nicely into the Present State/Desired State frame that he established at the outset of the meeting.

Present State	Desired State
shipping 2 weeks behind schedule	shipping on schedule

The GM's next move is a Precision Model procedure which we have only mentioned but not yet presented fully—one which many of the participants in our Executive Workshops intuitively recognize as particularly appropriate for this situation.

We call this *the Difference Procedure.*

> GM: What is the difference between the time when we used to meet our schedule and our situation now that might account for the difference in shipping?

The Difference Procedure is appropriate at any point in the process of eliciting high quality information where the manager has identified both (a portion of) the Present State and (a portion of) some desired state or desirable situation which has a positive characteristic which could be used as part of the Desired State. The question itself simply requests information about other characteristics of the desired state or desirable situation which may help to explain the presence of the positive characteristic in the desired state and its absence in the Present State.

An examination of the table showing the Present State and the Desired state reveals the context is appropriate for the Difference Question—that is, the GM has identified a portion of the Present State and a desired state from the recent past of the organization. In addition, he knows that the historically available desired state has a positive characteristic which could be used as part of the overall Desired State—namely, the shipments were on schedule. He, therefore, requests further information about the difference between the two situations using the Difference Question.

We distinguish this Precision Model question from the others we have thus far presented as there is no consistent immediate language cue to inform the information processor that the question is to be asked as there is in all of the other Precision Model questions. The

cue or test for appropriateness for the Difference Question is whenever both a present state and some possible desired state (one which
has some positive characteristic that would be desirable to incorpo-
rate into the Desired State) have been identified. There are, however,
a number of language cues which signal that this appropriateness test
for the Difference Question is satisfied. Specifically, these are:

1. Immediately following the Universal Blockbusting.
2. Immediately following the Precision Model questioning of a
   comparator question.
3. Immediately following a statement using the word(s) *except,
   with the exception of, different, difference, not the same as, not
   counting.*

We offer an example of each of these three language signals followed by the *Difference Question:*

1. following the PM Universal Blockbusting:

GM: . . . on what specific part of the inventory?

DM: Well, primarily on all those motors.

GM: On *all* those motors?

DM: No, not really on all the motors.

GM: What is the difference between the motors in the inventory
    where you have high interest payments and those where you
    don't? . . .

DM: Well, they're the newer ones—the B's—and the sales reps
    aren't as confident about them as the old line—the A's
    . . .

2. Following the comparator pointer:

Sales Manager (SM): . . . and because of the higher number of
    quality rejects from our customers we're losing sales.

GM: Higher than what?

SM: Higher than we had last reporting period—hell, higher than we had any period in the last three years.

GM: Slim, what is the difference between the last reporting period or any of those other periods and now that might help explain this higher number of quality rejects? . . .

3.   Following a statement using the words *except, with the exception of, different, difference, not the same as, not counting*

GM: . . . explain the delay on these reports? Controller (C): I think it may be the report itself—none of the divisions ever get them in on time . . . except Brandon's division.

GM: Simon, what is the difference between Brandon's division and all of the other division with respect to getting this report to us on time? . . .

The reader is cautioned against using *only* these language markers as the stimulus or occasion for the use of the Difference Question. These language markers simply guarantee that the Difference Question is appropriate. There are a large number of contexts where these language markers will not be present where the Difference Question is appropriate—that is, the language markers are a sufficient but not a necessary condition for the use of the Difference Question. The Difference Question is an extremely efficient and powerful device for gathering high quality information which directly allows a comparison of the present state and desired state characteristics—its use is highly recommended.

An examination of the table showing the Present State and the Desired State reveals the context is appropriate for the Difference Question—that is, the GM has identified a portion of the Present State and a desired state from the recent past of the organization. In addition, he knows that the historically available desired state has a positive characteristic which could be used as part of the overall Desired State—namely, the shipments were on schedule. He, therefore, requests further information about the difference between the two situations using the Difference Question.

The GM receives an answer to his question which he, in turn, subjects to Precision Model questioning to get a more refined representation.

SM	GM
. . . produced and shipped 60 special units a month last year and we're selling 70 special units a month this year . . .	. . . Did we produce 60 special units a month *every* month? . . .

The SM says that he doesn't know and that terminates the GM's questioning of the SM. The GM now quite appropriately turns to the production manager for the high quality production information he needs to further define the difference between the two states.

GM: Did we produce 60 special units a month *every* month?

Richard: I don't know.

GM: Joe?

Joe: No, that's just an average.

GM: What is the most we produced in a month?

Joe: I think one month we produced 75 last year.

GM: OK. We know that it's possible for our equipment to produce more than we need so let's see if we can discover the differences between that month and our current production of special units. Joe, what are some of the differences that might contribute to lower production?

Joe: Well . . . you know how it is. In peak months everything just goes right.

GM: What things, specifically, went right in the peak month?

Joe: The biggest thing is low maintenance. And we had really low maintenance then. Good workers (pause) willing to work overtime. Adequate inventory so we don't wait for material. Those are the big things.

GM: Good, Joe—I want to explore all three of those factors. . . . (GM moves to a flipchart and draws the following figure:

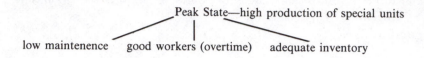

GM returns to seat and waves his hand at the chart.

GM: Just to help us keep track of where we are. OK, Joe, what specifically about low maintenance helps production?

Joe: (surprised at the obvious question) We don't have so much machine down time.

GM: Was maintenance higher in the current months than in that peak month?

Joe: I'm not sure.

Contr: Yeah, it was. Maintenance has been higher than last year and budget so far this year. We haven't had a month this year that wasn't higher than last.

GM: What maintenance, specifically, is up?

Contr: I don't know.

GM: Joe?

Joe: Well, the biggest maintenance job has been the overhaul.

GM: The overhaul of what?

Joe: Of line #1 assembly unit. That line doesn't produce any of our special units.

Joe: (continued)

(pause) Other than that overhaul, I don't think maintenance has been any greater.

Contr: Well, the numbers I have say it is.

GM: What numbers, specifically?

Contr: The costs of maintenance. Even without that overhaul, they're up.

GM: The numbers we are interested in are machine hours of down time on the line that produces special units. What do they say?

Contr: I don't know.

Joe: I think they're about the same.

GM: OK. Maintenance doesn't seem to contribute to the difference. Let's take the next factor, "good workers." Did you have more good workers in the peak month than the current months?

Joe: Yeah, we sure did.

GM: And these good workers—they're good at what specifically?

Joe: At working fast without making mistakes, coming in on time and not missing too many days of work. A guy like that is able to meet our work speed standards and experience.

GM: (after pause) What experience, specifically, does he need?

Joe: At least a year on this type of assembly and we need people with welding skills.

GM: What, in particular, is "this type of assembly?"

Joe: It means you need experience with drill presses and automatic cutting machines.

GM: OK. Do you have fewer of these skilled workers than you had in the peak month?

Joe: Yes.

GM: How many fewer?

Joe: Last year we had about 20 in that category, now we've got 14.

GM: You mentioned coming in on time and absenteeism earlier. Is this different from the peak month?

Joe: Yeah, it's way worse.

GM: How is it way worse?

Joe: I remember. We didn't have nearly so many people not showing up.

Contr: Our figures for paid non-productive hours are up 17% over last year.

GM: What are "paid non-productive hours?"

Contr: Mostly paid sick time.

Joe: We don't get any warning for those absences and we can't find anybody to fill in. It seems to hit line #3 the worst.

GM: What's the difference between line #3 and the others which might account for that?

Joe: I guess we have more pressure on that line because it's behind in production. We have more overtime there, too.

GM: OK. You mentioned overtime earlier. Did you work more overtime in the peak month than the current months?

Joe: About the same or a bit less. But that was just for a big month. We seem to be trying to get the men to work overtime regularly now. Some of them just won't do it.

Contr: Why don't you just fire them and . . .

GM: (interrupting) We aren't looking for solutions right now. We're just defining the difference between where we are and where we want to be. So, Joe, as I understand it, one of the differences is just that you can't get the overtime you need and you could before.

Joe: Yeah, that's right . . . but if we had good people we wouldn't need as much.

GM: The last thing you mentioned was adequate inventory. Inventory of what, specifically?

Joe: Parts to be assembled. If we have to wait for them it can really eat up production time.

The GM continues his precision tracking in Defining the Difference throughout this section of the transcript. Early in this portion of the transcript, he identifies and selects a previous performance period in the recent history of the organization—*the peak month*—which has the desired state characteristics of an adequate level of production of the special units tentatively as his target state. He elicits information from the production manager which indicates that there were at least three factors involved in this desired state. This section demonstrates the efficiency of the Precision Model as he establishes the Desired State Frame and tracks down the high quality information associated with each of the three factors which define that Desired State. All of the Precision Model questioning which the GM does in this section of the transcript are patterns which we have already introduced the reader to. The GM also puts the powerful Difference Question to good use in this section. We encourage the reader to follow the transcript quite closely so as to fully appreciate the technique in action.

The GM also uses a technique which we offer in our workshops. He recognizes that the production manager has offered him three different factors which are characteristic of the desired state that the GM established as his Frame. Wishing to insure that high quality information regarding each of these will be elicited for the purposes of comparison with the Present State, he uses a flipchart representation:

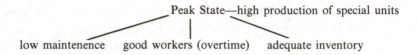

The effectiveness of such shared external visual representations in making a discussion—particularly those based on information which emerges during the discussion itself—both efficient and effective is immeasurable. We point the technique out here only in passing—the subject of effective shared representations itself belongs to the second phase of high quality information processing treated in a forthcoming book in this series.

It is instructive to note how, specifically, the desired state which the GM uses so effectively as an Outcome Frame (especially for the Difference Question) is arrived at.

SM: . . . produced and shipped 60 special units a month last year
. . .

DM: Did we produce 60 special units a month *every* month?

SM: I don't know.

DM: Joe? (the production manager)

PM: No, that's just an average.

DM: What is the most we produced in a month?

PM: I think one month we produced 75 last year.

The Precision Model Blockbusting questions have in common the function of drawing out from low quality information a distinction which is only implicit. They force the information source to refine their representation and detect and offer differences where previously they had things lumped together, making no distinctions at all. The visual representation we have associated with these patterns from Case Study I make the point nicely:

DM: . . . costs are up . . .

GM: . . . which costs in particular? . . .

DM: . . . my labor costs are the ones . . .

In words, as the DM mentions *costs,* the GM has inadequately precise information to appreciate the situation the DM is referring to. The GM, therefore, applies the Precision Model questioning thereby forcing the DM to identify which of the various possible components of overall costs in particular are up. The DM is directed by the question to refine the representation he is making to the GM —to make a distinction within the general category of costs, picking out precisely the piece of information needed. Statistical averages such as the one offered in the current transcript—*produced and shipped 60 special units a month last year*—are strikingly similar to the low quality word *costs* in that the statistical average is computed in such a way as to insure the loss of distinctions—they are designed to move away from the original sensory grounded experiences they are based on. Thus, we recommend to the manager using the Precision Model that whenever a statistic is encountered, he or she recognize it for what it is—a number which was arrived at by ignoring differences and distinctions which exist in the original experiences that the statistic was constructed from. In fact, we recommend that managers sensitize themselves to identify such statistics presented in the flow of language information and greet it with a certain enthusiasm. The argument for the enthusiasm we recommend is that if the statistical average represents a satisfactory or adequate performance in some operation within the business organization, then it follows that hidden within that statistic will be shorter term performances which will identify a standard of excellence. Using the Precision Model blockbusting question to penetrate a statistic will reveal precisely what the conditions were when that optimal performance occurred. The elicitation of high quality information describing such conditions gives the manager a well defined desired state which he or she may adopt as a target state with the full confidence that such a high standard of performance is within the present capabilities of the organization.

As we emphasized in the introduction, there is a direct correlation between the number of distinctions in the maps the business organization uses to plan and carry out its activities and the success with which those activities meet. In this particular case, the desired state that the GM uses so effectively as a Frame is reached only because he recognizes the statistic for what it is—a low quality representation. By challenging it with the Precision Model universal blockbusting question, he forces a more refined representation closer to the original experiences and by so doing, succeeds in discovering precisely the target state—*the peak month*—he needs to proceed effectively.

This portion of the transcript terminates with a Backtrack Frame by the GM. Note that in the Backtrack, the GM begins at the initial statement of the issue . . . *losing sales* . . . and then mentions only the tracks which lead to an appreciation of the differences between the desired state and the present one. In Backtracking, it is, of course, far more efficient to present only the track that led to differences between the two states. Tracks which were explored and discarded as not involving differences which are useful, are not recapitulated in a Backtrack. The single exception to this rule of thumb for Backtracking is in the case where the Backtrack is used to brief members of the organization who were not present at some or all of the original meeting. In such a case, the backtrack should also include the tracks explored and discarded to inform the new members that those possibilities were adequately considered.

GM: OK. Let's review what we've got so far. We're losing sales of special units at about 10 a month because shipments are going out about three weeks late. We have produced more units in a month in the past than we need to produce right now and the major difference seems to be that we can't get enough adequately skilled workers, we have increased absenteeism, and we can't get enough overtime from the people we have to get the production we want. Now, let's look at the things that might account for these factors. Joe, you said you have 6 fewer skilled workers than in the peak month.

Joe: Yeah, well, there were about six of them. George, one of my supervisors, told me three of them went to work for those new plants that were built on the West side. And we've had at least two retire since the peak.

GM: What are the differences between our plant and their plants which might get the skilled workers to go there?

Joe: I don't know, our pay is competitive.

GM: How, specifically, is it competitive?

Joe: Our hourly rate is about the same and so are our benefits.

GM: Which benefits, in particular?

Joe: Well, pension, sick leave, insurance, all that sort of stuff.

GM: What's the differences between the men who are still with us and the men that left that might explain why they went to the other plant?

Joe: Well, (pause) I know a couple of them a little. Bill lived on that side of town and doesn't have to fight the traffic anymore. And both Terry and Bill are older. They don't like to work the overtime we require.

GM: What other factors are different from when we had the peak month?

Contr: I'm having trouble getting good clerical and computer people and I was talking to Jim in Personnel yesterday, and he said that most departments were having trouble getting skilled people. He said those new plants have really made a tight labor market in this area. The traffic's way worse than it used to be around here and I think some of our people are getting sick of it. We used to be the only game in town but now those other plants are making it tough.

GM: OK. Can any one think of any other differences? (pauses) Let me summarize then and make sure we all agree. Right now we aren't producing enough special units to meet our sales and we're losing about 10 sales a month. We can't increase the production because we can't attract enough skilled workers. We want to make a change in our operations which will enable us to get the workers we need to produce enough to at least match our present sales. The most likely area for accomplishing that seems to be making some changes in our working conditions so that we can attract the people we need the most. The change in our situation which seems to have had the most impact is the start up of two new plants in our area. Adding to the problem is that our location is harder to get to because of increased traffic and those plants are easier to travel to than ours for many people. We also have so much overtime that it is unattractive for many workers. Are there any other factors which anyone thinks need to be considered? (pause) OK. I'm going to call a meeting in four days to see if we can find some ways to solve this problem. I think we should have a few more people in on it because it seems to be affecting most areas of the company and will involve Personnel as well. OK. That's it.

This section of the transcript begins with the Backtrack Frame— using this as our guide to information, we observe that the GM has elicited the following information:

Present State	Difference	Desired State
Sales	Down compared to (10 per month)	Sales
Shipments	3 weeks late compared to	Shipments
Skilled workers	Not enough compared to	Shipments
Absenteeism	Up compared to	Acceptable
Overtime	Difficult to get compared to	Overtime

The GM recognizes that the difficulty revolves around getting adequate skilled workers. He, therefore, focuses the group attention on this point from the opening—*Joe, you said you have 6 fewer skilled workers than in the peak month.* In the sequence of exchanges immediately afterward, he elicits exactly the information about the present state/desired state differences he requires—those differences which have placed additional demands on skilled labor pool in the immediate area. With the present state and desired state characteristics as well developed as they are in the beginning of this last segment, one might anticipate the extensive use of the Difference Question. An examination of this segment of the transcript shows that 5 out of the 7 questions the GM uses are Difference Questions. The GM terminates the meeting with a full Backtrack of the meeting, secures agreement from the members of the group that the Backtrack is an adequate representation of the effort—no essential pieces of information have been omitted in the Backtrack. He then chooses quite appropriately to close the meeting and to call another meeting which will include additional personnel. His decision is fully supported by the fact that in tracking down the difference (Present State/Desired State) he has uncovered high quality information which indicates that the situation is more widespread than originally thought and, more specifically, the personnel manager will be a necessary integral part of any satisfactory solution.

We trust that the reader will recognize the efficiency and precision with which the GM took charge, setting appropriate Frames and within those Frames eliciting high quality information sources and constructing from that information a high quality map or representation which precisely defines the difference.

We call the reader's attention to an interesting difference between the two case studies transcripts. While both are examples of the powerful and effective use of the Precision Model, the order in which high quality information is elicited about the Present State and the Desired State is entirely different. In the first of the two case studies, the GM tracks completely down to the adequately precise representation of the Present State prior to overtly considering any information regarding the Desired State. In the second case study, the GM moves quickly back and forth between the Desired State and the Present State information—comparing their characteristics almost in a pairwise manner. Visually, the movement can be represented as:

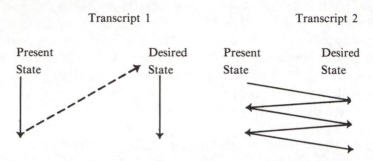

The success, effectiveness and efficiency of the communication in both transcripts shows the adequacy of either approach, thus, the difference can be attributed to style.

BACKTRACK

The majority of required business communication within a company deals with problems. That is, it deals with attempts to change a less than optimum present state to a more desired state. This may be in reaction to an emergency, a less severe chronic condition or a desire for excellence. To deal effectively with a problem, or to know whether one should deal with a situation at all, a clear definition of the difference between the present state and the desired state is required. This, of course, requires a precise definition of the two states themselves.

An explicit outcome based on high quality information is the requirement for effective business communications. Many problems are unrecognized or inadequately dealt with because of an illusion of shared understanding about the present or desired states. The language of business can hide many of the differences which would be useful to know. If higher quality information was available more appropriate action could be taken towards specific and agreed upon outcomes.

The Precision Model is a technique for obtaining high quality information from originally low quality representations.

It provides the tools maintaining a trajectory toward desired outcomes based on adequately precise information.

This chapter introduces the Outcome Frame. The Outcome Frame establishes and maintains the context of any particular segment of a communication so that the participants know what the task is and what is appropriate to it. It gives the manager control over meetings and, in fact, any discussion which is outcome oriented.

A second Frame introduced in this chapter is the Backtrack, of which this section is an example. The Backtrack Frame is used to reorient participants towards the topic or context desired and to access more of the individual representations or resources.

We introduce the Pointers or questions which are used to obtain the desired precision. A set of steps are outlined for recognizing when more information is needed and the specific question to formulate based on the initial statement. Each of these will move closer to direct experience which can be shared effectively, that is towards higher quality information. The Pointers allow the manager to direct the information source's attention to exactly the information he needs to know in that particular context.

Two procedures were also introduced to increase the efficiency of this means of information gathering. The first is the Relevency Challenge, the direction to state how a comment or question is relevant to the agreed upon outcome. It is a necessary companion to the Outcome Frame. The other is the Difference Procedure. This enables a manager to skip directly to a high quality representation of the significant differences in any situation or between two states or things. It can quickly extract the hidden elements of averages and comparisons.

The directive form of questioning introduced in this chapter along with the use of Frames guarantees that the information exchange will respect the need not to know.

Chapter 3

PATHFINDING

When my father was young, he lived on a farm in Alberta. Their community had to work hard to get a decent crop out of the tough soil. They were constantly having to spend resources on clearing new land. Continued prosperity required increasing the area available to them to plant seed for future harvest. They were in a constant struggle with nature and had to organize their resources to get the maximum sustenance from what they already had. At the same time, they had to use those same resources to get additional food from their surroundings.

The survival of the community depended upon maintaining the land areas which had already been cleared and claimed. In this province and under these tough conditions, hunting was serious business and not just the sport it is in most places today. Their comfortable existence depended upon successfully locating game. Having lived in communities where the results of hunting had been poor or inconsistent, my father knew that the key to success was knowing the paths and trails in the area to be hunted in fine detail. In these communities, conditions had been harsh and he remembered the successful hunts by the celebrations which had taken place. The community would gather and devour the game in a festival of high spirit as is the tendency of all people who have received a bit of unexpected good luck. His father told him that the communities were new and that others who were familiar with the area had moved on to different areas. The people who had stayed didn't explore new territory but were content to plow the fields they knew best.

When my grandfather arrived in the community where my father grew up, it soon became obvious to the others in that community that he was both a competent and adventurous man who was used to success. He was an excellent tracker and soon proved himself on a par with the best in the area even though he was less familiar with that particular part of the province. He could read the signs of what was around him and he seemed better able than anyone to get the particular knowledge of others which was most likely to end in a successful hunt.

This particular community was more successful at the hunt than many but its results were still erratic. The consistency with which my grandfather brought back game impressed everyone. The community soon began to take notice of his suggestions and, at his request, gathered to consider organizing the hunt for the whole community. He suggested that the community contained resources that were as yet not even dreamed of. If they shared all of their knowledge and skills in an organized fashion, they could be continuously and predictably successful at the hunt. The community had witnessed his success at hunting with others, which he always did, and decided to try this idea. After all, the results would soon be apparent and they could abandon the idea if it didn't work out. My grandfather was naturally selected as the leader of the hunt.

He would hold evening meetings in front of a roaring fire for a week before the hunting season was to begin. Any member of the community who might have something to contribute was invited. Others who had an interest in the hunt were welcome if they could attend and there was space available. All of the intelligence surrounding the movement of game in the area was shared. Any conditions which might change their habits or otherwise contaminate the original intelligence was reported. Most important of all, each trail in the area was placed on a huge map which covered a whole wall so everyone could see it. Each year the meeting would start with a fresh map of the area which showed only the major existing and well known locations. Each trail would then be entered on the map as it was remembered and treated as a new discovery. This helped some of the community to remember trails which they knew of but often forgot about when they could see the old familiar paths already laid out for them.

My grandfather had great respect in the community. As leader of the hunt, which year after year was successful, he was held in high regard. He loved his position and carried it well but had to take care lest it also cause him problems. Many members of the community were shy in his presence and would become silent. Some would even fail to tell him things that would be useful to him. Others would fail to provide him information in the area of their specialty because he seemed so much more knowledgeable than they. Fortunately, however, he had a way of dealing with people which allowed him to obtain the information he desired and, at the same time, put everyone around him at ease.

His ability to get information and put people at ease was especially important at the meetings around the fire. His value to the hunt, after all, was not due to his skills as a tracker but to his ability to get the shared resources of the community focused on the outcome they all desired—a successful hunt. He would suggest, at the meetings around the fire, that the most useful way for each and every person to proceed was to assume that any idea or piece of information he had might be valuable; that at least one other person in the room might need that bit of information to increase his own understanding of the situation they were about to face; to enrich it in such a way that quicker and better paths might come to mind which would ensure the success of the hunt.

Having been in his present position as huntmaster for many years, his father had come to understand that often the most important intelligence concerning the hunt would come from the most unexpected sources. He appreciated the fact that the skills required to be an excellent hunter were often very different than the skills required to talk about hunting articulately and many were unaccustomed to speaking out in front of others. They would be made to feel comfortable and would benefit from the verbal skills of my grandfather as he drew them out with sensitive care. Further, he understood clearly that often the precise piece of intelligence which would ensure the success of the hunt resided in the casual observations of the people of the community. The worth of this information was rarely recognized by the bearer of that information and, most frequently, they were unaware that they had such intelligence until, by his gentle yet precise questioning, he would draw it from them. They would be surprised and delighted to discover that they had contributed in ways which they had not imagined possible.

An apprentice to the hunt, who was not usually listened to by the others would provide information based on his own unique, if limited, experience which would often, after a few penetrating questions, yield valuable results. He might know of paths which he had discovered as a youth that were unknown to the older hunters. Others who were not experts in the hunt might have discovered unknown paths in their travels throughout the year. Each path, when added to the map, increased the flexibility of the hunters. It provided them with choices which they might not have otherwise had—many of which proved to be the difference between a successful outcome and failure. They all knew that the consistent success of their hunt was due to the detailed maps and intricate pathways that were created. Each little discovery of a new path could suddenly make previously useless paths valuable by providing new connections. The worth of this intelligence was proved time and time again by the successful outcome of the hunts.

Other communities heard of the success of the hunts in our area. Some of these simply put it down to a more abundant source of game and pursued it no further. Others copied our methods and began to hold meetings. Many even thought it necessary to hold their meetings in the evening around a large fire with a huge map on the North wall. These changes often improved their results if only in a sporadic way. None managed to extract the new information required for continued increases in success. They usually benefited from the first pooling of resources but seemed to level off after that—better, but never up to the standard of my grandfather's community. There seemed to be a difference in the intelligence available to our group which wasn't available to theirs.

INTRODUCTION

Pathfinding is the second phase of the overall model for business activity presented in the opening chapter.

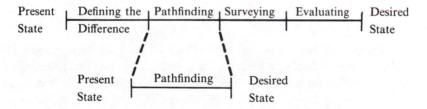

A winning race car driver, from the starting flag to the checkered flag which signals his win, will continually create a variety of tracks which he may drive his car along, depending upon the circumstances he encounters at each part of the track in each lap. These will be lightning fast and often out of conscious awareness. None will be rejected; many will never be used. The variety of alternatives increases his choices and ensures that he will complete the race with maximum safety.

Pathfinding is our name for the phase of information processing in business which generates alternative courses of action—alternative paths to eliminating the defined difference. There have been many attempts at establishing procedures which will elicit a rich variety of alternatives in a way which is suitable to normal business operations. Most attempted solutions have required many unusual procedures and have been rejected by many organizations as not suitable. The alternative has been to lose the creative resources of the people in organizations. It isn't, however, necessary to make that choice. The creative resources of individuals can be obtained within the normal procedures of business in an efficient and practical manner.

We will define the present state and the desired state of this phase to determine the requirements for processing. The course of action appropriate to this phase, its procedures, will be determined by the requirements of eliminating the difference between the present and desired states.

The theory of a double helix which opened the secrets of the DNA molecule was discovered by an image which was apparently created "by chance." The "chance" was a result of a clearly defined program of what was known and what was wanted, which provided the organizing principle for the discoverer's unconscious. The effort which went into the definition produced an "effortless" solution to a precisely posed question.

PRESENT STATE

To begin this stage, a problem has been defined, or more generally, a difference between a present and a desired state has been identified and defined to an adequate level of precision. The next step is to discover the possible ways to eliminate the difference. The best course of action to achieve the overall desired state is not known. All the alternatives are not even known. All of the potentially available information exists in internal maps and a method is required to share that information. The information must be elicited and organized in a useful way. At this stage, a set of explicit procedures are required to ensure that the greatest amount of relevant resources are available for finding alternate ways of eliminating the defined difference.

The content of the Pathfinding phase will be determined by the defined difference from the previous phase. To the extent the difference is defined to an adequate state of precision, the action taken to close or eliminate that difference will be most efficient. The precision of the defined difference will provide the organizing principle or basis for the Outcome Frame for this phase. If the difference has not been defined precisely enough, the attempt to reduce the difference will produce pathways which will lead inefficiently or not at all to elimination of the difference. An adequately precise definition will provide the context which ensures that the highest quality information available will be able to be obtained. Acceptable content in this phase is judged by its relevancy to the outcome desired. The specific content of this phase must be integrated or congruent with the overall desired outcome.

For example, a general manager may judge the performance of his sales manager unsatisfactory. The sales manager, however, using a different standard, believes his performance to be satisfactory. If the two meet to discuss how to resolve the difference in their views of performance and concentrate on whether "performance" is satisfactory or not, they may very well compound the problem. In the authors' experience, this is a common mistake. The kind of solutions which are generated are designed to improve "performance" by such alternatives as longer hours, more calls with sales representatives, reviewing call sheets, etc. The financial statements are generally taken to be the basis of performance as they are the only source available to the general manager. The difference is seldom defined to an adequate level which would show that the problem is one of different standards, not necessarily different performance. The general manager is using shipments while the sales manager is using orders. The present state is their different representation of the problem. If the solution doesn't include the standard of judgement, then the situation can be expected to recur. A more thorough representation of the difference would discover that the information needed was about the operations of the sales department related to point of sale activity and not to delivery schedules which in a manufacturing business may represent a delay of months. The solutions to this difference, now defined in adequately precise terms, would come from a whole new area of source information. The requirement is for the two persons involved in the difference to effectively use the same source of information regarding performance.

The present state of the Pathfinding phase is the defined difference from the previous phase. Other significant factors which may be part of the present state will include whether or not the composition of the individuals involved has changed since the first phase, whether or not there has been a time break between the phases, and if any new clarification of the difference or upgrading of desired state has taken place. These factors will tend to affect the process more than the content. Increased use of the Backtrack Frame will be called for if there has been a change in group composition or a significant time lag. The experience of the information processor will determine the most effective use of the Frames. The Precision model provides the tools to arrive at the desired quality of outcome. Excess use of the Backtrack Frame, for instance, may slow a meeting down but the desired end result will still be achieved. If the Outcome Frame is not used frequently enough confusion will result—but that same Frame may be called on to clarify the situation and return to the desired trajectory.

DESIRED STATE

Pathfinding is a descriptive term for this phase of the process. The outcome or desired state specific to this phase is to generate alternative courses of action which lead to the overall outcome in the most efficient or profitable way. The whole process is attempting to find a transition path from a present and less than satisfactory state to a desired state. At this stage the best possible path for eliminating the difference is not known. The requirement created by that condition is that as many alternative paths be discovered or generated as possible.

The emphasis on paths is to keep in mind that it is courses of action that are being concentrated on. The beginning and ending points have been identified. All efforts are now being focused on the actions required to move along a path which will lead from one state to the other.

The desired state or outcome of this phase is an extensive list of possible paths of action which will eliminate the defined difference. To meet the requirements of the Outcome Frame, the alternatives must be potentially capable of achieving the original desired outcome. The proof that they will do so and the practicality of their performance are tests which are left to later phases. How many alternatives would make a satisfactory list? The maximum number of possible alternatives cannot be known beforehand. The requirement for this phase, then, is to design a procedure which will elicit the greatest number of useful responses with the resources available. The procedure must be capable of eliciting the greatest number of alternatives from the available resources, of limiting responses to those which might achieve the outcome and it must establish an end point to the procedure. The problem for this phase will be to create a procedure which will generate an extensive list of alternative pathways from the present to the desired state.

What sort of procedures will they be? To find the answer we will have to consider where alternatives are generated from, the conditions necessary for getting access to them, and the procedures which will create and maintain those conditions. First, we'll consider the source of alternatives. Where are these alternatives which might be useful in the context and which are not immediately available?

All of the available information comes from the individual maps or representations of the world. Each individual has only his own experience to draw on. If no one present has any experience or knowledge of a piece of information which is required for the solution to a problem, the problem will not be solved. Each part of each potential pathway must already reside in the map of at least one participant. It is possible that no single participant has a complete path to the solution, but the individual parts must already reside in the various maps of some of the individuals. It is common for the pieces needed to construct the best path to be in different individual maps. When this is the situation, each individual with a piece tends not to contribute that piece because each has no way of knowing that it would contribute to an effective course of action. Knowing where the alternatives are and how to elicit them will provide a variety of pathways.

The outcome of this phase will be attained when all of the potentially relevant material from each individual map has been represented in a map which is shared. The limits to action which concern us are those that are self imposed, often unknowingly—but self imposed nonetheless. We live in a world of rich and varied experience and opportunity. The current business environment provides many options and alternative ways of achieving desired outcomes.

The authors recognize that there are laws which prohibit certain activities. Some of these activities may seem reasonable and profitable solutions to existing less than optimal states. We realize that there are conditions external to an organization which limit its ability to respond in a desired way to changes in environment. In our experience, however, there is always something that can be influenced to improve a problem situation, to reduce or eliminate a difference between any present state and a desired state in the world of business. Over and over, we have found that the limits which prevent an organization from moving toward its desired outcomes are limits which that organization and the individuals in it have inadvertently placed upon themselves.

What are the characteristics of individual maps which we must take into account? How can we promote the sharing of information, of the rich representation of each individual map? We have all stored vast numbers of details related to our own unique experiences. If these details were released without any organizing principles, we would get a meaningless jumble, intelligible to no one. All of the details, however, are hooked to experiences. To access information useful to the task at hand, we will have to access experiences which contain related material.

Imagine we have a microscope in front of us. If we cut a large piece of tissue and place it under our powerful microscope, we will see a detailed and active scene in front of our eyes. In fact, it will be so rich in detail and action that we won't be able to focus on any one part of it. We won't be able to make sense of what is before our eyes. To get useful information, we will have to limit the area or amount of tissue on our slide—put a boundary around the relevant material. If we are looking for a particular living cell in this tissue, we might have to put a color into the material which will highlight the particular type of cell we are looking for, filter out some of the detail. We end up with a coherent and fairly explicit representation of the cells we intend to study. The information we needed was isolated by establishing boundaries and highlighting detail from its irrelevant background.

Our internal representations are similar to the material under a powerful microscope. We can lose information which may be useful by wandering over a too wide area or we can get lost in detail. On the other hand, we can elect to examine the material relevant to our concern and choose to highlight the needed detail from its surroundings by putting it outside the boundary. We can also eliminate detail from the area under consideration. Both are necessary for normal functioning. Both can lead to a limited view of alternatives and a rigid and restricted way of operating. A requirement then is to be able to expand the boundaries and to sharpen the focus on the areas of maps under consideration as desired.

Business is often faced with the situation where there is too much area covered or too much irrelevant detail when problem solving techniques are tried. The rest of the time, the major problem is in too limited or restricted an area and not enough detail is available. The situation at first glance is a paradox. How can the desired amount of detail be obtained from an appropriate area? The solution is a set of procedures and questions which can elicit the desired material under controlled conditions. The manager must be able to access the areas they want an adequately precise amount of detail in.

Once the boundaries of individual maps have been expanded and their full richness made accessible, how can the detail which is relevant be elicited from these maps and be included in the shared map? To be included in a shared map, information from individual maps must be accessed and the shared information represented in a way that will make it useful to others. If the representation of an individual map is coded in such a way as to make it inaccessible or unintelligible to others, it will be unavailable for the shared representation.

The final condition is a constraint on the process. The original purpose provides a context for focusing resources. The richness of individual representations is the source of the alternatives desired and is also the source of a potential problem. Time and time again, attempts to access this rich material leads into a maze. It is easy and common to get lost in the richness and lose sight of the original purpose. The very richness and flexibility demanded provide their own trap.

One of the requirements is that the useful material not be buried and lost in the irrelevant. A constraint on the process is required to establish boundaries, determined by the desired outcome, which limits information to relevant material.

The conditions required to get access to individual representations and create a rich shared map will determine the procedures appropriate to the context. The first will be to expand the boundaries beyond the normal restraints and to focus on the material within them more clearly than usual. Another will be to generate material from each participant which the others can use to access more of their own maps. Another will be to ensure that the shared material is represented so that each participant has access to it. Finally, limits must be placed which accomplish the above within the context established by the desired outcome.

BRAINSTORMING

Brainstorming is the best known term for the particular models created to generate the maximum number of new ideas. Recognizing that expansion of boundaries was necessary to generate new material, a system was developed which removed all boundaries. It created conditions which removed any limits and invented numerous techniques to elicit new and creative responses to familiar situations. Many of the techniques are randomizers. They function to remove restraints and to provide the stimulus for accessing different areas of individual maps. The effectiveness of these techniques for generating new material is well known. Some percentage of organizations enthusiastically endorse this approach and create special groups and, often, special areas for this activity. A significant proportion of business has rejected the approach as being a waste of resources. They have concentrated on the negative aspect common to brainstorming, namely, that many of the ideas created are not relevant or are incapable of being put into action. Business, as an outcome oriented activity, has rejected an approach which seems to produce useful results on a random basis or not at all.

The fact remains that creative resources are not being tapped and that brainstorming, at least some of the time, generates new and useful alternatives. Additional resources are available which are going unused. The basis of brainstorming is that creativity is an unusual activity which can be carried out only with procedures which remove it from the ordinary world of business. Any procedure which, in the opinion of the manager, will stimulate the creative resources of participants may be included in a Pathfinding session. The outline which we present, however, is intended to create the necessary and sufficient conditions to generate creative alternatives for reaching a desired state. It will access creative resources in a manner consistent with ordinary business operations. The techniques of the Precision Model will elicit the maximum available resources from the individual maps of participants. The greater part of creativity is gaining access to existing material which has not previously been in conscious awareness as being relevant. The process dealt with in this book is the generation of high quality information. The method presented is designed to access the richest possible detail from each individual map or representation and to create the richest possible shared map. Any effective mental process which the participants go through to generate more material is valued behavior at any step of the process. The ability to elicit these resources *in the context desired* is the distinguishing characteristic of the Precision Model. It is the missing function which has caused many to try and separate mental processes into special categories or stages of the information flow.

Observers of the process of generating alternatives noticed that when no questioning took place, the number and quality of ideas were increased over similar meetings which allowed questioning. The justification for forbidding questioning was further bolstered by theories which suggested that certain individuals would not contribute ideas under certain conditions. Some, who were less articulate and couldn't justify their ideas to the satisfaction of the group or its leader, would choose to remain silent or give up their ideas too early. Many would be afraid to appear stupid before their peers. Some could only criticize the ideas of others.

All of these, and more, seemed good reason for abandoning the potential benefits of questions given the choice which confronted them. A more refined analysis of language reveals that there are certain types of questions, appropriate to the context, which will elicit more creative resources than if they are not asked. Questions can reinforce a creative atmosphere, they do not have to be treated as shutters which close off resources. This approach recognizes that there is often more information which might be useful behind an initial representation.

One of the results of removing all questioning, of opening the boundaries totally, is that the alternatives generated are often not able to be translated into action. Many ideas can be outside of the context of the desired outcome. Some are solutions to problems which weren't under consideration. Many move past the defined difference or desired state and propose paths leading to outcomes beyond the scope of the original goals. Each alternative is accepted as equally valid. Minor or partial solutions may be side by side with major operating policies. In this situation, it is often difficult to extract a useful alternative even when it is generated. There are two problems. The first is that good suggestions may be buried in a long list of impractical ideas. The second is that the process of turning the list into a form appropriate for consideration of action requires very different circumstances than the ones which generated the list. The lack of appropriate questioning has allowed items to appear on the list which may need much more explicit representation before their utility can be known. Many of these will turn out to be useless. Unless the alternatives elicited can be turned into action, they are of no use to business. The effort of turning a list of suggestions into alternatives that actually lead to the desired outcome can be a major task which is often prohibitive.

Expansion of boundaries is only one of the requirements for generating the maximum number of alternative pathways. An effective process must also extract the potentially available information for a shared map.

The problem of accessing the rich resources from each participant's map of reality is often a question of how it is represented to the external world; in this case, the others present at the meeting. There are some who have valuable experience and creative ideas but who are usually called inarticulate. These individuals may have rich variety of experience to call on but are unable to represent it to others in a way, namely, sentences of English, that the others may share. The foreman who can solve any problem at his machine but can't tell others how to do it is familiar to us all. The systems analyst or economist who can represent solutions only in a specialized language that we can't understand, is at the other end of the spectrum, still, however, effectively inarticulate. These individual resources become unavailable for generating alternatives even though they may have been the very ideas needed in the situation.

The expert or specialist is often prominent in a meeting to generate alternatives. He has special areas of knowledge which would not be ordinarily available to the group. Often, however, his knowledge will be theoretical and will not have enough grounding in experience, in his way of representing it, to enable the other participants to grasp its significance. If this is the case, the minimum value will be obtained from his input, if, in fact, any at all is realized, because it will not be represented in a way that connects with the experience of the other participants.

A precise technology is required to ask the specific kind of questions which will elicit the maximum resources of each person in the group and will avoid the pitfalls recognized by those consultants who observed the difference in outcomes between meetings where questions were and were not allowed. The model that we are presenting here allows the leader of the meeting for generating alternatives to make precisely the distinctions required.

Some problem solving approaches which reject brainstorming completely suggest that there is a class of problem which does not call for the creative generation of new ideas. They claim problems in this category will be solved just by gathering enough information. These are problems which are defined as a change in circumstances from a previously existing acceptable state to an unsatisfactory present state. Here, where the goal is a return to a specific state which previously existed, the gathering of high quality information at the problem definition stage will lead to the required path of action. This type of problem is encountered most frequently with machines or systems.

One such system involved a grain milling machine which produced material that couldn't be made into pellets in certain end products and was being investigated for worn or faulty parts. The machine was blamed because it was old and seemed a likely cause. When a more detailed investigation was made—after significant amounts of unacceptable products were produced and repairs were made to the machine to no avail—the difference between materials going in and machine operations was compared to when acceptable results were obtained. The difference was found to be that a particularly hard grain was used in some mixtures and not others and that the problem occurred only in those with the hard grain. The solution was a change in pre-processing before milling. Another instance with the same company involved a similar problem which occurred apparently randomly in all products. The old machine again took the blame. Upon further investigation, the difference turned out to be that oats from a particular area had a moisture content significantly lower than other oats which were bought as exchangeable products. The difference was discovered with astute questioning. Once the problems above were adequately defined, that is, once enough high quality information was obtained, the company could move immediately to action. There seemed to be no particular need for generating alternatives. The immediate problem could be readily solved.

The best long term solution, however, is seldom apparent from this type of approach. The desired state is often less than optimal if it is only to restore conditions to a previous state. While solving an immediate problem, a great deal of high quality information will be generated which could provide a base for a more aggressive and creative approach. In the above examples, there were simple and immediate solutions.

The second situation served to get the company to take a more serious look at the longer range situation. Instead of setting a goal of returning to previous performance, the company sought to make a lasting improvement. The new defined difference would require a new product or process. The potential solutions ranged from simple formula changes to complete new products, from process time alterations to new equipment. The final solution introduced a product which combined pelleted and non-pelleted material. This entirely new product is now a staple of the industry. It solved the manufacturing problems and was highly successful in the field. Instead of merely reacting to a problem and returning to an old situation, the company used the high quality information needed for problem solving to generate a state better than the previously existing one.

Business is often thought of as being conservative. The justification is assumed to be based on the production process. Business is required to produce and any existing business has a history of production. "It worked before" is commonly heard from companies which are marginally profitable as well as many more successful ones. Any change which is potentially profitable is also potentially risky. The authors believe that conservatism has been a justifiable approach for another reason. Survival and "good enough" aren't normal standards of business. They strive to grow and increase profits continually. It is our belief that if a change is going to be made, it should be aimed at improvement not just reinstatement of a status quo. What, then, prevents business from taking these risks? Why does business appear conservative? As the chain of information flow gets longer and the manager gets more removed from direct experience, he must rely on information sources and his ability to elicit appropriate detail. As the chain gets longer the quality of information gets lower and a manager will realize that a decision based on that low quality will be increasingly risky. We believe the answer lies in the lack of information processing skills. A model which provides appropriate information processing technology provides management with the knowledge to proceed along new paths with confidence. Adequate information reduces the risk and increases confidence in the reward.

A company getting unsatisfactory results from its computer installation hired a consultant to recommend a solution which was to include a new computer. The aggressive general manager thought that if major programming changes were being considered that was the time to improve total capabilities with a new computer. The consultant did a study and recommended a more powerful machine produced by the same manufacturer, one of the largest. The resulting installation finished with a more expensive piece of equipment doing basically the same job as before. The gain which might have been realized was lost because the general manager did not have the ability to ask the right questions of the experts. A conservative choice was made, which later cost additional capital, for lack of high quality information. A more adventurous choice was rendered too risky by the inability to obtain adequate information to ensure reasonable confidence in another choice.

The risk to a manager or company of any new idea is largely a function of the quality of information available. With the highest quality information, the only risks relate to the changes in future conditions which are never totally known to any of us. As the quality decreases, less and less is known about present conditions which may provide assurance about the future. The richer our internal representation about a situation, the surer we feel regarding decisions about it. The closer our representation is to experience, the more likely it is to reflect actual conditions. The ability to obtain high quality information is the necessary tool to provide adequate confidence in new ideas. Conservatism has been justified to the extent these skills were not available. This kind of conservatism is no longer justified. The technology presented here will give the manager the necessary tools to get precisely the high quality information needed for successful change and improvement.

The Pathways phase of information processing for business is a part of normal business operations. It is a special case of the whole process of information processing. Each phase of the process has its own set of appropriate procedures which are determined by the context. The context is determined by the particular outcome desired for the particular phase. Although some of the requirements are different in this phase, all are parts of the Precision Model, and therefore, within ordinarily acceptable business operations. A manager, as an information processor, is required to elicit the resources of those around him. His function is to draw on those resources, not to be the expert himself. The techniques presented here are designed to provide the technology for him to perform that function effectively.

Let's return to the outcome desired for this phase. We want to generate the greatest number of alternative pathways from the present state to the desired state as specified in the phase Defining the Difference. The most desirable outcome would be to end with a list of alternatives every one of which would lead to the desired outcome. The future phases would then merely identify and select the one with the best results, including side effects. The outcome requires that two variables be considered. The first is the number of alternatives generated. The second is the context—the overall outcome desired.

Imagine you are planning a trip from the state you are in to a state which you have never been to. You have a road atlas in front of you. First, you would identify where you were in the atlas and next where you were going. The starting point and the desired destination would be your parameters for determining which roads might be appropriate. As you look at the map, you see that there are only a few alternatives which are available that will lead in the appropriate direction. As you follow these, each in turn, you find more and more branches are possible which will all lead to your final destination. Then, as you near your destination, you find that the options available narrow once again. When you see the whole map at once, you discover that some of the roads which appeared to go in the most direct path at the start didn't necessarily end up being the shortest route. And a route that appeared to veer off turned out to be the most direct. You might also find that a number of roads would get you to your destination in about the same amount of time but some go through much more interesting country than others and some would be much more comfortable drives. By considering a larger area than presented by the more obvious straight line between two points, you might discover possibilities that you would have missed completely had you not expanded the boundaries of the area under consideration.

However, suppose your planning was being done in the middle of a family reunion. As you get out our atlas and begin to discuss your plans, some of the relatives get interested and begin to gather around. A nephew says, "Wouldn't it be nice to go to a lake which is fairly near that area." Another says, "Yeah, there's one that's even better further south. You could stay and have a holiday." An elderly aunt tells you of a fine trip she took along a road which doesn't start or end along your path and recommends you travel on it. An uncle who has had a little too much to drink insists that you can better spend your time in another area. Another aunt suggests a shortcut she took on the same general route once. Soon, you are so buried in information, some of which may have been helpful, that you pack up your atlas. You decide to find your own route at another time and place without the help of others.

The problem of expanding boundaries while maintaining a relevant context requires a model which can define the boundaries and enforce them in a way which supports new ideas. The brainstorm approaches tend to lose the context in their efforts to remove the boundaries. Many of their idea generating techniques are useful and need not be rejected provided an appropriate Frame or context can be maintained. Familiarity with the Precision Model, its use as a standard technique of controlling the context of any meeting, provides a Frame which can elicit the maximum benefit from idea generation techniques. Without the model, much time and resources can be wasted generating unique ideas which do not result in achieving the desired outcome.

The focus of the Pathways phase is on actions. In the experience of the authors at our management workshops, the most effective pointer in this phase is the Action Blockbuster. The defined difference passed from the previous phase will contain a series of unspecified verbs or action phrases. The outcome desired will be to find as many alternative actions as possible which will lead to the desired result. Each will be a specification of the original action phrase. A visual representation of the original information which will determine the desired outcome might look like the following:

- Increase return on invested capital
  - Increase margins
    - Reduce costs

Each node represents a course of action, a direction which could be pursued for elimination of the defined difference. The above representation indicates that the difference defined was narrowed down to reducing costs as the most likely way to increase margins which, in its turn, was the best way to increase return on invested capital. The defined difference in this case is an instruction to generate alternative courses of action to reduce costs. If the level of authority is high enough and the situation seems to warrant it, the information processor may move up the structure and generate alternatives for higher or less specified nodes, such as "increase margins" in our example. The statement passed, however, is a clear directive to concentrate on reducing costs. The concept of accountability, discussed earlier, can be used here as a tracking device for the information flow. The highest level of authority represented while generating alternatives will decide the appropriate level of action at which to generate alternatives. The defined difference represents a specific statement directing attention to a specific area. The definition will have contextual information which may indicate that a wider area should be considered. The Backtrack Frame would normally be employed before a consideration was made to change the level of concentration. The level of detail chosen for consideration and passed to this phase was chosen after a specific procedure. New information or a higher level of authority may be adequate grounds to change the area to be considered. The intervention point will be determined by the highest level of authority involved.

What procedure seems best for eliciting the alternatives desired? We suggest that each action phrase be specified as fully as possible before moving to another. The manager will decide whether to stick to that procedure or whether he will accept alternatives which are further specifications of one of the other actions represented.

The manager has full power to decide which procedure to follow. He may accept alternatives or put them on hold. He may also determine whether to accept or reject an alternative proposed which addresses a higher or less specified action. The differences in approach can be compared to the style differences referred to at the end of the preceding chapter. Visually this might be represented as:

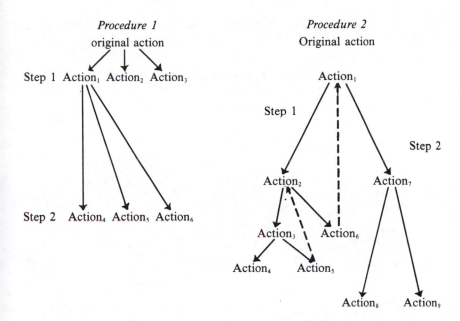

Following the preceding representation of the defined difference statement and procedure 1, we might get three alternatives which can be visually represented like this:

- Increase return on invested capital

- Increase margins

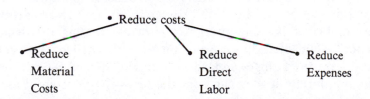

The next group of alternatives might be elicited by asking for specification of each of these in turn. No alternatives for reducing direct labor might be accepted until reducing material costs failed to produce any more alternatives. The information processor may then choose to elicit alternatives for each specific item under Reduce Material Costs before proceeding to Reduce Direct Labor.

A visual representation after eliciting for the first such item might be:

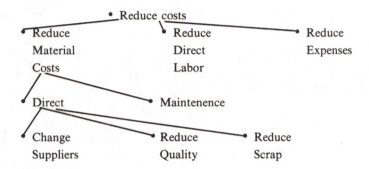

- Increase return on invested capital

- Increase margins

- Reduce costs

| Reduce Material Costs | Reduce Direct Labor | Reduce Expenses |

Direct   Maintenence

Change Suppliers   Reduce Quality   Reduce Scrap

The style difference referred to above is merely personal. The Precision Model will get the desired results. The major consideration for this stage is whether or not it maintains the trajectory toward the desired outcome.

POINTERS

Each pointer has specific contexts which make it appropriate. The test for this section will be, "Will this question lead to an increase in the number of possible alternatives for eliminating the defined difference?" The preceding discussion of verb challenges (Action Blockbusters) used this standard continually. Noun Blockbusters will be appropriate if they can pass the test—the Outcome Frame. Most of these pointers will not often pass the test in this phase for the simple reason that they will not be adding new alternative courses of action. The test must be applied to each situation individually. There will be some appropriate Noun Blockbusters, however. Whenever a situation is so unspecified that others involved in the meeting cannot relate it to their own maps or experience, some clarification is called for. This clarification may indeed result in further ideas being generated. A proposal which has no reference to experience, which can't be understood, isn't a useful contribution if left in that state.

Two other cues which would normally invite Precision questions can usually be ignored in this phase. Comparative deletions (better, worse) and universal quantifiers (all, every), if unchallenged, will seldom constitute blocks at this point. These pointers would normally not be appropriate in this phase because the answer to them is not likely to increase the number of alternatives. Statements such as the following constitute acceptable or adequately precise formulations of alternatives for consideration, that is, they lead to the outcome desired, even though they may not be totally accurate.

"*All* of the machines need fixing."
"*Every* salesman needs some training."
"*No one* should be fired or laid off."
"It would be *more profitable* to speed up the line."
"Company Y is a *better* source of raw material."
"We should copy Smith; he's *the best.*"

To challenge these statements at this point would demand justifications which would not increase the number of pathways and might decrease contributions from others who felt inadequate to provide support.

Another form of statement which may appear will be one that something is impossible, that an action can't or must not be taken. In this phase, the appropriate response to such a statement is ignore the claim in favor of including the statement under question as an acceptable alternative and to return to the action being specified. Rejecting a statement for impossibility may remove a potentially profitable alternative from consideration. To challenge such a statement at this point may reduce the willingness of participants to suggest alternatives. A statement that something can't be done usually reflects a representation which has imposed boundaries which are not absolute necessities but merely a reflection of individual experience. The purpose of this phase is to generate many possible alternatives, not to evaluate the degree of possibility. A common example of this type of statement arises when policy is believed to prevent an alternative. Often, in these circumstances, the idea never surfaces in a meeting because "everybody knows" it's against policy. It is often possible, of course, to change policy and ideas rejected at this stage will hide the costs of that policy. Better to consider the idea and let it be rejected after costs are considered.

The above comments regarding Pointers and the following ones on appropriate procedures are given with the understanding that the non-verbal components of communication are always more powerful than the verbal. Non-verbal communication is outside of the scope of this book and will be presented in a forthcoming work. We believe the verbal component of communication is the most effective place to start a full system of communication. Much of business communication is, after all, verbal. We introduce the non-verbal factor here as a caution to ensure that the user of the Precision model be aware of the outcome desired. If a manager really wants to elicit the resources of employees and peers, his non-verbal behavior will most frequently support that intention. Combined with the appropriate questions, that behavior will likely generate the desired response. The skilled use of non-verbal behavior will, with or without questions, elicit the appropriate responses with greater ease and elegance.

PROCEDURES

The next area of the Precision model we will consider is the one referred to as Procedures. Each Procedure was designed for specific uses at specific stages of information processing. The Procedures appropriate to the Pathways phase are the Relevancy Challenge, the Missing Link, and the Recycle Questions. The Relevancy Challenge is simply a request for the information source to identify how his statement is relevant—how it may help to achieve the outcome. This challenge can obviously be misused to defeat the purpose of this phase but it must be included for the information processor to ensure his ability to maintain control. The challenge can yield benefits other than control. If an idea is apparently irrelevant, it cannot be used effectively by others. Also, in the evidence produced for support of relevancy, there may be a chain of unspecified actions which lead back to the original source unspecified action and which contains links outside of the representation of the others present. The requirement of evidence of relevancy suggests this is the case. A Relevancy Challenge such as, "I don't understand the connection between your suggestion and the desired outcome. How, specifically, would that achieve the outcome we're after?" may elicit a favorable response which indeed provides useful new representations. Such a challenge may produce more alternatives and will eliminate alternatives which don't lead to the desired outcome.

MISSING LINK PROCEDURE

The Missing Link is a refinement of the relevancy procedure especially for this phase. We stated earlier that the approach to Pathfinding is to continually more fully specify verbs until adequate precision is achieved. The function of the Missing Link question is to retrace some of the node structure presented earlier to determine if there is a relatively less specified action than one already on the chart which is between the next highest or less specified action on the chart. In the Relevancy Challenge we asked for further specification because the relation to the desired outcome was not apparent. Here we are asking for further specification, not because we don't understand the connection but because there might be a relatively less specified action which would indicate a new direction for alternatives.

Let's return to a previous example of a sales manager and his general manager. The defined difference statment may have been "to create a new reporting method which would increase the control over sales." The first suggestion might have been to keep logs of sales call activity. A visual representation of this stage might look like the following:

> •Increase control over sales
>> •Create new reporting system
>>> •Keep logs of sales call activity

Now, if the *Missing Link* question, "What will keeping logs do to attain the desired outcome?" were asked, the response might generate the less specified verb phrase, "Use information not contained in the accounting system." That is, the purpose of keeping and using sales logs for reporting is that the sales manager is using that information to judge his salesmen and their efforts and he would like to be judged on the same basis. A more general statement of this possibility has now been added.

•Increase control over sales
  •Create new reporting system
    •Use non-accounting data in the reporting system (new)
      •Keep logs of sales call activity

This new representation provides the opportunity to direct the search for alternatives into the area of common performance criterion and will lead to the likelihood of discovering a better solution using orders taken.

RECYCLE PROCEDURE

The Recycle Procedure is appropriate whenever a word or phrase is so rich with potential hidden material that it might be profitably returned to. This procedure can be used when:

1. An action (verb) phrase is being pursued to develop a number of alternative courses of action or pathways, or,
2. A sentence or phrase has a number of words or parts each of which can be profitably developed.

The Recycle Procedure is like a memo to return to a particular point. It ensures that the manager won't get lost in following a particular track and fail to return to a place which he selected as potentially profitable. In our experience, many managers fail to return after one track leads to a dead end and lose opportunities to solve problems effectively. We have found that making a visual representation or note can be the most effective way to learn this procedure and that many experienced managers continue to use the technique of making these notes.

A whole tree structure can be developed and will help to keep everyone involved aware of the alternatives and where they are in the procedure. A simple procedure of writing down the action which is being specified as a reminder of the return point may be sufficient: For more complex problems, a list of verb phrases can be made and each item circled as it is being developed and checked when complete. Any of these procedures can be effective when the purpose is to generate a maximum number of alternative actions such as in this Pathways phase.

Each action should be returned to until all possible alternatives have been generated. A variation of the Action Blockbuster will be appropriate here. After the first Action Blockbuster, the Recycle Procedure will be accomplished by the question, "How else might we . . . (verb)?" The word "else" will be repeated until no more alternatives are offered. A visual representation of the *Recycle Procedure* with a verb phrase might look like the following:

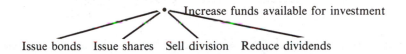

Issue bonds Issue shares Sell division Reduce dividends

Each of the items generated can, in turn, be further developed in the same way.

The Recycle Procedure is also appropriate when applied to an initial verbal representation. The initial statement is a highly coded representation of a complete map or representation. For instance, the statement, "We need to get rid of slow moving inventory" has a number of elements which all need to be expanded to be of high enough quality for an action plan.

Each of the following questions *for this particular example,* needs to be answered before any precise understanding of what has been proposed can be assumed:

1. Who, specifically, needs to take the action(s)?
2. What inventory, specifically, is being considered as "slow moving?"
3. How, specifically, is it to be "got rid of?"

All of these individual parts need to be considered to arrive at an adequately precise understanding before action is taken. Missing any one of them will leave a gap which could result in unwarranted action or the inability to obtain feedback or maintain accountability. A full specification will provide full control.

During a planning meeting, for which we had been asked to provide process consulting, the marketing vice-president stated she thought they needed "a new product to sell." All the information needed was contained in this initial statement in a highly coded form. We used a flip chart to demonstrate this visually to the meeting. The original was presented as:

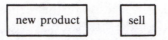

After the first question, "Sell to whom?" we had:

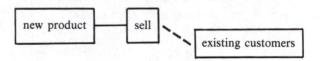

Next, we chose to track "New Products" with the Noun Blockbuster and developed the following:

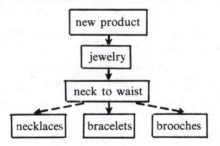

We then chose to track "sell" and developed the following:

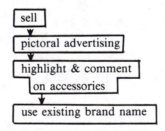

Finally, "existing customers" was tracked into the following:

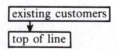

The final representation from the original statement looked like the following:

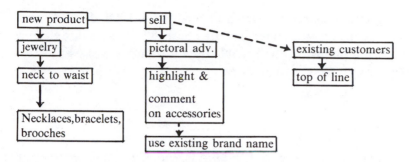

The Recycle Procedure was used to develop a high quality representation from the original statement "need a new product to sell." Each element of the original was developed to produce an action plan. The final verbal representation was a request to develop "a new product line of jewelry limited to necklaces, bracelets and brooches which would be sold to existing 'top of the line' customers by using the existing company brand name and existing advertising format." We recommended that the flip chart be passed on as part of the problem definition to the next phase. This would provide the participants with a visual device for demonstrating the source and development of the idea — a sort of snapshot Backtrack Frame for the next meeting.

FRAMES

The third area of the Precision model, the Frames, are all applicable to this stage. The Outcome Frame runs through all phases and is the mechanism for maintaining control of the process. It ensures that the manager knows where he is at all times and that contributions are relevant. It can be used to reorient participants to where they are or should be in the process. The Backtrack Frame is a device for refreshing the representations which may be valuable for the purposes of any particular outcome or phase of the process. It can be used at any time in this phase and will often help to access parts of maps which are relevant but were not elicited on previous runthroughs. It may be used as a summary of the content or where you are in the process.

We introduce the third and final Frame of the Precision Model in this phase. It is not restricted to this phase. Like all the Frames, it can be effectively employed in any phase. The Frames are the powerful techniques which will enable the information processor to access the maximum resources *in context* at all times.

AS-IF FRAME

The purpose of the *As-If Frame* is to make it possible to elicit the information and/or behavior required for the Desired State to be reached as effectively as possible given the present resources of the group.

The As-If Frame is appropriate whenever the manager determines that there is a condition in the actual present situation which is blocking access to information or behavior which moves toward the intended Desired State. The As-If Frame is the establishment of a contrary to fact context or Frame in which the desired information or behavior becomes available. This includes typically the assignment of roles or characteristics to various members of groups or the creating and establishing of information contrary to fact which shifts the context in which the group is operating to one where the information or behavior required is made available.

The exchange in the following transcript offers an example of the As-If Frame:

GM: . . . as a way of getting started, let me pretend to be naive about this margins-inventory situation. Specifically, see how many ways you can describe to me that this problem might be solved.

DM: I'm not sure what you mean, George.

GM: All right, Tom, act *as if* you had the ability to change any part of this operation. Now tell me how many ways you could change something which might solve the problem that we've defined here this morning—namely, to . . .

The GM has made the determination that an As-If Frame would be useful at this point in the discussion. His motivation in this case was that the DM typically assumed that the GM had information about the division as thorough and detailed as the information that the DM had. Operating with this assumption, the DM would typically allude to complex portions of the divisional operation for which the GM had little or no high quality information. Thus, to prevent a recurrence of this low grade information exchange situation, and to establish a temporary relationship with the DM which would make the detailed 'no-assumptions' Precision Model questioning more understandable to the DM, the GM assigns himself a characteristic . . . *let me pretend to be naive* . . . and the DM, a role . . . *act as if you had the ability to change any part of the operation* . . . Hence, the elicitation of the high quality information proceeds and as the reader will note, the GM succeeds in creating an environment where the resources of the DM are fully engaged in creating solutions to his own problem. The GM does not create any solutions, rather by his timely use of Frames and Precision Model questioning, he creates an environment in which the individual who has the fullest amount of high quality information, the richest internal map, does so—a splendid example of the art of managing.

There is a wide range of uses of this powerful Framing technique —some of which will occur in other segments of the transcripts. We offer two further examples at this point.

In a high level planning session, the CEO determines that one of the plans for achieving a Desired State is much more attractive than the others—particularly, in terms of the payoffs. He also has the intuition that this particular plan involves a high level of risk, specifically, the risk of an expensive sales and advertising campaign being co-opted by a particular competitor. In order to upgrade his intuitions regarding the risk of a campaign take-over by the competitor, he turns to one of the members of the executive planning committee:

CEO: Jim, didn't you once tell me that you have made a hobby out of predicting the responses that Driver (the CEO of the competitor in question) would make to our plans?

Executive: That's correct—I've gotten quite accurate over the years.

CEO: Excellent. I've got something here I believe would be extremely useful for our meeting. Jim, I want you to act as if you are Driver and, further, that you have received informa-

tion that we are about to initiate the campaign we've been
discussing. Your task is to develop as many ways as possible
that you could take over the campaign for your own purposes.
If we can build in safeguards to your attempts at a take-over,
I know we can defend it in practical terms. Are you game?

Another common and extremely powerful use of the As-If Frame
is one in which a group of business people in a meeting are exploring
specific ways to achieve some desired state. As they pursue one
particular possibility, one of the group members makes the following
objection:

Controller (C): . . . look, it may look like a time saver to your
people, but let me tell you that if we do away with the Special
Stores way of accounting for tools, the employees will steal
us blind. Can anyone tell me how we're going to keep them
from stealing the equipment? Huh? I'm just not going to buy
it.

CEO: Orville, you've raised a very important issue—accountability, and frankly, I don't have an answer to your question at
this point. However, I do know two things—first, there are
companies similar to ours which have successfully done away
with the Special Stores method of accounting for tools; and
secondly, this possibility looks like just the solution to a number of our difficulties if we could solve the accountability
problem. So I'd like to pursue it right down to the specifics
to determine whether it is as good as it looks. Orville, just
suppose for a minute, that we could come up with a system
which satisfies the accountability issue you've raised, would
you then buy it? Would you have any objection at that point
to the proposal?

In this instance the As-If Frame isolates an information deficit.
None of the individuals presently available can offer the high quality
information required to fill this information gap. The CEO has information that leads him to believe that with some research and planning the objection that the controller has raised can be dealt with
effectively. Thus, he uses the As-If Frame to isolate the information
deficit and instructs the other members of the group to act as if a high

quality solution is available. This frees the group to continue their detailed examination of this possibility. The alternative would, of course, be to drop the otherwise promising proposal until the information deficit has been filled and reassemble the group at that time to continue the discussion of that alternative. The savings in time, energy and money is obvious. The CEO will, of course, prior to the termination of the meeting if the remainder of the discussion of that alternative proves it to be otherwise viable, assign responsibility for eliciting information of a high quality to fill that information deficit.

The model just presented has demonstrated how a context can be maintained within ordinary business procedures *and* information can be effectively elicited at the same time. There need be no inherent contradiction between these goals. Many individuals have rich representations stored internally which they are unable, without skilled assistance in the form of questions or other techniques, to convert into verbal representations. The ability to access this material is provided by the questioning format in the Precision Model. The individual representations must be converted into a form useable for shared representations for this phase of the process to be most effective.

We have presented the Pathfinding phase in considerable detail. Now we present some dialogues which will demonstrate its use. We recommend that you identify the Precision Model cues and the appropriate question or statement within the context of this phase for yourself as you go. A commentary at the end of the dialogue will highlight some of the more significant points.

CASE STUDY I (SEGMENT 2)

GM: OK, Tom, I agree we've tracked it down—now let's figure out how many ways we might solve this margins-inventory problem . . . and as a way of getting started, let me pretend to be naive about this margins-inventory situation. Specifically, see how many ways you can describe to me that this problem might be solved.

DM: I'm not sure what you mean, George.

GM: All right, Tom, let us act as if you had the ability to change any part of this operation,—now tell me how many ways you could change something which might solve the problem that we've defined here this morning—namely, to get your margins back up and interest charges on inventory reduced.

DM: You mean, like dropping interest charges on my inventory of type B motors?

GM: OK, that's one—go ahead, I'll keep track.

DM: Well, let me see. . . . I could boot old Larry in the pants and tell him to push the type B motors. . . . but he's already doing one hell of a job and I'd hate to. . . .

GM: (interrupting) That's all right. Don't worry at this point about evaluating each possibility. Just come up with as many ways to solve this problem as you can—we'll evaluate each one in turn for feasibility later—go ahead.

DM: Well, obviously one solution is to cut back on producing the type B motors until inventory levels are appropriate, but realistically I. . . . well, we can discuss that later, I guess.

GM: I agree—let's discuss it more specifically later. Any other ways that you can think of?

DM: Hmmmm, . . . nothing occurs to me at the moment.

GM: OK, let me remind you of where we are. We are generating alternative ways that might logically solve the problem that we've defined here this morning,—specifically, how to raise profit margins which have slid in the last reporting period due to high interest charges on your inventory of type B motors. So far, you've come up with three possible solutions—I'll list them on the flip chart here where we can easily see them.

1. drop interest charges on inventory
2. increase divisional sales (on type B motors)
3. cut back production of type B motors

DM: Right! I'm with you.

GM: All right, Any other ways to handle this problem occur to you?

DM: Hmmm. . . . not really.

GM: OK, let me try something here, Tom. Pick one of the alternatives listed up there—maybe the one that you presently favor without being really specific about why you favor that one.

DM: All right, I guess that I favor the second one at the moment.

GM: OK, now, Tom, what outcome does increasing divisional sales of type B motors achieve for you? What is the result of increasing sales of the type B motors?

DM: Well, obviously, increasing divisional sales on that item will move inventory so that the interest charges will drop, . . . and my margins will rise.

GM: Right! Now, let me just repeat what you said—increasing divisional sales on that item will move your inventory. . . .

DM: OK. . . .

GM: in other words, the outcome you achieve, the result you get by increasing divisional sales is to move the inventory. Another way of saying it is that increasing divisional sales on that item is an example of one way you might *move your inventory.*

DM: All right, I think I understand. One way to attack the problem is that I've got too many type B motors in stock—so anyway I can move them will solve my problem.

GM: Right—getting Larry to increase sales is one way to move your inventory. Can you see any other way to move those B's?

DM: Yeah, I was just thinking while I was listening to you that an inventory transfer would be another solution—yeah, maybe some other division is short on the type B's and would welcome that.

GM: All right.

DM: Or even a special head office sales advertising push—in fact, didn't I hear that the Phoenix division was negotiating a major sales of B's to Stonewall's (a major client)?

GM: Could be—we'll check that out shortly. Any other ways to move that inventory occur to you?

DM: . . . Well, how about a package?

GM: What specifically are you packaging?

DM: I was thinking—the SX power units are moving faster than we predicted. They're our hottest major item—What if we offered a special package: SX power units with a type B motor at a special price?

GM: You mean—package the sales of the SX power units with the type B motors and sell them together?

DM: (excitedly) Yes, that might work real well.

GM: OK, got it. Any other ways you see to solve the margins-inventory problem?

DM: . . . (pause) . . . I guess that's it—How did I do?

GM: Really well. I'll put the rest of the possible solutions you came up with on the chart.

4. inventory transfer
5. special sale by head office
6. re-package—specifically an SX power unit and type B motor

DM: You know, when I look at those six alternative solutions, I feel a lot more confident about solving my margins problem.

GM: So do I, Tom—good start on the solution.

COMMENTS

The GM establishes the context of the meeting by stating the required outcome. He asks: "How many ways can we solve this problem?" The answer to this question will be the necessary input to the next step of the process. He restates the problem for which alternative pathways are to be found for solution. This might be represented as follows:

>1 increase margins
>2 reduce interest charges
>3 reduce inventory of type B motors

Either of these verb phrases may be used as a starting point. In this instance, the manager allows Tom to pick what he thinks to be the most likely starting place and proceeds from there. The context for the meeting has been explicitly established at this point. It may be referred to later to ensure that the meeting follows an appropriate course. The GM further refines the context by suggesting a procedure which may help Tom to access more of his experiential maps. The authors refer to this as an As-If Frame. That is, "act as if you had the ability to change any part of this operation."

This Procedure generates some alternative paths of action which can be represented in the following manner.

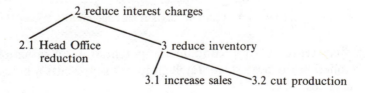

When Tom runs out of suggestions, GM uses the Backtrack Frame to refresh Tom's memory. When that fails to generate any alternatives, he decides to select the Missing Link Procedure to create a verb which is less specified than the alternatives already generated but more specified than the original set passed from defining the difference. He allows Tom to pick the most likely alternative and goes to that one. He could use this procedure on any one of the suggestions where he thought it might produce results. The question he then asks is, "What outcome does increasing the divisional sales of type B motors achieve for you?" He is requesting a higher level of action not included in the present structure. The response he gets is, "It will move my inventory . . ." After this response, the structure could look like the following:

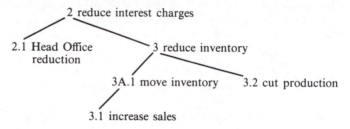

A new level of possible action has been introduced which may result in the creation of more alternative paths as it is further specified. The new node generates more alternatives and the structure created may be represented in the following manner:

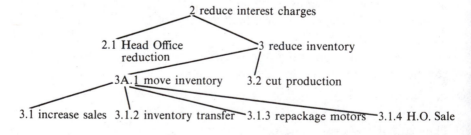

This final representation contains the potential paths of action to be developed in the next stage. Each endpoint represents a potential solution. These are:

2.1 Head Office reduction

3.1.1 increase sales

3.1.2 inventory transfer

3.1.3 repackage motors

3.1.4 Head Office sale

3.2 cut production

and are the starting points for developing alternatives which is the next stage. The outcome has been achieved in an efficient way. Both requirements of precision have been met. The paths of action generated all are different ways of achieving the Desired State. Each alternative has been adequately specified according to the intuitions or needs of both participants.

Many managers we have observed have difficulty in being precise about what stage of a process they are at. Present states and desired states are both often not clearly known to the participants in a meeting. When managers are carrying out their normal functions, they are often engaged in the processes we are presenting here. It is equally important in such informal processes to know where you are as it is in meetings set up explicitly for the process of problem solving, 'brainstorming,' or decision making. The Precision Model demands that you know where you are in the process and provides the tools enabling you to know. Failure to clearly differentiate where you are, that is, to be constantly aware of the context, often results in inappropriate responses to comments or information.

COMMON ERRORS

In contrast to the opening of our Case Study I, many managers will start with a representation which ignores the need to establish an outcome or inadvertantly set an inappropriate one. For many managers, jumping to the solution stage too quickly is common. They might start in the following manner:

GM: Let me make sure I've got this. Your margins are down because head office charges are up—specifically, charges on your inventory of type B motors. Right?

DM: Yes, that seems to be an accurate statement.

GM: OK, Tom, now let's fix it. What are you going to do about it?

Compare this opening to the case study, noticing particularly the phrase "how many ways we might solve" the problem. Instead of asking for *the* solution, the manager creates a context which will obtain full creative resources by removing the pressure for a single solution.

After some general discussion about the situation the following takes place:

DM: I'd like to get a more reasonable rate on those interest charges. If we could make an adjustment, only for . . .

GM: (interrupting) Hold on a minute, Tom. You can save your breath. The company policy on inventory interest charges isn't about to be changed. So let's be realistic about this and not waste our time. You'll have to come up with something better.

A second common and major error is to jump in with evaluation at an inappropriate time. If the objective is to get a number of alternatives, one which has already been proposed, however unlikely, can be accepted and the trajectory toward more proposals maintained. Notice that the original statement which suggests *the* solution be found will tend to require that judgement be applied to each one as it is proposed. The response to this particular proposal in the original transcript, "OK, that's one—go ahead", is much more conducive to getting more creative alternatives.

A third error which is common is pursuing an alternative to a degree of detail not required at this stage. Once a proposal is understood, it should be accepted and the momentum maintained by turning to new ones. Getting into excess detail will almost certainly lead to evaluation. Worse, the participants tend to get lost in the detail or validation of the proposal and often neglect to return to the original objective, namely, to generate as many alternatives as possible. For instance:

DM: We could cut back production and that would decrease inventory levels.

GM: How would you cut it back?

DM: I could set a date—say 6 weeks lead time and notify everyone involved. Tell them how much.

GM: Good point, Tom. How much would you have to cut back?

DM: I'm not sure. I'll have to work it out. It'd affect a few people. (pause) No. This is impossible. It would cause too many problems with personnel.

GM: Why? What's going on there?

DM: The situation has got kind of touchy lately. Some problems with foremen and discipline.

The meeting terminates without a solution. The excess detail has served to stifle creative resources and has also gone so far that the manager has lost sight of the original objective.

These types of mistakes can be overcome with consistent use of the Outcome Frame. Not knowing where they were in the process made it difficult to maintain an appropriate context. An explicit outcome would have prevented the tendency to judge and pursue alternatives past a needed point. The authors insist that information is precise only if it is in context.

The second part of the model which would have saved the meeting, although not prevented the waste of time of not having an explicit Outcome Frame, is the use of the Recycle Procedure. Recycling to the phrase, "decrease inventory levels", would have provided the opportunity to discover more ways that might be accomplished.

The model offered here presents the technology to move from a representation of a problem and a desired state to the world of experience where action needs to be taken. Each step of the process requires a step toward experience, until the final desired state can be realized by following a specific, high quality action plan.

Each unspecified action may be carried out in many ways. Each is a source of a variety of potential courses of action. The Precision Model is designed to elicit the maximum number of alternatives at this stage. A verb such as "reduce," when applied to costs, may generate alternatives ranging from across the board cost cutting or scrap reduction to firing all employees or ceasing advertising to reducing head office charges or changing allocations. All further specify the verb "reduce" when applied to costs.

When a particular course of action has been developed following the specification of a verb as fully as possible or desired, the next step is always the same. The desired state is maintained by returning to the original unspecified action and asking the Precision Model question, "How specifically might you reduce inventory?" Even tracks which end in rejection by evaluation will lead back to the original outcome of generating action alternatives.

We invite the reader to proceed to the next transcript and participate with us in applying the Precision Model to a meeting for generating alternatives.

In particular, the following elements should be noticed:

1. Any unspecified verb may be challenged with an Action Blockbuster question such as:
   "How, specifically, might we move the inventory?"
   "How, in particular, could we increase sales?"
2. Any statement of impossibility should be set aside and the alternative it refers to included in the list.
3. Each unspecified action should be challenged until no further alternatives can be generated for it. (The Recycle Procedure)
4. Any verb may be challenged to find another which, relative to the desired outcome, is less specific. (The Missing Link Procedure)

We suggest that you select the points at which you would apply the Precision Model and the specific questions you would ask at that point.

CASE STUDY II—VARIANT

Meeting called to generate alternative solutions to the personnel problem defined in the previous chapter.

Attendance: GM, PM, SM, Contr, PSup, CSup, Purch.Mgr, Personnel.

GM: This meeting is for generating alternatives to the way we are presently operating. We're losing orders and good customer relations because we're not producing special orders with options fast enough. We've narrowed the basic cause down to personnel problems. Let's see what kind of alternatives we can come up with. You all got memos summarizing the last meeting on this subject. (Memo says above plus there are problems in absenteeism, tardiness, morale, and discipline.) OK.

CS: Well, I know someone who said there were a lot of women who would work if we changed our hours.

Contr: We don't have any part-time work available, besides, they're more expensive to hire. Benefits don't change much you know.

GM: OK, Mary, you suggest part-time work.

PM: That might get us over our present problem if we can get the union to agree.

Pers: I've heard of a situation where one full time job was shared by two people. I don't know how it would work, though.

Mary: I can't see how it would work either.

GM: (writing) OK. Two people share a job.

Contr: How would they know what each other was doing?

GM: Save that for evaluation.

PM: Well, I don't think we need all these fancy changes. We just need to hire more workers.

GM: Joe, we don't want criticism here.

Pers: Besides, if we could hire more workers we wouldn't be having this meeting.

Joe: Well, we could pay more.

PS: We could change shift times, at least for some people. If it was easier to get to work it might cut down the tardiness and put people in a better mood when they get to work.

Contr: We could give some of our supervisors training in being more assertive.

Pers: Or courses in active listening. That might help improve morale.

GM: We could try flextime.

PM: What's that?

GM: It's a system where employees get to choose their own hours.

The meeting ends at this point. Valuable information which would have generated higher quality ideas was not obtained. The amount of criticism kept some individuals quiet, others were not drawn out enough.

Let's look at the points where a choice might have been made to apply the Precision Model.

The first choice point we would select is the unspecified verb "change." A question such as, "If we changed our hours, how, specifically?" would elicit higher quality information which would get the specific alternatives intended by the verb "change". The GM may have missed the point entirely when he used his own interpretation "part-time work" to classify the representation. Notice that his term is relatively unspecified and Mary may think it covers what she said when, in fact, it doesn't.

The exchange of criticism, both favorable and unfavorable, on Mary's alternative is the second point, the Relevancy challenge could have been used to enforce the context and reduce such future interventions.

The third choice point we would select in this transcript is the unspecified verb "hire." The question is implicit in the personnel statement, "Besides, if we could hire more workers we wouldn't be having this meeting." This statement served no useful purpose. The question, "How, specifically, could we hire more workers?" would get precisely the quality of information which might have provided more useful alternatives.

The fourth choice point we would select is the unspecified verb "change." The question, "How, in particular, might we change shift times?" also has the possibility of obtaining useful information. The argument attached to this verb "shift times" is more likely to seem obvious to those experienced in business. This makes the point that the Precision Model can be applied usefully as a strict model and not only when one believes himself to be unsure of meaning. It is often productive to ask questions as if one didn't know the meaning of the phrase used; mainly because that will frequently turn out to be true. We seldom are aware of the particular set of experiences or maps which the speaker is referring to.

The fifth preferred choice point is on the unspecified verb "choose." This particular verb is connected with concepts which are much more obviously outside the understanding of the group and other information gathering questions could be used with good results. In the context of eliciting action alternatives, however, we would choose the unspecified verb to get precisely the kind of information we want. "How, specifically, could they choose their own hours?" or "Choose from what?" are two examples of questions which would generate information which would allow the participants to connect the original alternative to their own experience.

Let's look at an example of a meeting to elicit action alternatives using the Precision Model. This is an example and we realize that different responses could have been made. We invite the reader to consider the distinctions and Frames presented so far and consider how different choices might have produced different outcomes.

CASE STUDY II

Meeting called to generate alternative solutions to the personnel problems defined in the previous section.

Attendance: GM, PM, SM, Contr, PSup, CSup, Purch Mgr, Personnel.

GM: The purpose of this meeting is to generate alternatives to the way we are presently operating which will result in a more satisfactory state of affairs. Specifically, we are presently losing orders and our good customer relations because we are not producing enough special orders with options to meet demand.

A satisfactory state will be when we are producing enough to meet scheduled demand within 3 days on a regular basis. The basic cause of this problem we found to be lack of adequate personnel. Further, this is being felt throughout our organization due to changing labor market conditions. All of you here today have been affected by this same set of circumstances and have valuable experience and ideas to contribute to solutions. You have all been circulated with minutes of the last meeting which defined the problem. Let me summarize those points and then obtain any further clarification before we move to generating alternatives. First, we have more competition for labor, particularly skilled due to the recent start-up of two plants in the area. Absenteeism and tardiness are increasing alarmingly. Labor costs and overtime charges are increasing while it is getting harder to get employees to work overtime. Are there any further facts which will help define the problem?

PS: Well. . . .

GM: Yes, George?

George: I think we have a morale problem which is part of the problem.

GM: How is it part of the problem?

George: I think the men could meet production just by working the way we used to.

GM: What way is that?

George: Well, they seemed to be more motivated.

GM: More motivated to do what?

George: To get the job done. They needed the job and were glad to put in a full day . . . even extra time. Now they seem to be interested only in filling in time. There seems to be a lot of frustration, too.

GM: Frustrated about what?

George: They complain about the rush hour traffic, about overtime, about not getting jobs finished and having to do tooling-up over again. Stuff like that.

GM: (pause) Thanks, George. Anyone else?

CS: Well, I know someone who said there were a lot of women who could work if we changed our hours.

GM: Mary, that sounds like a useful alternative. Would you hold it until we find out if there is anything which will more clearly define the difference between where we are and where we want to go?

CS: Two of our clerks quit in the last two months because they needed more time. They needed to look after their families.

Pers: The union is beginning to sound tough on the issue of overtime. I think they realize that they're in a better position and have us over a barrel.

GM: Better than what?

Pers: In past years their members didn't have anywhere else to go. Now they do.

GM: Anything else? . . . . OK. Let's start generating some alternatives, paths we might reach our desired state by. Specifically, our objective is to generate as many alternatives as possible. I'll record them here on the blackboard. Mary, you had a suggestion earlier.

Mary: Well, I know there are a lot of women out there who would work if they could work part-time.

Contr: We don't have any part-time work available, besides . . .

GM: This part of the meeting is for generating alternatives. Evaluation will be done at a separate stage of the meeting. I want any ideas, no matter how unlikely they may seem at first. That way we can combine our resources and find new and better ways which none of us might come up with individually. Mary, we would organize some jobs so that they would be done, say, between the hours of 10 and 2 as a permanent part of our schedule. (writes down suggestion as Permanent Part-time)

Pers: I've heard of a situation where one full time job was shared by two people. I don't know how it would work, though.

Mary: I can't see how . . .

GM: At this stage we only want to generate ideas, not evaluate them. How, specifically, did they share the job, Ellen?

Ellen: Well, some women who didn't want to work full time, a woman writing a book and two guys working on getting degrees, all shared jobs so that they had some money and lots of time off.

PM: What were the mechanics? I can't get a picture of how it might work.

Ellen: One of the pair worked in the mornings and the other in the afternoon.

Contr: It wouldn't work if they needed to share information.

GM: Evaluation later, Alan.

PM: Well, I don't think we need all these fancy changes. We just need to hire more workers.

GM: How, specifically, might we hire more workers, Joe?

Joe: Well, we could advertise in other counties. This is a pretty good area and some people might want to move here from worse jobs somewhere else.

PS: We could change shift times, at least for some people. If it was easier to get to work, it might cut down the tardiness and put people in a better mood when they get to work. It takes me a half hour to relax after fighting traffic.

Joe: We could raise wages. It might make it easier to get the men to produce and I'm sure we could attract more men that way.

Pers: I've read about some stuff but . . .

GM: We don't want evaluation now, Ellen, even on yourself. What have you read?

Ellen: I've read that flextime has reduced absenteeism and tardiness and increased morale and production at the same time. It might solve all our problems.

PM: Oh, yeah? What's this magic?

Ellen: Well, I only said what I read . . .

GM: (with a look at PM) Ellen, tell us more, particularly what flextime is.

Ellen: It's a system where you install special time clocks which accumulate the number of hours worked over a day, week, or month. It has an earliest starting time and a latest quitting time and employees can choose their own hours within that time period.

GM: How, specifically, do they choose their own hours?

Ellen: There's what they call 'core time' when everyone has to be there. That's so you can count on attendance at meetings and share information and things like that. Other than that, they have total freedom.

Purch Mgr: I like the sound of that. Why does it have to be fixed hours and core time though? And time clocks. . . .

GM: Larry, we don't want to evaluate here. Can you add an alternative to the one just presented?

Larry: Uh, . . . I'm not sure what you mean.

GM: It sounded like you had an alternative in mind.

Larry: Well, I just figured maybe we didn't need all that structure. We could just have a kind of informal system where everyone just made sure he got the job done in his own time. Sort of an informal flextime, I guess.

GM: OK, let's add that to the list.

Ellen: How about 4/40?

GM: If you think there's any possibility of the idea being useful for consideration, I'd like to hear it. I don't know what 4/40 stands for though. What, specifically, is 4/40?

Ellen: Well, it means a 4 day forty hour week.

GM: (starting to write) OK. 4 day 40 . . .

Ellen: Well, I'm only proposing that we could change the total hours per day.

GM: How, specifically, could we change total hours per day, Ellen?

Ellen: I don't know enough about our manufacturing operations to propose 4/40 exactly.

GM: What would you need to know?

Ellen: Well, the idea is to fit the schedule into the requirements of the production process and at the same time match the particular needs of your employees. My idea is that . . . well, actually the idea I read is that we have a shorter work week with longer working days.

GM: Thank you. (after a lengthy pause) Are there any more possibilities?

Purch Mgr: I've got one.

GM: What is it, Larry?

Purch Mgr: Is it OK to combine some ideas?

GM: Sure. Yes.

Larry: I can think of combining flextime and job sharing and also shift changes with job sharing. I'm kinda excited about the possibilities for my employees.

GM: (writes those two) Anything else come up?

PM: I might consider staggering shift starting and stopping times over a longer period, something like flextime. That might help for our longer processes.

GM: (after long pause) Anything else? (another long pause) OK. Let's move on to the evaluation.

If the leader of a caravan across the early plains of America was faced with the task of choosing his path before he started out, what might he do? He realizes that there may be others in his company who have greater knowledge than he does. Some of them, particularly the scouts whom he has hired for their expert skills, have crossed the area he intends to cover more frequently than he has. Others, drivers hired by the settlers who hired him, may have been to the territory they intend to reach by different ways. What kind of things would he have to say, what kind of questions would he have to ask, to be sure he would arrive at his destination safely and in the shortest possible time? The ability to find the most profitable route would depend on his ability to know of all the possible trails he might take.

The first step would be to give precise descriptions of the starting point and the desired end state. He would need to be sure that those who might have useful information knew specifically where they were starting and where they wanted to end up or a shortcut or newly found trail might not be mentioned.

The manager begins by presenting a clear statement of the present state and the desired state. He summarizes the issues which were relevant to arriving at the descriptions of these states. Then he states that the area to be improved, the actions to be taken, will relate to the lack of adequate personnel.

Each participant now has a precise and explicit framework to use in accessing experiences and resources useful in reaching the desired outcome of the meeting.

The manager may refer to this context, which will have been already established for the participants, at any future point in the meeting. This is the first step to ensure that one of the requirements for precision will be met. Any actions or words which do not lead from the present state to the desired state will be recognized and terminated. The meeting will not be led down paths which are not useful to it.

The leader of the caravan will have determined the starting point of the trek and the final destination with his employers. The scouts and drivers, however, would not have been involved at that time. Some background, in the form of a summary of the original discussion, would begin to access appropriate parts of their experience. They might also have pieces of information about the starting or ending points which would influence the decision about the best path to take which could be useful to others as they accessed their own maps of the territory.

The manager summarizes the pertinent experiences discussed at the meeting in which the difference was defined and asks for any further experiences which might assist in finding alternatives. There are individuals present at this meeting who weren't at the previous one and the background information will help them to begin to access relevant experience and to provide intelligence that may not have been available at that meeting. The Backtrack Frame will begin to access the appropriate areas of experience for those who were at the first meeting. It will refresh their memories or begin to activate again the appropriate resources.

Notice that the manager uses only Action and Noun Blockbusters for the statements which are presented to him. He is using this step of the meeting to access chunks of maps and his overall purpose for the meeting is to generate many ideas which need not be specific.

The leader must get the scouts and drivers to inform him of any paths or trails which might be useful for their trek. They each may know of paths which none of the others are aware of. Some of these paths, when considered by those who know of them, might appear to be unrelated to the known destination. Some may even seem to lead away from the destination. Any one of these paths, however, might be the very one needed to find the best route from the starting point to the desired ending point. It may be the necessary connecting path between two others which are rejected because no one knows how to connect them. None of the scouts or drivers, or even the leader himself, can know which path might prove the best until all of the potential paths are displayed on a common map. The information required at this point is of all the paths which can possibly be traveled. Questions of terrain or of relative difficulty are not important until the most likely combinations of paths are assembled.

So he drew in the dirt the beginning and end and each man added trails which might help. And as a trail was added, others made connections of their own, and soon they had many alternatives to choose from.

The manager now specifies the specific outcome or desired state for this particular stage of the meeting, which is "to generate as many alternate paths to our desired state as possible." He again makes clear for each participant the framework for obtaining the objective. No deviations from this path are accepted. Each time one occurs, the participants are directed back to the original framework with a restatement and a specific question.

Each path suggested is related to the specified outcome and accepted if it is a potential way to achieve that outcome. If a suggestion is at a logically higher level, the manager will be at a choice point. He must consider whether he wants to remain in the previously established Frame or open to a relatively less specified verb. This decision will depend on his assessment of the likelihood of its success and the time and effort available for attainment of the desired state. It can be appropriate to reject such an alternative and/or to defer it to a later date or time.

This meeting ends with many new alternatives being generated: More than might have been imagined possible and many not considered by this company before. The arguments passed to the next stage, evaluating alternatives, are a list of paths of action with verbs specified to the level of detail considered necessary by each participant in the meeting.

DIAGRAMMING

The information passed from the meeting for Defining the Difference is precise. The present and desired states have both been defined with precision and the action areas required to eliminate the difference have been specified. The statement passed to the last dialogue is specified as "improve working conditions so we can attract more skilled workers to increase production and eliminate lost orders of special motors." For the purpose of finding the maximum number of paths from the present to the desired state, we select all the unspecified verbs and construct a model according to their level of specification.

1. eliminate lost orders of special motors
2. increase production

3. hire more skilled workers
4. improve working conditions

The manager will make a diagram similar to the above and use his experience and level of authority in deciding which specific verb phrase he intends to develop. In defining the difference, an initial problem has been increasingly narrowed until an adequately precise formulation has been reached. Each major chunk of the path which was traveled to arrive at the adequately precise formulation will be reviewed. Each of these chunks is a point at which further specification may be profitable.

The particular point selected will depend on the manager's evaluation of factors outside of the original selection process. The most promising area for action, the planning time frame for impact of results, the duration of the particular solution desired and the time and effort available for generating and investigating alternatives are all factors which will be evaluated. The manager may select any point. The Precision Model will provide him with the tools to pursue a solution most efficiently from any point he selects and will also provide the means to go to another logical level if it is later required.

One of the major determinants will be an assessment concerning the cost of information. All information has a cost. The time and effort required to develop alternatives for the first unspecified verb in the above chain will be substantially greater than to develop alternatives for the last. The definition of the difference has been done to arrive at the specific differences which account for the original difference which was considered a problem. Many other paths could be developed which might turn into more profitable and longer range solutions. They are ones which appear to require longer chains of capital investment or time and were therefore ones which are more risky and had longer periods before the benefits would be realized. The chain which was received in the form of an adequately precise definition of the difference already reflects an assessment of the problem.

An example of a map of the problem which might be developed from the original specification might look something like the following:

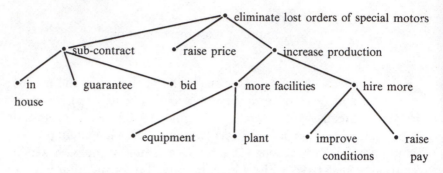

As can be seen in the above diagram, which is far from exhaustive, the time and effort required to investigate each alternative is geometrically increased. The manager will make what in his judgment is the best decision. If he finds no satisfactory solution to eliminating the difference by pursuing it from the level he started at, he may move back up the structure and try from another level. Notice that movement will always be to a higher level because each lower point will be included in his investigation. A suggestion may be made which logically deals with a level higher than the one selected. The manager has the option of moving to that higher level or of placing the suggestion aside and remaining at the level he originally selected. The development of our last dialogue might look like the following after the manager selects the last node "improve working conditions" as the most likely area.

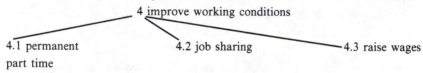

At this point in the transcript, the production manager gives a suggestion which is at a higher level on the original structure, namely, (3) hire more skilled workers. The manager, having information about previous efforts in this area, decides to put that alternative on hold and returns consideration to (4) improving working conditions. At this point, the manager decides to make a test to determine if there is a node which may fit between (4) and (4.1). His question must be phrased to indicate the unspecified verb he wants to follow and the particular specification which indicates the path. The Missing Link question asks for an unspecified verb phrase, or node, in between the two existing ones. Using the structure above, we can ask, "How, in particular, will starting permanent part-time (4.1) improve the working conditions (4)?" This question is searching for a category or type of action which includes the more specified verb in the existing chain and which might include other ways of arriving at the same desired state. The answer yields the following structure:

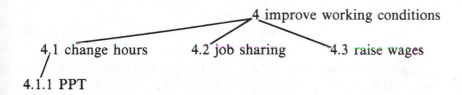

4.1 change hours   4.2 job sharing   4.3 raise wages

4.1.1 PPT

As the meeting progresses, the structure grows to look like the following:

The manager has paused and received no further alternative pathways to reach the desired state. He Backtracks to elicit any additional ideas. This step will ensure that each unspecified verb has at least two nodes if it has any. No specification will be useful as a separate node (alternative) unless there is another possible way of accomplishing its objective. As the structure is reviewed, he finds that (4.1.3) has only one specification. He will request another or

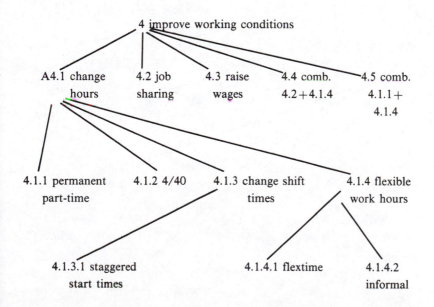

consolidate the one given (4.1.3.1) into the original (4.1.3). The result from this summarization, which generated some new alternatives as well, looks like the following:

The meeting ends having arrived at its desired outcome. An adequate number of alternative paths of action has been generated. All participants have contributed everything available from their own maps of experience and they now share a composite of the richest representation of alternatives possible to them. They have achieved what they planned to in an efficient manner.

Applying the tests provided by the Precision Model, we find that the context has been maintained. The meeting requested that the maximum number of alternatives be generated and that each be a potential move towards eliminating the difference so that the desired state can be attained. The test of adequate precision has been met by restricting the information processed to continually refining the unspecified action phrases into the variety of more specific actions which might be required to achieve the desired state.

The structure which represents the desired state of the meeting to find pathways provides the present state definition for the next stage. Each endpoint node represents the specific action which might achieve the desired outcome. Each must be developed into an action

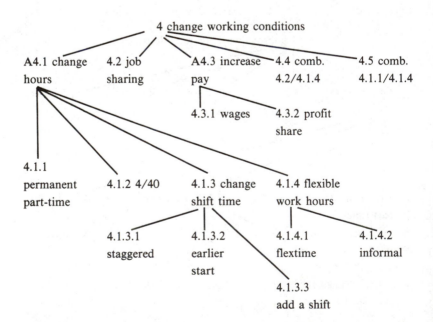

plan which can be evaluated and carried out with specific feedback built into it.

Each step of the process needed only the Precision Model to achieve the desired results. The intuition of the manager may enhance the speed and power of the process, as it will in all activities. We recognize and respect the skills which managers have developed to generate alternative paths to desired outcomes in the absence of any explicit technology to assist them in this task. We offer this technology to enhance these abilities, and specifically, as an explicit set of tools, a set of tools which will provide the manager the means to follow through on his intuitions in an efficient manner.

The frustration of knowing what needs to be done but not being able to get the appropriate resources or responses from subordinates is familiar to every manager. The feeling of having to do everything yourself eats up the time and stomach of every manager at times: The pressure of having your resources spread too thin to leave time for the more important planning which you know should be done. The Precision Model will reduce these concerns and enhance the existing powers of each individual manager.

Managers who lack the experience or intuitive skills of the most powerful and creative individuals have been required to depend on a finite set of procedures which have been, at best, inefficient and at worst actually harmful in attaining the outcomes they desire or were instructed to get. Not having tools available to provide them with a process to obtain adequate precision in the information they required, they must develop their skills in a way which involves great risk to their companies or attempt to duplicate previously existing states. They must also be heavily involved in the content of any problem or be at the mercy of opinions which they have no way to assess confidently. The Precision Model provides these managers with a process which ensures that they are able to reach an adequately high quality of information. They may use the model to obtain more precision than a highly experienced and intuitive manager would require but they need only err on the side of safety. There is no longer any need to act without precise information.

The Precision Model not only enables a manager to know where he is at any time in the process of problem solving, it insists that he know where he is. Maintaining context and specificity will be accomplished only if a manager knows where he is in the process. And the tools provided ensure that he need only follow the model. Variations which are moving successfully may be pursued to their desired end. At any point when doubt arises as to the success of the current path, the Precision Model may be returned to or invoked and used to find where you are and where to go from there.

A new manager has a great need to be able to benefit from the accumulated knowledge of his predecessor and other successful managers in a company. At present, there is little ability to accomplish this transfer of the refined resources potentially available. A benefit of the Precision Model is that a manager who is unsure of his intuitive abilities knows exactly where he is in the process and may request the precise intelligence that he needs. He will have the power to represent the present state and desired state in precise terms and ask for the specific experience required in the current situation. He will have access to the individual resources of his employees as well as his peers. In addition, he will have the ability to learn from the process of the more experienced manager by appropriately precise questioning to reduce confusing chunks into manageable pieces.

BACKTRACK

The pathfinding phase presented here starts with a definition of the difference between a present state and a more valued desired state and develops as many alternative courses of action as possible which might eliminate that difference. This phase will be productive to the extent that existing arbitrary boundaries are removed from individual representations.

A second and often seemingly contradictory requirement is that the alternatives be within the context of the desired outcome. The problem has been to widen the boundaries to access new creative resources while maintaining enough control to elicit potentially useful alternatives.

The distinguishing characteristic of the present state is the definition of the difference. Many attempts at generating alternatives founder on the lack of precision of the problem statement. The Precision Model provides the tools for ensuring that the information which is the present state of this phase will be precise enough to provide a context for generating potentially useful alternatives.

The objective of this phase is to create a shared map from the rich individual maps available as resources. Each individual may have a part of an alternative or one which was previously unknown to other participants. As these become part of a shared representation, more resources may be accessed—resources which the individual source may not have known he possessed. Part of the task of this phase is to elicit resources of participants which are not known beforehand. Many techniques have provided unique ways of accessing creative resources but, until now, none has provided the means to ensure that these resources are accessed within an appropriate context. The Frames provided and cues identified by the Precision Model provide the ability to elicit information without requiring previous knowledge of the specific piece of information being sought.

One of the techniques which the authors have found particularly useful at this stage is to create visual representations. A more detailed shared map is the source of new and creative alternatives. Making some kind of visual representation can be an effective means of assisting each participant in that process.

The sensitive use of personal skills, as well as the specific parts of the model presented here, will produce great benefits. Many theories dealing with generating ideas are particularly concerned with this issue and develop elaborate techniques to ensure full cooperation of participants. These concerns are valid and the authors acknowledge their importance in accessing the various resources of participants. We take the position, however, that the sensitive use of personal skills will enhance cooperation in any human activity. We recognize that an environment which is antagonistic will likely inhibit access to individual maps. The resources of others are required in all business activity. We believe that the requirements at this phase for rapport are equal to those at other phases and believe the losses at any stage will be too significant to ignore.

The powerful new As-If Frame was introduced in this chapter. It is appropriate that we introduce it here, even though it may be effectively used in any phase, because the set of procedures for this phase commonly known as brainstorming is itself nothing but one possible As-If Frame. The limited reception of brainstorming reflects the weakness of a procedure, even one as powerful as the As-If Frame, without a technique for maintaining context such as the Outcome Frame.

All of the Frames can be used at any stage of information processing and are powerful tools for maintaining the trajectory toward a desired outcome.

The As-If Frame has much more variety than the usual brain-storming one of "pretend there are no limits." These include:

- act as if a particular stumbling block is already solved
- step into someone else's shoes and act as if you were that person
- think as if the desired state were already attained and find what had to be done to get there
- act as if the organization were twice as large.

A new Procedure was introduced in this chapter—the Recycle Procedure—which has uses throughout information processing. Its unique application in Pathfinding shows the full power of this Procedure. The Procedure is a memo to return to any particular part of a statement which may yield richer or additional resources. The particular application in this phase is to fully develop each action alternative proposed. The desired state is an extensive list of alternative actions. Returning again and again to a relatively unspecified verb will produce a variety of courses of action which may accomplish the original goal. Many potential paths are never discovered because a particular train of thought ends unproductively and the information processor doesn't return to its starting point.

The Recycle Procedure, whether as a mental or written note, provides the reminder to return. The authors strongly recommend a visual representation be made to ensure that all such points are fully explored.

The Pointers are precisely contextualized at this stage. That is, we have previously defined the cues and uses of Pointers. The stress in this chapter was placed on the contextual test to determine whether a particular Pointer is appropriate or not. The test, of course, is the Outcome Frame—will this particular question move me closer to the desired state? The ability to distinguish between types of statements and appropriate responses provides the opportunity to question, at any time, any representation in a manner consistent with the outcome desired. All theories which the authors are aware of have been unable to make these distinctions and have had to forbid all questions when the desired state is to generate as many alternatives as possible. They have sacrificed the power available to the information processor for lack of the ability to make explicit distinctions. The Precision Model restores power to the executive—and increases the creative resources available to him.

The desired state of this phase is an extensive list of alternative courses of action which will eliminate the previously defined difference. How is an information processor to know if an adequately extensive list has been elicited? The first assurance is provided by using an explicit model which provides the techniques which will access rich individual maps. The assurance is an appropriate elicitation procedure. The second is a test for completion which satisfies the information processor in terms of efficiency and his own intuitions. The end point for any particular creative task will be determined by time available and importance of outcome.

The Recycle Procedure is one method for assuring that the process is continued while there is still potentially rich unexplored material.

The outcome will be a list of alternatives, all of which can attain the desired final outcome. Each alternative will require development to determine whether it will, in practice, attain that outcome within the overall operating constraints of the total organization. The test for practicality is a separate phase which would unnecessarily limit the boundaries for creative generation of alternatives. The list produced, then, will be the richest possible within the economic or efficiency constraints imposed by the information processor.

Chapter 4

SURVEYING

As I reminisced with my son the other day about his basketball team's state championship victory, we recalled how uncertain he had felt three years previously starting with a new team. We'd just moved to a new city and he had the usual concerns about making friends and starting school in a new place. He had a greater concern this time, though, because he had started playing basketball the year before and was anxious about making the team. He knew he could do it at his first school but this one had a bigger reputation in basketball.

When he went out for the team the first year, he discovered his coach had been a top college player a few years back. His awe of the coach began to wear off as the season progressed. Although a skilled expert player, the coach couldn't always pass these skills along to the players. Some developed very well with the excellent skills coaching they received but others, who had different personal styles, couldn't always learn as well. It seemed that this coach knew only one style and could only teach by example. This method was highly successful with some of the players and less so, and frustrating, for others. The coach discouraged these players from attending clinics or getting assistance from other experts. The team learned a style of playing which was quite effective but which never seemed to have that extra bit of flexibility required to beat the really top teams. Their season record got them to the play-offs but they lost in the first round. My son remembered being disillusioned by the end of the season. Only one style of individual play and one team style, a zone, had been tried all year. This coach could only repeat an experience which had worked well for him in the past. The boys had become stale and, with no new stimulation, without the ability to test new approaches, they were beaten by teams which didn't always have players with as highly developed individual skills.

168

The next year we remembered as a disaster. He started the season with a new coach. This man had come in a little unsure of himself and had told the team that he wanted to let everyone play, to have each boy enjoy himself and to really develop a team spirit. It had sounded good at the start and they had liked the coach. They had seemed to spend more time than usual working out differences of opinion in practices but they all got a lot of practice and experience in the exhibition games. As the regular season started, however, they began to notice some tension. My son actually began to dislike the coach. For my son, the reason to get on the basketball court was to win basketball games. For the new coach, it was to create team spirit and promote each boy's enjoyment. As the season wore on and the team lost to schools which they all felt they could have beaten, there was more and more bad feeling. Even the players who were playing more than they otherwise would have were unhappy with the situation. As my son recalled this coach getting fired in mid-season, a big smile came on his face.

His smile didn't last long as we talked. The replacement was not an experienced player or coach and was uncertain about his status. The boys never did find out how much he knew and he never got their cooperation to find out how much they knew. They had been playing together for some time and had information about themselves and the competition. My son couldn't remember any particular hard feelings generating revenge; it just never seemed appropriate to suggest things. The reason, as he looked back, seemed to be that the coach had always asked the star player of the team for advice and only seemed interested in his opinion. He didn't seem to have the ability to judge, with accuracy, the information offered. It seemed he thought the safest policy was to listen to the best player. My son remembered that the best player had wanted to make the all star team and had a tendency to suggest plays or strategies which favored his own particular talents. This player seemed to be thinking of the team all right—but from his own perspective. This would have been no problem if the coach had the appropriate skills for obtaining and assessing information. That particular year, his team finished out of the playoffs altogether.

As we started to reminisce about his senior year, his body began to take on the tension we associate with excitement and challenge. Each time we talked about this exciting year, a marked change came over him. The thrill of achievement was still strong in him. He started the season with the fourth coach in three years; a situation which would seem to be less than optimal. The players sensed right away that there was something different about this coach. He obviously didn't have many skills as a player yet he appeared supremely confident in his ability to do the job which was expected of him. His manner and particularly his way of asking questions made it apparent that he was interested in the contributions of each player. Yet all the boys knew he would consider each opinion without being ruled by it. Each player knew that he could offer his opinion and have it considered if it was appropriate. He also would leave with a better understanding of his own idea even though the coach often had done nothing but ask penetrating questions. Usually a player would know whether his idea was a useful contribution without having to be told.

The new coach started the season by stating his position—the task at hand was to win the state championship. What was required to accomplish that was to win enough games to get into the playoffs and then win the playoffs. He wasn't going to worry about particular losses along the way. Each set-back was to be a learning experience. He wasn't an expert player but he knew the process required to produce winning teams and he would use the required time to get the results he wanted. He asked for the team's agreement to his goals and, getting it, proceeded towards the selected target.

My son remembered with respect how he had obtained scouting reports, had got just the information he needed from the scouts (whose written reports he seldom used), and filled in the missing pieces from information which the team members had. These sessions were a new experience for most of the players and many would use them when they later became coaches.

As my son recalled the season just completed and the actual championship game, his manner changed to one of the relaxed confidence one sees in members of a winning team who have been together for a long time. He remembered how each member of the team had put more energy than they knew they had into the effort and how they had barely noticed how hard they had worked. The same team which had not made the play-offs the year before had been changed, almost miraculously it seemed, into a championship team. Each player had developed some strategies for good ballplaying which were uniquely his own and were useful to the team in individual ways. Each member had increased his skills without knowing how it had been done. The feature my son remembered most vividly was the amount of information this particular coach had been able to obtain, the way he could organize it and the accuracy with which he could predict what kind of defense or offense would be most effective against a particular team in a particular situation. His team always seemed to have the extra something; that slight edge. The result had been not only a winning season but one in which each player had grown and could look back to with satisfaction.

INTRODUCTION

Surveying is the third phase of the overall model for business activity presented in the opening chapter.

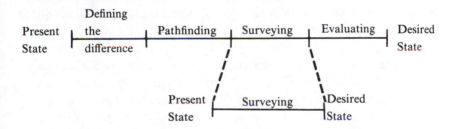

The particular process of developing alternative pathways into actions which will reduce the difference between the present state and a desired state we refer to as Surveying. Surveying is an activity which fills in the details of an area of known interest. A path for a road between two points will be selected from a few known possibilities only after the terrain over which it is to be constructed is precisely known. The original selection of possibilities will have been made with *some* existing knowledge of the terrain. The specific route selected for construction requires that the particular qualities of the terrain be precisely known. Grades, settling qualities, water courses and land composition all need to be known for each particular section of road. Notice that the adequacy of information is directly related to the purpose of the final desired state—a road. Potential information for a survey, say, about types of trees, or elevation, will not be useful and other areas of information such as weather patterns will be considered irrelevant as well. The survey will be adequately precise for its purpose only when the specific line of the exact path is obtained. No final decision will be able to be made until the precise formations are known.

"The value of any information system must be ultimately measured by the quality of management decisions. Anything less is inconclusive, and anything more unnecessary".

Russell, Kennecot Copper/Curt Symonds
A Design for Business Intelligence

The surveying stage of the process produces the high quality information about each potential pathway to enable decision makers to arrive at effective decisions confidently. The quality of management decision will be judged by the outcome achieved. Having specified the desired state to an adequate level of precision and generated alternative pathways within an appropriate context, the full development of each alternative will provide the necessary and adequate basis for sound decisions.

". . . the raw material of management is information. This is all that any manager has to work with—He has to to know what information he has about any problem, what information he doesn't have and how he can get it, and how he can use all the information he has to the best advantage in getting the problem solved.

Kepner and Tregoe
The Rational Manager

The specific information required is the answer to the question "What do I need to know to make a decision about this particular alternative?" The "need to know" will be in two specific areas. First, a specific action plan exists which is explicit enough to provide assurance to the decision maker that it will, in practice, accomplish the desired outcome. Second, the process used to arrive at that plan has been thorough and grounded in information that is adequately precise. If both are not met, the next requirement is to know what specific information is not available at an adequate level of precision and how to obtain that information.

The "need to know" information must be explicitly and precisely defined. One of the significant failures of 'brainstorming' sessions is that they generate ideas, some of which, if translated into action, would provide profitable solutions but which never get translated into actionable plans. The problems of translating potential ideas into actual pathways is often insurmountable if appropriate tools aren't available for both the stage of generating alternatives and for converting these ideas into action plans. The Precision Model provides the tools.

Without an explicit and appropriate model, the difficulties are enormous. The lack of context referred to in the previous chapter and the inability to extract ideas consistently of a high enough quality as defined by the Precision Model provide an uneven quality for the present state of this step of the process. The brilliant solution for another problem, the practical solution buried in a long list of major reorganizations and the incompletely specified solution which can never be brought to a specific enough level in action, all these are familiar to those who have had some exposure to 'brainstorming'.

The internal requirements for generating alternatives are similar to those for developing alternatives into action plans. Both call for creative resources. Both call for the ability to extract information from individual maps and create a richer, fuller shared map. By placing the generation of ideas into a special category of action removed from the practical operating world of business, the ability to access creative resources throughout the information processing has been lost. The idea that certain mental processes are valuable for one phase of information processing but should be removed from another phase suggests a less than optimal fragmentation of the whole, creative individual. Each stage of the process is characterised by the attempt to create a shared map which is the richest possible representation of contextual information possible. A requirement for obtaining the fullest possible representation is that each individual bring his own fullest resources to the process.

The Precision Model provides the techniques which can access these resources to their fullest at every stage of the process. The ability to elicit the richest variety of alternative pathways depends on the same set of skills as the ability to elicit the richest representation of the terrain of those pathways. Each requires the verbal patterns to extract high quality information. The ability to elicit this variety in a context appropriate to eliminating the difference between present state and desired state also depends on the same set of skills as the ability to elicit the details for surveying those pathways. Maintaining context and eliciting high quality information are required throughout the stages of information processing.

The context which the Precision Model provides for creating pathways provides a specific subset of the total model appropriate to opening the boundaries and restrictions commonly found circumscribing individual maps. The boundaries are opened in a way which allows any internal representation full sway and demands only that the external representation be within the established context. The Surveying stage, to make maximum use of the pathways generated, must maintain the ability to draw on the same resources. The primary difference between the two stages is that the context is more focused in Surveying. That is, it is closer to experience and therefore information of higher quality.

This stage of information processing unpacks the relevant, detailed operations necessary to yield the most efficient route to the specified outcome. The prior stage of development is to find plausible paths to a goal. During that stage, pathways aren't specified in detail although each is required to have the possibility of achieving the desired outcome. Some necessary and intricate parts are known and are referred to by name and others, necessary but not known are assigned to 'block boxes', or information deficits. The parts may require detailed analysis to determine if they will actually perform the task necessary with an adequate amount of precision. Each part must be exploded into its component parts before this judgment can be made. The 'black boxes' require a different procedure. The necessary functions to be performed at that point must be detailed and then answers found for the specific problems presented. Sometimes the answer becomes apparent from the analysis of the particular, precise requirements. Other times, the 'black box' remains an information gap which needs to be filled before a decision can be reached about whether to go ahead with the plan or not.

Creativity and full access to each individual map is as important here as at any other stage. The ability to identify information gaps in an efficient manner will depend partly on knowledge of content, as mentioned earlier. The Precision Model will get all the information required and, in the hands of skilled managers, it will get it faster and access the maximum creative resources.

PRESENT STATE/DESIRED STATE

The present state for the Survey stage will be a set of alternative pathways which may lead to the elimination of the difference defined in the first stage. These will be of high quality information in that they are adequately precise for the stage of development and they are all in the context specified at the beginning of the process. The desired state, or outcome, for the Surveying stage will be a set of alternate pathways which will result in the desired outcome and which are specified to an adequate level of precision. An adequate level of precision will be one which has a detailed action plan which could be carried into operation with no further information required or an action plan which contains known information gaps, which, when filled, will provide such a plan.

An example of such a plan many readers will be familiar with is a completed PERT chart. This chart is a visual representation of all actions which need to be taken to complete a construction or computer project on time. It shows the area of responsibility, the allowable time frames, and the specific actions to be taken. Anyone can look at the chart and know whether it will reach its objective and whether it is on time. An appropriate outcome for each specific path considered might contain such a chart with gaps for missing information to be filled in and a similar chart for obtaining that information.

The most efficient use of available resources will be to eliminate as soon as possible any alternatives which don't lead to reduction of the defined difference or do so at too great a cost to the organization. There is a danger in this criterion. Ideas which may in fact be profitable when fully developed or which may be profitable if combined with others being considered may be rejected too early. On the surface, an idea may seem to be obviously too costly or bound to have unacceptable side effects. A proposal requiring a major new investment in equipment seemed out of the question until the information was elicited that the machine it would replace was old and due for replacement in any case. A proposal to cut accessory products from production appeared on the surface to be bound to reduce sales of the primary units. It was later found to be a profitable alternative when the option of buying from an outside source was suggested and tried. This is a similar problem to the 'brainstorming' paradox. If evaluation is applied too rapidly, valuable potential will be lost. If not applied soon enough, valuable resources will be wasted.

Efficiency is a standard applied throughout business operations. Any procedure designed to get an outcome will be judged by its efficiency. That is, it will be efficient if it gets the desired outcome with the minimum use of time and resources. A fast procedure which doesn't reach the outcome isn't efficient. An expensive and time consuming procedure, relative to what is possible, isn't efficient. The overall desired outcomes of business always include the minimum necessary expenditure of resources. Efficiency often means in practice the quickest or easiest way to a *minimal* outcome. The emphasis is generally placed on the time and resources side because it can be relatively easily quantified and measured. This emphasis ensures that only minimal results will be obtained. Obtaining results closer to the optimal requires a method of determining the optimal. To be efficient, the method must be known to produce continually higher quality results as it proceeds and before the particular results are known. The Precision Model is designed to provide the assurance of efficiency while creating the conditions to reach optimal outcomes.

The original paradox is the view that there is a standard of judgment, other than intuition, which would determine in a particular instance what was too soon or late. Quantity of information or time spent are not the criteria. The answer to the paradox lies in stepping outside the context of too soon/too late and looking to procedure itself. A procedure which controls the quality of information and its context is required. The safeguard against potential waste of resources lies in focusing the flow of information on the contextually most significant area not yet examined.

FIFTH POINTER-*BOUNDARY CROSSING*

In this phase of the overall model, we will encounter the last of the Precision Model questions—the Boundary Crossing question. One of the general characteristics of the set of Precision Model Pointers thus far offered is their consistent ability to search out distinctions and refinements which did not exist in the initial information presented. These distinctions expand and enrich the shared maps or representations of the information processors using the model—the greater the number of contextually relevant distinctions available in the map, the greater the number of choices which the information processors involved have available to accomplish their goals. The effective use of any of the Pointers creates such distinctions, and the overall effect is the transformation of low quality information into high quality information—an excellent base for success in business.

The last of the Precision Model Pointers is particularly powerful as it challenges the boundary of the information source's internal map.

Some specific examples of Boundaries and related Boundary Crossing Pointers are:

Boundaries	Pointers
. . . not even bother to consider the possibility of increasing production. It's impossible –I just can't do it!	– what stops you from increasing production? or – What would happen if you did increase production?
. . . raising (lowering) prices— that much would be disasterous! We can't do it.	– what would happen if we did? or – What stops us from raising (lowering) prices that much?
. . . just that we have to meet the requirements that were set down.	– or what would happen? or – what would happen if we failed to meet those requirements?
. . . that the plant is simply unable to meet the quotas agreed upon.	– what prevents the plant from meeting the quotas? or – what would happen if the plant met quotas?
. . . that the employees must have a physical once a year.	– or what would happen? or – what would happen if the employees failed to have a physical once a year?

Whenever there is a claim either that:

1. something is impossible, can't be done,   or
2. something must occur, is necessary

use the Boundary Crossing Pointer.

Such phrases are a clear indication that the speaker/writer has reached the limits or boundries of his or her map.

The point is that all too often practices and procedures which were appropriately developed during one phrase of the growth of an organization will become such a habitual part of the everyday routines that they are carried forward into new phases in the growth of that organization where they are superflous. Left unchallenged and therefore not updated, they may seriously reduce the set of choices available to the information processor. In other cases, the use of the phrases and words like those in the examples—*it's impossible, can't, have to, unable and must*—signal that the speaker has some limitation or boundary in his or her representation which is unconnected with the business practices of the organization but indicates a refusal or, at least, a reluctance on the individual's part to consider representation in this area. This refusal may in fact be substantiated when investigated. That is, when an individual indicates by one of these phrases that they do not wish to explore the facts in some area of business possibility, it may be that they have reason to believe that if the thing they are claiming to be impossible is attempted, the results will be highly unprofitable—or conversely, if the thing they are claiming must be done is not done, likewise they believe the results will be negative. What they sometimes seem to fail to note is that talking about some business activity is not the business activity itself. During a directors' meeting one of the authors attended, a statement that all of the customer's related needs *must* be met was challenged by the general manager. Several directors immediately attacked the manager with an obvious display of emotion. It was apparent that their response was appropriate only in the context of taking action—not simply to discussing a possibility.

The Precision Model allows the rapid development of high quality information in any area of business. Thus, if the off-limits, out of bounds areas of possible business activity can be penetrated, the information lying behind the individual's reluctance can easily be determined.

Very often in the authors' experience, the gains by penetrating such areas are enormous. For example, during a discussion centering around the possibility of producing a more refined product, the controller adamantly stated it was out of the question,—wholly impossible. Finally, after several refusals to even consider the possibility, the CEO asked the Boundary Crossing—*what would happen if we did decide to produce the new, more refined product?* The controller answered that the more refined product would require a new machine—none of the machines presently on line were capable of the refinements under discussion. The controller went on under Precision Model questioning to explain that the return on the investment for the new machine would not be adequate. As soon as the production manager heard the underlying reason for the controller's initial refusal to consider the possibility of the new product, he pointed out that at least two of the present machines were due to be replaced in the next three month period for reasons of age. Thus, the new product was demonstrated to be a viable alternative—specifically, the fact that while the new machines required only for the new product would not be cost effective, new machines required for the new product *as a replacement for a machine being retired* were quite cost effective.

Note that the point is not that the new product became a profitable choice for the organization, but that the choice would not have been available without going outside the boundary of the area of activity that the controller initially refused to consider developing information about. The issue here is not the competence of the controller but the information engineering skills of the manager. The Precision Model Boundary Crossing pointer avoids entirely the issue of the competence of the individual who claims something is necessary or something is impossible—rather the issue is eliciting high quality information to be used in the construction of the shared map which the information processors involved may use to take effective action. By avoiding personality issues, the Boundary Crossing pointer automatically converts the initially reluctant member of the group into a valued information source from which ultimately high quality information is elicited.

As in the case of the other Precision Model questions, the skill of using the Boundary Crossing pointer can be usefully represented as a two part process:

Boundary Crossing Question

1. a perceptual recognition program—in this case the Precision Modeler hears the Boundary Crossing cue word, recognizing it from the short list of such words in English:

can't   have to
impossible   necessary
unable   must

2. a response program—the challenge to the representation. If the Boundary Crossing cue word comes from the left hand list, ask either one of the following two questions:

what stops you?

or

what would happen if you did?

If the cue word identified comes from the right hand list, ask either one of the following two questions:

or what will happen

or

what would happen if we failed to

We wish to caution the reader that there are a number of idioms in use which have the same effect as the cue words for Boundary Crossing listed above—idioms such as *it's out of the question, no way, it's got to be, absolutely essential. . . .* We rely on the native intelligence of the reader to recognize such expressions as equivalents of the standard cue words, especially as these rather colorful expressions tend to change rapidly and have a wide variation in different parts of North America.

In the surveying procedure, pointers are a particular set of cues and related questions which can be used effectively at this point. The pathways presented as input to this stage were developed by using mainly one portion of the model, namely, the unspecified Action Blockbusters. No challenges of evaluation were employed at that time except the Relevancy Challenge. Any Boundary Crossing cue words such as "can't, impossible, won't work" were treated simply as termination points for particular tracks and the 'impossible' alternative was retained. The most efficient use of the Precision Model at this point will be to ask for factors which appear to demand that an alternative be rejected. The Precision Model provides the technique to elicit the material behind the challenge to an alternative in a way which will enrich the shared map of everyone involved. The challenges at this point will result in potentially useful paths or rejection based on the high quality information which will be elicited by the Precision Model. If they are retained, the shared representation of that path will already have been more fully developed and useful progress will already have been made.

Many managers consider a request for more specific information a risky venture. Such a request, which may cause rejection of an alternative, is considered particularly dangerous by many. Curt Symonds has accurately reflected this concern in the following statement: "(the manager is) frequently at the mercy of the system itself. He often has neither the time nor the talent required to challenge the validity of the information he receives, and in many cases might even consider it imprudent to do so."

The management of conflict is approached in three distinctly different ways at present. One is to avoid it at all costs. Another is to force it into the open and deal with it as a primary issue. Both of these approaches have at their base that conflict necessarily means strong emotions, bad feelings, and unproductive energy. The first approach attempts to avoid these by ignoring the issue entirely; by attempting to create conditions which will remove it or by simply overriding it. The second approach recognizes the emotions as facts in the situation and elevates them to the same level as the original desired outcome of the meeting; sometimes to the point of replacing the original desired state. The third approach accepts conflict as a normal part of business. It is often referred to as "conflict management" and uses a matrix style which actually fosters these conditions. This group is generally less concerned with the emotions which may lie behind conflict and deals with the issues rather than emotions. This group, however, states that a manager must have expert knowledge of the content to deal with conflict effectively.

"(Managers) need influence based upon perceived knowledge and competence"

Lawrence and Lorch,
Developing Organizations.

The authors agree that managers require special knowledge to effectively deal with conflict. The special knowledge required is not expert knowledge of content, however, it is knowledge of the structure of communication—specifically, language—and its effective use. The Precision Model provides the technology required to deal with the complexity of increasing specialization. The demand for expert knowledge is an impossible one in the context of management growth and effectiveness.

A manager should insist that his people have more expert knowledge about their operations than he does. His primary task as a manager is to elicit that information in a way most useful to the outcomes of the organization. Precision Models, Inc. has a specific model for what is commonly called conflict or matrix management which includes the sensitive use of the Precision Model to obtain the most effective allocation of a company's resources.

Each individual has experience which is not immediately apparent to others and the authors maintain that this is a primary source of business conflict. Conflict arises when the individual maps are not shared. Intercompany conflict is often simply a result of the inability to elicit high quality information. The ability to elicit the differences in representations in an efficient and respectful manner will add greatly to the effectiveness of any manager.

A common term which appears in any discussion of meetings or potential conflict situations is "hidden agenda". Obstacles to proposed solutions, or even to the process itself, are attributed to these hidden agendas and elaborate methods for recognizing their existence and smoking them out are constantly being devised. Recognizing their existence is comparatively easy; smoking them out is extremely difficult. After all, the agenda is hidden internally and hallucinations about its content are less than reliable guides to action. The issue here is clearly also one of inability to elicit high quality information. A hidden agenda is nothing more than a portion of an individual's map or representation of a situation which is not shared by the others involved. The Precision Model provides the procedures to elicit the information which is not presently part of the shared map and determine whether it is relevant or not. Notice that no special concern for the motives of individuals is required. Any statement will be accepted as a potential portion of a shared map and subject to the tests of the Precision Model without regard for the existence of hidden agendas. Every statement is subject to the same conditions of being adequately precise. A potential obstacle to an alternative may be a personal bias, an emotional outburst, a conflict with larger goals or a practical consideration. No special procedures are required depending on which it is. Fortunately, all that is required is the ability to track each statement back to its source in the individual map; the ability to elicit high quality information.

EFFICIENCY PROCEDURE

The Efficiency Challenge is appropriate whenever the outcome of a process requires that a specific list of items be developed to greater precision for a known purpose. The most common occurrence will be when the result is to be action plans toward a desired outcome.

The Efficiency Challenge is part of the Outcome Frame. It is appropriate at the start of a Precision Model process before the statement under consideration is further specified. Once the Outcome Frame has been established, it is a request for conditions which indicate that the high quality information about to be elicited would be out of context in some way. This will occur if the proposal is known to be impossible to execute. In a meeting to consider alternative building sites, one of the participants knew the site had recently been sold. Obtaining information regarding costs, dimensions and zoning laws for that particular site would have been a waste of resources. Or, during a meeting where various plans for increasing sales of a particular product were being developed, and a participant new there were plans to replace it with a new design, the Efficiency Challenge saved a great deal of time which would have been wasted. The purpose of the Efficiency Challenge is to direct resources toward the outcomes sought by developing only possible alternatives.

The first two conditions specified for Surveying are precisely those conditions related to the *Efficiency Challenge*. The first Procedure will test each alternative against the Outcome Frame. The question "Does anyone know of specific factors which prevent this alternative from reaching the desired outcome?" Will immediately elicit any information which might demand rejection of the alternative as not eliminating the defined difference. This statement will be subject to all appropriate Precision Model pointers until the adequate level of precision has been reached. An adequate level will be one which has enough high quality information to reject the alternative or enough to know what additional information is needed. The second challenge will test each alternative against meta-outcomes. An alternative which would reach the desired outcome but would prevent other essential higher level outcomes from being reached will also be rejected at the earliest possible time. The question, "Does anyone know of specific factors which make this alternative impractical in relation to organizational goals?" will elicit objections with statements of necessity or impossibility. These objections will be subject to Precision Model pointers until an adequate level of precision has been reached to reject the pathway or to overcome the obstacle and pursue the alternative further. The test against organizational or overall outcomes, the second condition for extending the gathering of high quality information in the Surveying stage, has precise limitations in its use at this stage. A pathway will be rejected only if it is contrary to overall organizational goals which are the direct responsibility of those doing the rejecting. The defined difference will never include an explicit statement of the total context. One of the most frequent terms accompanying a statement of necessity or impossibility involving pathways to a desired state, which is not simply a return to a previous state, is a reference to company policy. Company policy is a low quality term which requires specification. The only policy or overall outcome which may cause rejection of an alternative is one where the ability to determine the specifics of a policy, what it is intended to accomplish and the costs of changing it can all be examined in adequately precise terms. Adequate precision would be where the person with the authority to change the policy, who is involved in the meeting, has adequately high quality information to make that decision at that time. Until it is known whether or not a policy can be changed and what the cost would be, it should not be a condition for rejection. If alternatives are rejected on the basis of policies of higher levels of management, those higher levels will never know the cost of the policies. It should also be apparent that an adequate level of precision cannot be attained if there is no access to anyone responsible for the policy or overall outcome.

A company manufacturing heavy equipment for metal fabrication had a policy of quoting on all jobs requested. Although they had their own production design, they did a great deal of custom work. At various times in the history of the company, a manager would propose that custom work be refused because it was too disruptive of the manufacturing process for their own production design. Any time this proposal was made it was immediately turned down by reference to company policy without consideration of cost to the company. In its early years, this policy had served the company well and it had grown at an impressive rate. At that time the use of manufacturing equipment was most effective with that policy. As sales of standard production units increased, the practice became more and more costly but management was forbidden to question policy. The company was saved from ruining itself only when an outside consultant, not bound by the policy rule, pointed out how costly it had become. The costs were determined only because of the appropriate questions being asked during the study being done for added production facilities. It turned out that the company saved a large capital investment by reorganizing its plant in a way which could fit its own production needs without consideration for custom work.

Whenever policy is used as an objection to an alternative, the As-If Frame can be used to continue development. Even when the organizational outcome is within the authority of those present, the As-If Frame will provide a fuller map for consideration of the cost of the policy before a possible useful pathway is rejected. Whenever it is outside the authority of the meeting, the As-If Frame will allow the fullest possible representation to be made to the higher levels of management upon which they can base their decisions.

The Efficiency challenges asked at the start of this phase will take care of an information gap created intentionally in the Pathfinding phase. Statements of necessity or impossibility were excluded from being challenged in the Pathfinding phase to encourage an expansion of the normal limits in individual models or representations. The first step of this phase is to pick up at the intentionally created deficit and proceed to obtain information of an adequate precision to accept or reject the objection. In the experience of the authors, a statement of necessity or impossibility is often simply a statement that an alternative is too costly. The cost may be in terms which haven't been quantified, yet they are still costs. The business world has an immensely rich and varied array of alternatives from which to choose both its desired outcomes and its methods of attaining them. The limits are seldom imposed by unchangeable facts.

Truly impossible outcomes or methods are seldom represented from individual maps. The objections are due to the limits of the individual maps which are available to a meeting. Many of these limits may be shared by each participant and only the Precision Model challenges will elicit the experience behind those limits which may provide the path to removing them. Potentially profitable alternatives which are not developed because of acceptance of these limits are never known.

A major project for job enrichment in a large, multi-division organization was almost rejected because it was believed that the unions would never accept it. As the project progressed and the unions began to support it, the higher management was surprised to find that the resistance came from lower levels of management and some of the projects were failures on that account. The limits of the models of the original decision makers were similar and they didn't have the resources available to access deeper material which would have expanded their representation. Neither the anticipated problem nor the one which surprised them were necessary conditions of reality. Each could have been handled in a variety of ways had the original planners had the ability to access higher quality information before they generated their program. There is a wide variety of ways to reach any goal and a detailed examination of the terrain between present state and desired state will yield the most efficient one.

DESIRED STATE

Once the Efficiency Challenges have been presented and any information elicited has been incorporated in a way that hasn't caused rejection of the alternative, the quality of information regarding each alternative will be at a comparable level. That is, the deficit from the Pathfinding phase caused by not using the Boundary Crossing Blockbuster will have been made up and each alternative will be ready for specification to the adequate level of precision for an action plan to be developed. The first two conditions have not been fully met at this point. It will still be possible for information to be accessed which will prove the alternative to be inappropriate to the desired outcome or to overall outcomes of the organization. Each further specification will produce richer material for the map which may demonstrate that it is too costly or which will indicate solutions that are potentially profitable. The reason for the specification, for the increased precision, is that both of these types of intelligence are equally valuable.

At this stage of Surveying, all of the Precision Model challenges may be appropriate. There are no restrictions imposed by the Outcome Frame of this section. The requirement is to develop an explicit set of action plans for each alternative which will be the basis for later evaluation, decision making and actual performance. The full facilities of the Precision Model are required to complete the task. The precision requirements are determined by the acceptable outcomes.

There are four acceptable outcomes for each pathway at the completion of this phase:

1. An adequate level of specificity is obtained which demonstrates that the alternative will not achieve the desired outcome at all.
2. The alternative will achieve the outcome but only at the cost of other organization goals. These overall-outcomes will include company policy, marketing strategies and cost-benefit analysis. If a level of management is involved who can make policy changes at the required level he may accept or reject the alternative. Otherwise, it will be passed to the next stage.
3. An adequate level of specificity is obtained to produce a complete action plan which can be carried out according to a timetable with assigned responsibilities.
4. An adequate level of specific action is obtained which precisely specifies the information gaps which prevent the completion of the action plan and can also specify a timetable with responsibilities for obtaining the high quality information necessary to fill those gaps.

It will be usual at this stage not to have adequate high quality information available to complete an action plan. If the alternative pathways include any creative new suggestions and the Survey phase follows immediately then it would be reasonable to assume that there will be substantial gaps in information.

If each information gap was treated as a termination point for a particular line of investigation the information returned to a subsequent meeting would often be inadequately precise and require further assignments and interruptions to the investigation. The specific kinds of information which will need to be known cannot be predicted with this abrupt termination. A number of well known management books attempt to get around this type of problem by proposing a standard list of questions to be answered. A standard list of questions might bring back higher quality information than otherwise but might also bring back irrelevant information or far too little specification for an important item. The answer to the question "When?" may bring anything from a month, week or day to a shift, an hour or a minute. The level of specificity required will not necessarily be apparent from the initial context until the gap is being closed, particularly if it is a large gap. As we have demonstrated in previous transcripts, it may take a series of challenges from the first unspecified phrase before an adequate level of precision is reached.

A high powered rifle with a scope and a shotgun are both effective weapons. They are designed for different uses and each has appropriate functions related to its use. The most efficient use of each gun will be when the purposes of the gun matches the purpose of its user. Each can be used in situations which call for the other if the preferred choice isn't available. In these circumstances, the result may be the desired one but it may also be detrimental to the user.

Using a shotgun for hunting deer will reduce the amount of edible meat considerably, if any game is taken at all. Using a high powered rifle with a scope when the target is small or cannot be seen clearly won't provide the choices which may be required. If, however, only one tool is available it will have to be used. Some hunters are unable to afford the appropriate variety of weapons. They become adept at using the single weapon that they possess for a wide variety of purposes—for some of which the weapon was never intended. They develop their skill with this weapon so highly that they can outperform many who have weapons more appropriate for the job. They often take great pride in their skills. A pride which is, of course, justified, for they have worked hard, developed great skill and proved the worth of their activity with the only worthwhile proof—food on their tables. They never are able, however, to obtain the success of those who have also developed their skill and who have the appropriate tools available. For those same abilities combined with the appropriate tools will provide their owners with more food for less expenditure of time and effort. The first step of precision in any circumstance is to know the weapon which is appropriate to the task. The basis of selection will be determined by the specificity of the task. When the target area is broad, the weapon to use will have to cover a wide range and will hit many things which are irrelevant to the outcome. When the target can be clearly identified the weapon which can concentrate its power precisely where it is needed will yield the most predictable results. A high powered rifle with a scope has two advanced tools combined. The scope provides the information about the desired target and the rifle concentrates the power on that same target.

Effective communication requires the ability to detect feedback and respond to it appropriately. The manager who wishes to be effective and move ahead in his organization needs a model which is responsive to the context. A catalogue of general questions— "who", "where", "what", "why"—will not get responses with precision related to context. A detailed catalogue, like shopping catalogues, will provide many times more questions than needed in any particular situation. These catalogues are sometimes useful for people with expert knowledge of the content of the area of interest. The Precision Model provides a tailored set of contextual language cues which enable the manager to obtain the desired specificity for his particular context.

"Why", a question which is still included in most lists, yields information which is uniformly of the lowest quality. The question gives no indication of the type of information desired in the answer. A manager needs to know what type of information or response is desired to formulate an appropriate question. If the purpose is unknown, if a specific type of information is not being sought, the question and its response are likely to be of the lowest quality. Knowing what is sought will allow a precise question to be formulated. The question, to elicit the highest quality response, needs to be formed so that the information source recognizes specifically the kind of information wanted.

Compare the precision in the following responses:

Statement	"I think we need to increase sales."		
response	"Why?" or "Why do you think that?"	to	"How specifically might we increase sales?" or "What would happen if we didn't?" or "Sales of what, in particular?"
statement	"We can't change that policy."		
response	"Why?" or "Why not?"	to	"What might happen if we did?" or "What stops us?" or "Change it how, specifically?"

The responses in the left hand column don't indicate what type of answer is expected, what sort of information is being requested. The answer may be anything from a discussion of causality to a statement of internal processes to a defensive reaction. "Why?" is often taken as a demand for justification rather than simply for higher quality information. Being specific about the information being requested will make it much easier for the information source to respond appropriately.

The As-If Frame mentioned in the preceeding chapter will be particularly useful in the Surveying stage. In a situation requiring information from someone not at the meeting, an assignment to the most likely individual to act "As-If" they were the missing information source can elicit valuable intelligence. Sometimes it will elicit information that persons were not aware they possessed. The As-If Frame can be used where a proposal has a part that cannot be accepted by a participant. He can be requested to act "As-If" his particular objection can be solved. This will continue the development of an alternative and maintain access to the objector's rich, personal maps at the same time.

The quality of information will be higher than otherwise with the creative use of Frames. As pointed out in the discussion of the As-If

Frame, an information deficit will often be created that must be filled. Each time an As-If Frame is used, an assignment for obtaining information to verify the tested material should be made. The As-If Frame will have allowed the pathway to be further developed and information gaps at more detailed levels may be discovered. Using this Frame, a complete path can be developed. The ability to subsequently obtain the necessary high quality information will be greatly enhanced. The consequences and implications of the path being surveyed will be known in much more detail and relevant information more easily determined. The individual assigned to gather the information will also have been trained in what is required by having been through a complete process already.

Using the full power of the Precision Model, let's look at its effectiveness in the following dialogue.

CASE STUDY I

GM: OK, Tom, lets take a careful look at each of the alternatives that you came up with to get your margins back up. Let's see, the first one you mentioned was to drop interest charges on inventory.

DM: Yeah! I like that solution—getting interest charges dropped on inventory would really help me get my margins back up.

GM: I agree. There are a number of repercussions of dropping interest charges on inventory. Your inventory represents capital and capital costs have to be absorbed by divisions. We also keep control of division inventories this way. (pause) Let me be quite blunt with you about this alternative. The issue of interest charges on inventory is a company policy. If you had been able to convince me that dropping rates was a reasonable course of action, I would be willing to pursue it. But since I'm not convinced, let's use our time and energy efficiently and move on to consider other areas.

The GM has established the present state and desired state for this part of his meeting with DM which is a continuation of the same session as the Pathways phase. He immediately introduces the efficiency challenge to point out his own objections to the plan. Because he has the authority to change this particular policy and he hasn't been persuaded to do that, he moves to the next item. This tactic can be used effectively at any point in the meeting, including the beginning where it appears here, without danger of losing the cooperation of the DM. The setting of the Frame to begin and the continued use of the Precision Model will ensure that the only relevant issue is to obtain high quality information.

DM: OK, I'm with you on that one, what's next?

GM: The second alternative you mentioned was kicking old Larry in the pants— that is, getting old Larry to increase the sales of type B motors.

DM: Yes, I remember.

GM: All right, how specifically can you get Larry to increase sales on type B motors?   Action
                                                                                                            Blockbuster

DM: Well, that brings up the thing I started to mention before—I really think that Larry is doing one hell of a job for us.
With the number of sales people he has, I think he does a fine job—I've examined the number of calls his people make—the spread between old accounts and developing new accounts, right on down the line. They're all doing a great job for us . . . of course, they're doing a better job on selling the older models, but . . . .

GM: (interrupting) Older models . . . older than what, Tom?   Comparator

DM: You know, the old standards, the type A series, as opposed to the newer type B's.

GM: I understand . . . you said that they were doing a better job selling the older models, right?

DM: Right! They sell a lot more of the older models than the new type B's. They

can't seem to move the newer ones as well as
they move the older models.

GM: Tom, what specifically stops them
from moving the newer ones as well as they
move the older models?

DM: Damn, George, if I knew that I'd be
able to solve the inventory problem.

At this point GM is told that there is no more information available in the trajectory which is being followed. Pause for a minute
and imagine your own response to this situation. How are you
going to elicit some useful information? Or are you going to send
the DM out to find solutions and report back? Or suggest your
own alternatives?

GM: OK, let's do it this way—you step into Larry's shoes and
     I'll question you about this so that. . . .

DM: What? Step into Larry's shoes.

GM: Look, Tom, we're after information which will allow us to
     discover how specifically to get your margins back up,
     right?

DM: Right!

GM: More specifically, we're tracking down information about
     the difference between Larry's ability to move the older type
     motors and the newer type B motors. Are you with me?

DM: Yes.

GM: You have spent a lot of time with Larry and have un-
     doubtedly picked up a lot about the way that he thinks and
     reacts to situations. So I am asking you to pretend to be him
     and react like you think he would. Got it?

DM: All right, I'll give it a whirl.

GM: OK, Old Larry there. I understand that you and your reps have been moving a lot of the series A type motors—my compliments.

DM: (in role as Larry) Yeah, we've got an excellent product and we know how to sell it.

GM: I also understand that you haven't been able to move as many of the newer type B motors as you hoped to.

The As-If Frames are effective for drawing out information which is not available under usual business procedures. The more that an atmosphere is established which provides a context for the As-If Frame, the more effective it will be. Notice in the preceding section that the GM explains the purpose and also creates an appropriate context by calling the DM Larry and opening with a comment rather than immediately resuming the questioning—As-If this was a different conversation.

DM: (in role as Larry) Yeah! Well, that's basically true. The customers just don't seem to trust their performance like the older models.

GM: Which customer specifically doesn't trust their performance?

Noun Blockbuster

DM: (in role as Larry) Well, there are a number of them, you know.

GM: Sure, but just go ahead and pick one that will be a good example that we can talk specifically about.

Noun Blockbuster repeated in a different form

DM: (in role as Larry) All right, one of my bigger accounts would be a good example— take Waldrup's, for instance.

GM: OK, Waldrup's. What specifically doesn't Waldrup's trust about the performance of the newer type B motors?

Noun Blockbuster

DM: (in role as Larry) Well, you remember that they got burned on their very first shipment of type B motors.

GM: Yes, remind me, Larry, of what in particular happened with that first shipment that they got burned on.

As-If Frame— simple frame saying, "pretend I don't know anything"

DM: (in role as Larry) They hooked the newer type B motor wrong and it blew out some major circuits—even started a fire, they had to close down the line for a couple of hours. They were really unhappy.

GM: Who specifically hooked up the type B motors at Waldrups?

Noun Blockbuster

DM: (in role as Larry) The guys who did it were Waldrup's own people.

GM: Where was our sales rep when all of this was going on?

DM: (in role as Larry) That was old Bob. Bob was out at the plant earlier in the week and told those guys how to do the hook up. You know, a couple of incidents like that and even my sales reps begin to mistrust and lose confidence in these newer models. Especially, some of my older reps.

GM: Some of your older reps what?

Noun Blockbuster

DM: (in role as Larry) Some of my older reps what? I don't understand.

GM: A second ago you said "especially some of my older reps".

DM: (in role as Larry) Oh, yeah! Especially some of my older reps have very little confidence in the newer type B models, compared with the older models. I make calls with the older ones. I make calls with them all and they just aren't as assertive in their presentations with the type B motors, compared with the older series motors.

GM: OK, Larry, I'm beginning to get the picture. Let me back you up a minute here. A few minutes ago you said, "especially some of the older reps", I take it that the situation is different with the younger sales reps. Is that true?

Difference Procedure

DM: (in role of Larry) Yeah, well, not exactly, it's not the young/old difference. It's more how long they've been on the job.

GM: All right, I take it that the longer that one of your sales reps has been on the job, the less assertive and effective in moving the newer motors.

Mini-Backtrack

DM: (in role as Larry) Yes, it seems to fall out that way.

GM: Now, consider this question carefully. I want to know whether there are any exceptions to that statement. Are there any of your reps who have been on the job, say, as long as Bob and who are assertive and effective in moving the newer series?

Universal Blockbuster Q.—Are there any exceptions

DM: (in role as Larry) No . . . I don't think so . . . Wait a minute there's Ken—he's been around as long as Bob but he's really effective with the newer stuff. I wonder . . . . .

GM: (interrupting) OK, hold on, there old Larry. I want you to ask yourself the following question "Besides his effectiveness with the newer motors, what distinguishes Ken from my other sales reps who have been around for as long, like Bob?"

Difference Procedure

DM: (in role as Larry) Uhmmm, well, he lives over on the . . . no, that wouldn't make any difference. I really don't . . . wait . . . there is one thing, less than a year ago he attended that voluntary . . . . (interrupting himself and coming out of his role as Larry) . . . son of a bitch, I told Larry that that school was important and to get his people over there and . . .

GM: (interrupting) Hold on, Tom. Slow down a second! Ken attended what voluntarily?

Noun
Blockbuster

DM: George, you remember about ten months or a year ago the division managers arranged that special school for familiarization with the type B's when they first came out. You remember, all of our sales reps got on the job training on the B's but we thought that it would be useful to have a more thorough training school offered. Well, I was in favor in requiring all of our sales reps to attend but I let old Larry talk me into requiring only the newer sales reps to attend and making it optional for any reps who had been with us for three years or more. Ken was the only one of the older reps who attended . . . and look at the difference it made.

GM: I agree, Tom . . by the way, my compliments on the way you were able to step into Larry's shoes. We got really useful information doing that.

DM: (smiling) You know, I guess that I know old Larry better than I realized . . . yeah, that did work pretty well. OK, what happens now?

GM: Excellent question. Tom. What happens now?

DM: I have no doubt about one thing. I
want that school run again, and this time
everyone of those sales reps who haven't been
through it will be there with bells on their
toes.

The transcript presented here details only the evaluation of the
first two of the alternatives generated by the DM through the process
of using the Precision Model tools. Subsequent to the point in the
transcript where we left off, the GM and the DM, using the precision
of the model, made a thorough evaluation of the remaining alternatives.

3.   cut back on production of type B motors
4.   inventory transfers
5.   special sale by head office
6.   repackage i.e. a new package SX power units with type B
     motors.

In summary then in a relatively short period of time the following
results were obtained.

The third proposal—cutting back production on the type B motors was initially rejected out of hand by the DM as the extracted
portion of the transcript reveals.

GM: All right now, Tom, let's take a crack at the next alternative
     —cutting back production on the type B motors.

DM: Well, let me be really up front about this one, George, like
     I started to say earlier, it's impossible. I really can't cut back
     on production. Let's go on to the next alternative—we'd just
     be wasting our time to consider this one. I can't do it.

The reader might, as an exercise in communication, adopt the
perceptual position of the GM in this mini-transcript and determine
for yourselves what response you could make to this rather forceful
and completely unequivocal communication from the DM. The
reader will likely have all too familiar sensation of being trapped in

a dead end communication. What choices occur to the reader when faced with the task of responding effectively to the DM's last communication? The most frequently occurring responses to the kind of communication that the DM has made, which participants in our management training workshops offer are:

A. if you trust the manager (you believe him fully competent in the area of business under discussion), you accept his judgment at its face value and go on to the next alternative.

B. if you have some hesitation about his judgment in this area of business, you demand that he justify his judgment with the appropriate arguments and figures. This demand for justification of his judgment most typically takes the form of asking the question, "why not?"

The typical outcome of making the first choice—accepting the judgment—is, on the upside, that the manager has the experience of being supported; that is, his judgement regarding his own operation is accepted without question. On the down side, the discussion is over—the alternative is never explored, and a potentially profitable and effective maneuver is lost. The result being the loss of one of the alternatives for the company—a net reduction in flexibility. The typical outcome of the second choice involves again, both advantages and disadvantages. The advantage is that the option is explored and thus, feasible solutions emerge and potential benefits from manipulating the production quotas are made available. The primary disadvantage is typically the demoralization of the manager whose judgment about his own operation has been challenged. There is also typically an even more debilitating consequence. In this second choice, the employee whose judgment about his own operation is being challenged will provide only very low quality information as he is pressed to justify his judgement. Thus, the superficial advantage of this choice evaporates under closer scrutiny.

This analysis leaves the GM in an untenable position. Neither alternative yields the desired outcome—specifically, that of evaluating the alternative using high quality information as the basis of the evaluation. The Precision Model tools provide a resolution of this dilemma.

DM: . . . wasting our time to consider this one. I can't do it.

GM: Tom, what would happen if you did cut back production of the type B motors?

DM: Well, the cut back would force me to lay off some of the people involved in production. Our relations with the union is already under severe strain and. . . .

The outcome which results naturally from the Boundary Crossing Pointer is optimal. The DM is invited by the question to provide high quality information regarding the consequences of the action he is reluctant to take. There is nothing in the question which challenges his competence in making the judgment which he previously announced: hence no defensiveness arises on his part. The GM has requested that he provide high quality information regarding his understanding of the consequences of a cutback in production. The Precision Model accesses precisely the high quality information needed for a thorough examination and evaluation of this specific alternative from the individual who has that information regarding the situation without any challenge to his competency. Indeed, in this particular instance insuring discussion of this re-opened alternative revealed that the disastrous consequences feared by the DM could be avoided simply by maintaining overall production quotas for the division but shifting a portion of the labor force from the production of type B motors to the production of additional SX power units and type A series motors.

The preceding dialogue demonstrates the efficient use of Frames and Pointers. The dialogue flows easily and smoothly along a trajectory toward a desired state. The two parts of the Precision Model are reflected in the use of the Frames to maintain context and the Precision Model questions and procedures to elicit high quality information. A professional communicator, which a manager must be, has to know two things. The first is the answer to the question "What information do I need?" The second is specific techniques to be able to elicit that information. The Frames establish and maintain the context in response to the first question. The questions maintain the Frame or context and elicit the high quality information required. The definition of precision presented and applied here, covers these two needs of the communicator.

A test for the precision of any communication sequence is its connectedness. Connectedness is the condition of having a word or phrase in a response which is the same as or refers to a phrase in the preceding sentence. Notice that all the Precision Model questions have this feature. Each question is, of course, a direct response to the content of the preceding statement. If you have ever sat through a meeting which appeared to have no direction, you could have given yourself something to do by keeping track of the noun phrases to see how little connectedness there was.

The problem of connectedness is particularly noticeable in meetings of more than two people. The task of maintaining context or relevancy is much easier in larger meetings if explicit and precise tools are available. Many prescriptions for making meetings work have sections on what is often called gatekeeping. The term refers to giving everyone present the opportunity to speak and closing off those that speak too much. The basis of judgement is left unspecified. What is too much? Is it really necessary for everyone to speak? If so, how much? These questions are left to the intuition of the manager in charge. These directions, however, fail to give the manager the tools to actually be in charge. To reach his goals efficiently and maintain control of a meeting requires a specific set of skills. Rather than using the feelings of each participant as a guide, as a contextual frame, the Precision Model uses the context set by the purpose of the meeting and explicit skills to elicit information. It is beyond question that there are circumstances where it may be useful and even necessary to solicit information from a potential but silent source. The Precision Model provides possible openings and, more important, the techniques to elicit the information desired from that source.

The purpose of "gatekeeping" is to insure that the resources of all participants are available to the meeting. By demonstrating that all input is valued and by using the questioning methods presented here in a sensitive way, the authors contend that the richest possible shared map can be created. A manager's intuition about who might have the information most wanted at a particular time will, of course, speed the process if used in conjunction with the Precision Model. The following dialogue represents the use of the model in a meeting with five people. We comment on the Frames used as the dialogue progresses to focus on the control provided by them. Rather than a concern with "gatekeeping", we present a dialogue which, in requiring adequate precision, uses context or desired outcome as the standard for action. As you read the dialogue, challenge yourself with two tasks. The first will be to identify possible Precision Model questions and note the one which was selected. Use a card or paper to cover the right-hand column. The second will be to notice if the sense of direction which is obvious seems likely to generate cooperation or not and whether the requirements of seeking information from individual participants are met or not. We call to your attention one particular feature of each Pointer. Every Pointer contains at least one word from the statement towards which it is directed. The authors have found in workshops and consulting that a common failing is to jump in with a question which is not clearly and directly related to a previous statement. The frequent result is that what appeared to be a shortcut led away from the original direction—sometimes, never to return.

CASE STUDY II

GM: OK, we've generated a list of alternative pathways all of which may get us to where we want to go. Specifically we want to change working conditions so that we can hire more skilled workers and increase production so we can fill orders and keep customers.

Backtrack Frame

I'll post the list of alternatives and we can consider them one at a time. We'll cover the production area and you can all keep in mind how the discussion might relate to your own departments. At the end of the meeting we'll have a list of alternatives which still appear feasible, the specific information we need before making final decisions on them, and specific ways of carrying them out. OK, Joe, which alternative do you want to start with?

Outcome Frame
—establishes
procedure

Outcome Frame
—specifies
desired outcome

Joe: (PM) Raising wages seems like the best alternative to me. Everyone wants more money but no one is going to want to work longer hours. Those flexible working hours might look OK to some people but I can't see how to make it work.

GM: Joe, let's take each alternative one at a time. The first one you chose was "raise wages" so let's look at that. Raising whose wages, in particular?

Outcome Frame —recalls established procedure

Noun Blockbuster

Joe: Well, I'd figured on everybody's.

GM: (with rising intonation) Everybody?

Universal Blockbuster

Joe: That's what I'd assumed. I don't think the union would allow us to change the rate for only the people we need.

GM: OK. We want to establish what further information we need to make a decision on each of these alternatives. Let's put that aside to be investigated later. If the union would allow us, whose wages would we raise?

Outcome Frame —specifies outcome for the next step.

As-If Frame—act as if the union would allow it.

Noun Blockbuster

Joe: Experienced assembly workers and welders.

GM: All experienced assembly workers and welders?

Universal Blockbuster

Joe: Yeah. We're having trouble getting skilled workers and if we only pay for line #3 work we won't be able to get replacements for the other lines.

Pers: If we can get the pay differential, I think it might work. Our company would be providing better prospects for those that came in at lower rates. Joe's right, though, the union won't allow it.

GM: What would happen if we proposed it?   Boundary
                                                                                  Crossing

Pers: They wouldn't buy it. . . . I know those guys, I bargain with them all the time.

GM: We don't have one of them here to question. Who is one of the influential ones that you know well?

Pers: I know Harry pretty well and he's on the executive.

GM: OK. I'd like you to put yourself in   As-If Frame
Harry's shoes and respond to my questions as
if you were Harry.

Pers: OK

GM: Well, Harry, we're considering pay-   As-If Frame—de-
ing higher wages to experienced assembly-   velopment of at-
men and welders who work on line #3. We'd   mosphere to get
like your cooperation in figuring out a way   greatest effect
we can do it. We need to be able to attract
more skilled people here and this way some
of the men already here can benefit. Can you
think of any specific objection to the proposal?

Pers: Well, Harry would object immediately and then . . . . .

GM: (Interrupting) this will be most effec-   As-If Frame—
tive if you actually step into Harry's shoes   reinforces
and answer my questions as though you are   original frame
he. OK?

Pers: OK.

GM: (repeats proposal) Can you think of any specific objection to the proposal?

Pers: (as Harry) You know we can't allow you to pay just certain guys more because you need some extra work. That's just bribery. We put a stop to that a long time ago. Each pay difference has to be a defined category that anyone could obtain.

GM: OK. If we found a way to create categories that would be acceptable to both of us, is there any other objection?

As-If Frame—act
as if problem
solved within the
previous As-If
Frame.

Pers: (back in pers. role) No. He won't object to paying somebody more as long as it fits into their system.

GM: We know whose wages we want to raise. The next question is "How much?"

Action
    Blockbuster

Pers: I would guess about 15%. When we've tried it in clerical areas to attract more people, anything less doesn't seem to have enough impact.

Contr: Fifteen percent! We're already over labor standards. Our profits will disappear.

GM: Over how, specifically?

GM chooses to pursue Controller's statement. He could use Outcome Frame to return to personnel

Action
    Blockbuster

Contr: Well it's taking more labor hours per unit of output and the costs are higher than standard too!

GM: How, specifically, are they higher?

Action
    Blockbuster

Contr: Well, our rates are the same as standard so it's all in overtime.

Joe: If we got the people we needed we wouldn't have nearly as much overtime. It might pay to raise wages.

GM: There are some specific pieces of information which we'll need before we meet to decide on which alternatives to follow.

Outcome Frame —establishes outcome using backtrack as well

Let's set out what information we need, specifically, and how we're going to get it. First we have to establish what rate would attract the workers we need. Personnel can look after that. Second, we have to know how much, in total dollars, that raise would cost both if we gave it to all production workers and if we only gave it to experienced assembly workers and welders. That will come from accounting and we also need from them the current cost of overtime. When accounting has those figures, Joe, you'll estimate how much overtime might be saved with each plan and the cost of additional skilled workers. Then the three of you can get together and calculate whether either plan is financially feasible. Third, if the selective raise might be feasible, Production and personnel will construct a category that might be acceptable to the union. Fourth, meet with a union representative and attempt to sell him on the plan which appears most attractive. (At the end of this section of the meeting, the GM had drawn a representation of the situation that looked like this.)

RAISE WAGES   establish % raise required (pers.)
                   calculate costs (Acct)
                      calculate potential net cost/benefit (Prod
                                                        /Acct)
                      create special category (Prod/Pers)
                      discuss with union (Pers)

The time frame for these activities will be determined at the end of the meeting when all information gaps are represented.

Let's consider flexitime next. Flexitime is a formal system of flexible hours which uses a time clock to keep track of total hours. Joe, in what way, specifically, might your hours be flexible?

Outcome Frame
—next step

Joe: Well, I don't know. I've never heard of this system and I haven't given it much thought.

GM: Ellen, you're familiar with this idea. Why don't you give us an outline of how it might work.

Ellen: Well, one of the main things is that people have to work a fixed number of hours per day, or sometimes per week, but they can choose their own start and end times and take lunch breaks whenever then want. There is a time clock which accumulates hours so they know and we know they work the required number of hours. They all have to be available during core time.

GM: What, specifically, is core time?

Noun
Blockbuster

Ellen: There are fixed times of the day when everyone has to be there.

GM: Which times, specifically?

Noun
Blockbuster

Ellen: That depends on the business. It's usually around the middle of the day and it's to make sure everyone is available for meetings and there during peak load periods.

GM: OK, Joe, how, specifically, might your hours be flexible?

Action
Blockbuster (GM directs attention to the participant likely to have the most useful information)

Joe: I don't really know where to start. We have to have people there when we need them.

GM: Need them for what, in particular Joe?

Noun
Blockbuster

Joe: For set-ups, for production decisions, for disputes, for emergencies, for maintenance (pause).

GM: Is that everything?

Joe: Yeah, I guess so. (shrugging)

GM: (listing items) OK, Joe, let's take them one at a time. Who, specifically do you need for set-ups?

Outcome Frame
—establishes procedure (after making visual backtrack)
Noun
Blockbuster

Joe: We need the experienced assembly workers.

GM: When, specifically, do you need them?

Joe: We need them all the time.

GM: *All* the time?

Universal
Blockbuster

Joe: Well, not all the time. But it could be at *any* time. I can't predict when the set-ups will be except for the start of the day.

GM: What is different about the start of the day.

Difference
Procedure

Joe: Each assembly unit needs a set-up at the beginning of the day because the automatic cutting programs can't be left operating and have to be reset.

GM: What, specifically, stops you from predicting when these assembly workers will be needed?

Boundary
Crossing

Joe: It takes 3 hours for regular units to go through the assembly area and 5 hours for special units. We only work an eight hour day and that means jobs are in various stages of production.

GM: OK. Let's step back for a minute and look at the situation as if we were already using flexitime. Let's assume that the board of directors had decided this is the way to go and the union has already agreed. Our task is to find out the best way to make it work. How might you solve the problem of scheduling people for set-up?

As-If Frame—act
as if we are in
future situation.

Joe: Well, we wouldn't be restricted to an eight hour day, would we? So we could complete two special units a day and three regular units. We wouldn't need to leave any jobs in mid-point of assembly overnight and that would reduce the total number of set-ups required. Hey, this could really work! If a new job was started each morning, the set-up men would know when they were needed and could schedule their time around that.

GM: OK. Let's consider the other points assuming that flexitime is already our system. Who, specifically, do you need for production decisions?

As-If Frame—reinforces above frame.
Noun Blockbuster

Joe: Supervisors.

GM: All supervisors?

Universal Blockbuster

Joe: Well, I suppose not as long as there is at least one around.

GM: When, specifically, do they need to be around for these decisions?

Joe: All the time. (pause) It has to be all the time because we can't predict when there's going to be a problem and the line needs to be stopped.

GM: What would happen if they weren't around to stop it?

Boundary Crossing

Joe: Well, foremen aren't allowed to stop the machines but they might have to be stopped . . I guess they'd be stopped anyway.

GM: OK. That's a point to be reviewed. Let's look at the next item. Who needs to be around for disputes?

Noun Blockbuster

Joe: A supervisor.

GM: Who needs to be around for emergencies?

Noun Blockbuster

Joe: A supervisor.

GM: Who needs to be around for maintenance?

Noun Blockbuster

Joe: The maintenance crew.

GM: The whole crew?

Universal Blockbuster

Joe: No, I don't think so. We need some around and maybe some on call. I guess we'd have to see how it worked out.

GM: OK. I think we've covered the major points. Now let's drop the idea that we already have flexitime and find out what we need to do to make it a workable plan that a decision can be made on. Joe, you've sketched out a plan here, what specifically would stop you from carrying it out?

Outcome Frame steps out of As-If Frame and establishes procedure.

Efficiency Procedure

Joe: Well, I can't think of anything we haven't covered. I'd have to get together with some people and work out a specific plan to see if it'll work. We haven't done anything like this before.

GM: OK. We'll deal with the planning later. Does anyone else have anything to say on this alternative?

Outcome Frame —establishes procedure, requests information.

PS: I never thought this wild idea could work but as you talked about it, I began to think it had some good points. A lot of my doubts have been cleared up. I think we'll still have trouble with the foremen, though.

GM: Trouble with the foreman over what?

Action Blockbuster

PSup: They'd have to work really long hours. The plant's going to be open 10 or 12 hours a day.

GM: What would happen if they didn't work long hours?

Boundary Crossing

PSup: The men would be working without any supervision some of the time.

GM: Is foremen working long hours the only way the men could have some supervision at all times?

Recycle procedure—How else . . .?

PSup: Well, I guess we could schedule so someone was there all the time. Yeah, I guess we can do it.

Richard (SM): I don't have any real problem in this area because my staff is OK the way it is . . .

GM: (seeing signs of uncertainty) But?

Richard: You've got to keep customer relations in mind when you consider this sort of thing.

GM: You're absolutely right, Richard, and I've invited you to this meeting for that reason. Your ideas and experience will help insure we have a most profitable outcome. What part of customer relations specifically, are you concerned about?

Noun Blockbuster

Richard: Our customers need to know they can depend on someone here.

GM: Which customers are you concerned about?

Noun Blockbuster

Richard: All of them.

GM: Every single one of them?

Universal Blockbuster

Richar: Well, the big ones and all our regular West Coast ones.

GM: Which big ones?

Noun Blockbuster

Richard: State and Seegers are really stuffy and they raise hell.

Purch: Maybe you could make special arrangements for them.

Richard: Yeah, maybe.

GM: (Noticing uncertainty) What, specifically worries you about our West Coast customers?

Noun Blockbuster

Richard: With the time difference they already have shorter service hours. Some of these proposals might make it worse.

GM: Which proposals, specifically?

Noun Blockbuster

Richard: Those flexible working hours are what worry me.

GM: What, in particular, worries you about them?

Noun Blockbuster

Richard: Everyone might go home early and that reduces the available service hours even more.

Contr: With staying open longer we might be able to increase the service hours. It would be possible to do that with flexitime.

Richard: Maybe, but those kind of changes affect everybody, you know. And customer relations are important.

GM: That's why we have all departments here. What about customer relations, specifically do you want us to consider?

Noun Blockbuster

Richard: Well, we've established certain relationships with our customers to keep them happy.

GM: What specifically, have we established with them.

Noun Blockbuster

Richard: We have the same person for them to contact, mostly. We try to do it that way although we don't have quite enough staff to do it completely.

GM: What would happen if we changed them?

Boundary
Crossing

Richard: That would depend.

GM: On what?

Noun
Blockbuster

Richard: What specific changes were made and how we approached them with the changes.

GM: I'd like your recommendation on changes, Richard, and I'm sure your skill at marketing will enable us to present any changes we make in a positive light. What changes might we make to improve customer relations and realize the kind of gains we're investigating at this meeting.

Outcome Frame
—reminder of
context.

Richard: If we improve shipping schedules and have our phones open longer it would help. I'm still worried though.

GM: What specifically, are you worried about?

Noun
Blockbuster

Richard: Our competitor has excellent customer relations because they always have the same person handling the same customer. We couldn't do that with the proposals we are considering here.

GM: Does having that kind of contact necessarily get good customer relations?

Boundary
Crossing

Richard: No, I guess not. Not if shipping is on time and some kind of good contact is available.

GM: What, specifically, prevents having good personal contact in the proposals we've been discussing?

Outcome Frame
—reminder of
context.
Boundary
Crossing

Richard: With flexible working hours we couldn't predict contact hours in the proposals we've been discussing. With flexible working hours we couldn't predict when individuals would be in and who would be handling different customers.

GM: Necessarily?

Boundary
Crossing

Richard: No. I guess it would be possible to set up schedules so they would be predictable. We could set our procedures and then let our customers know.

GM: Do you see any other obstacles to good customer relations?

Recycle
Procedure

Richard: No. It looks as though it might work pretty well as long as we have good coordination. I'm here to look after our customers.

GM: Good. I'm glad we got your ideas so that we can take them into account as we develop these ideas.

Anything else? (pause) OK. Let's list exactly what has to be done.

(The details needed to arrive at a decision on this proposal were worked out and the following representation resulted.)

FLEXTIME: 1. Research with actual operations (pers)
               2. Schedule—tentative (prod)
                    A. Production needs— assembly
                                    maintenance
                                    emergencies

B. Other demands— customer service
                     intra-department communi-
                     cation
C. Foremen & Supervisors
D. Mechanics— core time(s)
                 earliest start/latest quit
                 accumulation basis
                 minimum manning basis
3. Meet with union (pers/prod)

The value of having the ability to access full representations from all participants is apparent here. The possibility of reducing requirements for the missing skilled labor in accord with production line needs, once discovered, was available for use in other plans. Creating a fuller, shared map of all participants ensured that the richer representation was available to all participants for all the alternatives under consideration.

The consideration of attracting more skilled workers was expected to be less of a problem because production, particularly of special units was expected to increase due to fewer extra set-ups. This area did however present a problem. We pick up the dialogue when this point arises during discussion of the 4/40 option.

PM: Well, I can see how it would really help our production but I'm concerned.

GM: Concerned about what, specifically?   Noun
                                                   Blockbuster

PM: People quitting and we'll be worse off than before.

GM: Who in particular might quit?   Noun
                                                   Blockbuster

PM: Most of our experienced assembly-men.

GM: What's the difference between them   Difference
and the rest of the men?   Procedure

PM: They're older.

GM: And?

PM: They're the ones that complain about overtime the most and some of them refuse to work it at all. They don't need the money any more and they'd rather stay at home.

PSup: I think they'd like it. Most of those guys like to hunt and fish and I think most of them would like long weekends.

GM: OK. We might have a special consideration here. One of the missing gaps in our information is whether the people we want to keep and attract will like 4/40 or whether it will drive the ones we want away.

The primary objective of this meeting was to develop alternatives that would change work conditions to attract more skilled workers. If the change would attract more young workers only and most of the ones they required were older, they would be defeating their original purpose while meeting the first stated needs of attracting more workers. The other issues were defined and a list of required information was developed.

A major factor in the choice of As-If Frames will be a manager's judgment of the critical abilities of the individual and his congruence when making a statement. The Precision Model provides the method for eliciting high quality information. The responsibility for knowing when that high quality information is necessary rests with each particular manager. A subordinate who has been reliable in the past and has established that he normally bases his opinion in the area of concern on high quality information can be depended upon when he presents his opinion in the same manner on a current issue. The ability to distinguish when one can depend on the opinion of others and when one can't is a skill which can be learned.

It is also the skill which often, in the past, has been the distinguishing one between adequate managers and really successful ones.

The meeting ended with a list for each alternative showing what information was required, how it was to be obtained and who was to obtain it. It represents the desired state which this particular meeting was supposed to reach. The highest quality information obtainable at this point has been reached and is being passed on to the next meeting. Included in this chart are the specific information gaps and what kind of information is required to fill them. The next meeting will start simply by making sure those gaps have been filled in the precise manner required by the plan.

The previous dialogues demonstrate the full use of the Precision Model. An entire range of its Frames, Procedures and Pointers were used. This stage of the information process requires the highest quality information for all areas of the shared map be elicited. The issue of management is information. All of the leading management books refer to the activity of processing information as a primary requirement for, and shortcoming of, existing management theories. All of these models require an information processing base which they do not provide. Further, they apparently are not aware of the existence of such a base. There are existing models for specific parts of the management process which are highly refined. Kepner and Tregoe in *The Rational Manager* provide a model for solving problems, particularly those relating to physical processes, which is useful and efficient. Curt Symonds in *A Design For Business Intelligence* provides a model for developing management information systems which is creative and powerful. Davis and Lawrence in *Matrix* present a model for matrix management which clearly identifies the requirements for a new concept of organization.

These books, which are three of the most powerful models available in their respective areas, have one thing in common. Each requires a set of communication skills which they do not provide and which they recognize as lacking in existing management.

This lack of adequate precision seriously weakens their models, except in the hands of those individuals who have developed effective communication skills on an intuitive level, or who have learned the Precision Model. The individuals who have developed these models are personally skilled in their application. They cannot, however, transfer their skills along with their models. The dialogues show that these skills are available and can be learned by anyone who desires to become precise in their own processing of information.

"Unless he has both the inclination and the authority to challenge, to question, or to take leadership in demanding change, he will gradually subvert his managerial talents to the less exacting role of administrator. He will, in effect, end up serving the system rather than meeting the needs of the business."

Curt Symonds,
A Design for Business Intelligence

This passage deplores the lack of adequate information processing skills. As Symonds points out, these skills are generally lacking and their lack creates the kind of attitudes mentioned above. Lacking skills and feeling too intimidated to try for information, the manager feels insecure. The models which have been proposed to fill this gap have all been shotgun approaches. Lacking an understanding of the requirements, or even possibilities of precision, they have provided whole catalogues of questions. As with any catalogue, the items of interest may be contained in it. In any catalogue, however, there are a vast number of items which are of no interest whatsoever to its reader, particularly if that reader has a predetermined purpose.

The dialogues in this chapter demonstrate that information may be elicited in a systematic way with a set of precise tools. No issue of emotional conflict or intrusion need arise and respect for participants is maintained. The model requires only that it be applied systematically. The existing personal skills of the manager using it will further enhance its effectiveness.

The major case studies we have given so far of applying the Precision Model have dealt with situations having a common characteristic. The manager using the Precision Model has been eliciting information which the participants in the meetings recognize as being needed to eliminate a defined difference. The participants have been in agreement that more precise information has been required for each of the desired objectives. The model presented is not restricted to such a situation. The full power and effective use of the Precision Model will be realized when it is applied to all outcome oriented communication situations. When a subordinate proposes a plan of action intended to reach an outcome which has never been accomplished before or to reach an expected outcome by a new path, the manager needs the same skills for the situation presented to him. A skilled manager will use his intuition and knowledge of the subordinate to determine the level of precision required for the plan being proposed. He will use the Precision Model skills to obtain the appropriately high quality information he requires.

In the authors' experience, the enthusiasm of a manager for his own plan has often led to an inadequately developed plan which can have consequences which would lead to disastrous results even though the basic idea is good. It is not the basic idea but a specific set of actions which will be carried out. A manager who allows too much slippage between his idea and the action plan will likely fall flat on his face.

The development of computer systems often falls into this kind of trap. The systems analyst, knowing virtually anything can be done on a computer, often ignores the costs of development or the practical effects on the other side of the computer room doors. Requirements for input or the ability to actually use the output produced are often based on assumptions about operating conditions for which the system analyst has no experiential base. In conjunction with a potential user of information, the analyst designs a system which appears to be the answer to the prayers of a manager. Before approval is given for such a product, some Precision Model application is likely to be in order. We present an example of part of such a session based on our experience.

CASE STUDY

The sales manager and systems analyst are meeting with the GM to get his approval for a new program to produce sales reports. They've outlined a plan which will report orders received instead of the accounting sales which represent orders shipped. The sales manager points out that sales as now reported reflect only history and such information is not a useful guide to action. He is excited about the prospect of knowing current business represented by orders. The information will allow him to plan sales strategies based on business they are generating independent of production and shipping. After explaining the benefits of the system and showing the systems flow chart which tracks the information flow from its source, the sales manager asks for authorization to proceed.

GM: Before we go any further, I'd like to get some more information. The plan does seem promising and I'd like to find out what other areas it might affect. I also want to make sure that we realize the full benefits which this system might offer us.

I like the idea of managing based on order information but we haven't done it before and I'm not sure it would work. The source of the orders is available and you've handled that pretty thoroughly. I still count success by the profit on what we actually ship out of here; and the numbers on the financial statements. How will your reports tie into that?

SM: Well, orders get shipped sooner or later and so we just have to reconcile the difference each month.

GM: How, specifically, can we reconcile the difference?

SM: We can keep track of orders cancelled and we know the shipment figure so the reconciliation is easy.

GM: How, specifically, can we keep track of orders cancelled?

SM: It can be done by the computer. We can have a report which shows new orders, cancelled orders and shipments.

GM: OK. I'd like a layout of that report and its systems flow done before final approval. The next thing that concerns me is that you'll be using the sales orders report for operations but I'll be holding you responsible for the sales reported by accounting. How can we work that way?

SM: I'd like to persuade you that you should use the same figures I'm using. I can't be held responsible for whether or not orders are shipped.

GM: What will happen if you are?

SM: Well, I am now and it isn't working too well. I spend a lot of non-productive time justifying and explaining what has already happened. I also have to spend time with production problems which don't really allow me to concentrate my efforts on selling. I can't hold my salesmen responsible for their performance because I don't really know what it is. These reports will be valuable to me whether you use this order method or not.

GM: How specifically, will they be valuable?

SM: I'll be able to keep track of current sales activity of each salesman and I'll be able to investigate lost orders as they happen.

GM: OK. You've convinced me of the value of the reports to you. I'm interested in the idea of working those reports in with our regular ones so that I can use them, too. I'd like you to have a meeting with the controller and come up with a solution for that. I don't want you to write the program and then have to start again because of any changes that might cause. I'll give final approval after you've worked out the order reconciliation problem and met with the controller.

In this case, the original programs had to be modified when a method which included production cost figures was included. The company ended up with a model which allowed them to keep on top of their current business. The original plan would have created a problem with reconciliation to accounting figures which was not anticipated in the original plan. Worse, the sales manager would have been working with information which was not available to, or understood by, the GM and they would have spent many bitter hours attempting to find a common base for accountability. Many systems in the authors' experience have been scrapped or poorly used for these kinds of reasons. The application of the Precision Model at the beginning of development of any action plan can mean the difference between a profitable venture and a failure.

BACKTRACK

The surveying phase presented here covers overall business information processing from a point of having a list of potential courses of action to full development of these paths or rejection. This is the final phase before evaluation and decision making and, as such, requires that each potential alternative be converted to a fully specified action plan. The next phase cannot proceed with any reasonable degree of certainty without high quality information regarding how, specifically, a course of action is to be carried out. The authors have seen many business operations head for serious trouble when they neglected this phase. Computer data centers which have assumed they could program an application which cost much more than anticipated, or in some cases couldn't be done at all, because of inadequately specified methods of solution. Many computer systems are sold which can't perform the work they were sold to do—for lack of adequately precise surveying. A large hotel was constructed with few problems but had to be sold and turned around from bankruptcy caused by failure to use the same kind of surveying in determining market factors as was used in construction planning —in this case financing requirements and the construction of others (a highway) beyond their direct control. All of these situations, and thousands like them, could be prevented by applying the Precision Model for adequate surveying.

Surveying starts with a list of potential action pathways. Each of these has been contributed as a possible way to reach the goal, it is possible that some will not and others will reach it only at a prohibitive cost. The list of pathways was created with no constraints as to practicality. The only constraining factor was that if it could be done, it might reach the desired outcome. The start of this phase is optimal so far as the list is rich with alternative possibilities for reaching the desired state.

As the list was created without concern for practicality, the first step will be to test these conditions at this point. Maximum efficiency, in this phase, is to reject alternatives which don't meet the practical condition as soon as possible without rejecting any which, if adequately high quality information were available, would prove to be acceptable alternatives. Any objections at this point will be Precision Modeled to insure that no alternatives are rejected based on unacceptably low quality information.

Each path which survives will be developed to a specific action plan. As it is developed, it may be rejected for impracticality, as higher quality information is elicited. If not, it will result in a complete action plan or an incomplete plan with a specific plan for obtaining required and missing information. The increasing specificity will reveal information gaps which need to be filled before adequate precision will be attained for a particular path. Some of these gaps will be filled by guesses or intuitions which will need to be verified before evaluation.

The issues of conflict and emotion, insofar as they are problems, have been shown to be functions of the inability to elicit high quality information. These become problems when the differences in representation are not known and participants are unable to operate from shared maps. The Precision Model, by establishing a framework which is outcome oriented and providing the tools to elicit high quality information, creates a positive environment for obtaining the rich resources which are available from the individual experience of each participant.

The complete Frames of the Precision Model have been presented in previous chapters and all are appropriate at this stage. Particular emphasis on the power of the Efficiency Challenge introduced in this phase, was made to demonstrate how information may be brought to a comparable level of high quality quickly and efficiently. The As-If Frame was also highlighted as a means of by-passing information gaps usefully, gaining valuable information without sacrificing quality. The Boundary Crossing Pointer was introduced in this phase and contrasted how the Precision Model can usefully focus information according to the context with how it can expand the area of awareness. Although the Boundary Crossing Pointer was highlighted, all Pointers are appropriate in this phase of information processing.

We note that much of the material in this book, and a common focus of most communication models, covers situations in which the information sources are not aware of their potential contribution to the task at hand. Eliciting information is frequently a painful process of extraction. We have shown our model equally applicable to a situation where an eager subordinate has developed a plan to improve some part of a company's operations. The same model is used to obtain high quality information whatever the attitude or position of the information source. Goodwill is enhanced with a precise model for eliciting information.

The outcome of this phase will be a number of alternatives all of which would achieve the desired state which started the process. The result will be similar to a PERT chart with actions to be taken, responsibilities assigned and time frames established. The analogy to a construction project is appropriate. The precision with which engineering and construction plans are formulated has, until now, been missing in ordinary business operations—missing but needed as much.

The surveying stage needs access to rich individual maps as much as any phase. Many potentially profitable alternatives are rejected because access to individual representations is limited by unnecessary boundaries—often the very boundaries which caused the original problem or limited the primary objectives. The Precision Model accesses individual maps in ways appropriate to the particular phase of information processing. The surveying phase requires that details in a particular area be highlighted to clarify the specifics of attaining an objective along a previously identified path. Boundaries are defined for this phase, yet precise tools are required to insure that any boundaries which are accepted are necessary, practical and have known costs.

An alternative will be rejected at this phase if it is in conflict with overall outcomes of the organization. That is, it is too costly in terms other than directly financial. Policies which the organization has established may prohibit certain alternatives. We maintain that alternatives which violate policy should be rejected only if there is a level of authority present which is capable of considering changing that policy. Too many high level executives never know the true cost of their policy statements. These policies become laws of an organization which often outlive their usefulness.

Desired states or outcomes exist at all levels of information processing. In the context of problem solving, each phase has desired states and each of these is determined by the overall desired state—the solution of a problem. The desired state of each phase is subordinate to the final desired outcome.

Each alternative which is passed from this phase—which constitutes the desired state—is a detailed course of action which will attain the final desired outcome. In most situations there will be a number of alternatives which could achieve the desired ends. The Surveying phase develops each of these to a level of precision which will allow this effect to be measured, the relative costs and benefits assessed, and give confidence that the specific actions required are known and can be carried out. The result will be maximum orientation to the outcome desired.

Chapter 5

EVALUATING

When I was a young boy about 9 or 10 years old, my family traveled to a small town in the Midwest where my mother's parents and many of her other relatives lived. It was one of my favorite summers—there were swimming holes, horses, a bunch of kids my age, and watermelon, and it stayed light really late. My grandma used to finish up dishes after supper and come out on the front porch and sit and rock. I remember one evening in particular, my uncle had come by to drop off some fresh fruit from his orchard. Although he was usually a calm man, this particular evening he was fretting and mumbling to himself and running into doors and chairs. I couldn't believe it was my very own uncle. Finally, my mom took him firmly by the arm and marched him home so as to leave the rest of us in peace.

After he had gone, I found grandma on the porch just rocking away and I asked her what was bothering Uncle Jed. She told me that the only thing that could really bother Uncle Jed was Uncle Jed himself. I was disappointed and told her that I thought that that was a silly answer and that I was asking her real serious like. She stopped rocking and said that she had been serious, and the way her eyes looked and her voice sounded, left no doubt in my mind that she was. I didn't appreciate what she meant until years later, but even then I could feel it was big and important. Then her face softened and her voice became gentle but I always remembered.

She told me that my Uncle Jed was in a dither because he had been put in charge of the town's annual pie baking contest. When I laughed, she chided me, explaining that while it might sound funny to my city ears, it was a very important event for the people of the town and all the country around, and it was a grave responsibility that Jed had to

226

make sure everything went well. Being only 9 or 10, I had no idea what even could go wrong at the pie baking contest, so I asked. She said that since there were people involved, there was no end to the things that could go wrong, and then she began to tell me about some of the things that had gone wrong in the past.

There was the time when neighbor Ellie, who had won the contest three years in a row hands down, got herself in a hurry carrying her pie up to the display table, and slipped and fumbled her pie right into the judge's lap. She lost, and everybody said that it was because the judge was upset about the way the pie was presented and never really gave it a chance—everybody but Ellie. She said that it was the man in charge of the contest's fault for not making sure the rug she tripped over was laid down properly. And then a lot of people blamed him, too. Probably, grandma said, because the judge that year was the head of the bank and you have to be careful about folks like that.

Then there was the time when a woman who lived right around the corner from the church brought her pie to the contest. And when you looked at the pie you could see right away that something wasn't quite right. It turned out that the woman hadn't made enough dough to make a top to the crust. Everybody who got to taste it later said that what she had there tasted real good, but it just wasn't a pie—you know, with a piece like the top missing and all. At first the judges didn't know what to do, and the woman was demanding that what she had baked be considered right alongside the pies others had brought. Finally, they thanked the woman for her efforts and said that they would have to set it aside, even though it showed great promise because it wasn't complete enough to be considered a pie alongside the others.

One year, the morning of the contest the electricity failed in the northern end of town. Grandma reckoned that none of the people who were baking pies on that end of town noticed because when it came time for the judging, every single one of the pies entered by people from that end of town was only half baked—and, as grandma said, any old completely baked pie is going to be tastier than any half baked one. And a lot of folks were unhappy because there were a lot of good bakers from that end of town whose pies were ruined. Some folks even said that we ought to postpone the contest because of it, and then, of course, they got mad at the man in charge of the contest who had to explain that no, they couldn't put off the judging.

And then there was the year that just as the judges were finishing congratulating the man whose pie had been judged best in the contest, some old lady came trotting up with the most scrumptous looking lemon meringue pie ever. She was so angry that the judge wouldn't taste her pie and consider it for the contest that she popped him right in the face with it, yelling that she was offering him a big bite. 'Course everybody started hollering for the man in charge of the contest again. Grandma told me that the day after that happened and things were just settling down again, the judge made the awful mistake of mentioning that he really thought the lemon meringue pie tasted better than the blueberry pie that had received the award, and just stirred everything all up again—and nobody was satisfied then.

The worst year of all was when half way through the contest they found out that one of the judges was allergic to coconut. The way that everybody found out was when the judge refused to taste a coconut cream pie Aunt Sarah made. Nobody knew what to do—if the judge won't even consider one of the pies entered, how could a decision be reached? The whole thing fell apart; the man in charge of the contest got yelled at some and everyone went home with a bad taste in their mouth.

I asked grandma why did the people still have the contest if it raised such a fuss. And she laughed and said that most years things went very well indeed, and that everyone enjoyed themselves. She had just been picking out the years when things had gone wrong. She said that she agreed with me and I asked what do you mean, and she said that if you looked at the pie baking contest like it was an occasion for catastrophe, then it probably would be better not to do it. But if you looked at it for what it was intended to be—an occasion for gathering together the best pies that could be put together by the best bakers in the area, then naturally your mouth would begin to water and a little smile would cross your face, and you knew that it was still the best way to get to the best pie that could be had in that county. She said not to worry about Uncle Jed because fussing was just his way of getting himself to take care and make sure that everything went right this year, and that when the day came, everything would be fine and he would present himself with dignity, knowing he had done his job as the man in charge by making the judging work. I said, "Good," but I was really just thinking about the pies and how many there would be and how good they would taste.

PRESENT STATE

We come now to the final segment of the model—Evaluating.

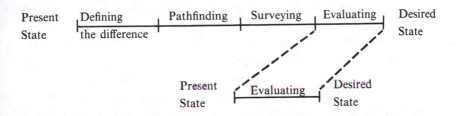

It is here that the payoff for the precision work will occur. This phase of the model begins when three conditions are met:

1. The set of pathways which were identified in the third segment —Surveying—as leading to the Desired State are made available. These pathways must also identify the high quality information gaps which arose during the third phase specification of the alternatives along with the name of the person who has been assigned responsibility for developing the high quality information required to fill the specific identified gaps.

2. The individuals who were assigned responsibility for developing the high quality information which is needed to fill the gaps in the various pathways are available and have indicated that they have secured the information.

3. The individuals who have the authority to render a decision regarding the issue in question are available. There must be present at least one individual from the highest echelon of the organization which will be affected by the decision. This person must have a thorough understanding of the overall goals of the organization. He or she will be called upon to pass on the ecological fit of each of the various pathways being considered. By ecological fit, we are referring to the fact that some pathways which represent solutions that are developed at levels of a business organization below the top level, may be in utter conflict with extended plans and goals which have been developed at the higher level. Thus, the need for a well informed and articulate representative of that higher level.

In terms of the model we have presented, when these three conditions are met, the present state conditions for the final phase are met. It is often the case that in the final phase of the model, individuals who have not been present for all or, indeed, for any of the previous discussions, will be included as an integral part of the team that will select the alternative(s) to be implemented.

The presence of such individuals is a signal to the manager who is in charge of the meeting that a skillful piece of Framing is required. Nothing is more disheartening and demoralizing to a group of business people who have worked long and hard on a plan or set of solutions to some less than optimal present state, than to enter a meeting ready and eager to select and implement a choice, and have to spend time listening to someone who has not been present at the earlier discussion slowly and painfully (to the informed members of the group) track down the information needed to satisfy themselves that all of the viable alternatives were considered—essentially recapitulating the earlier discussions. Yet the individual(s) new to the issue and charged with the responsibility of rendering an excellent decision must satisfy themselves that all of the viable alternatives have been explored. This is simply their legitimate demand for the high quality information they require to execute their responsibility. Fortunately, the Precision Model offers an elegant solution to this dilemma—the Backtrack Frame. The Backtrack Frame is a verbal recapitulation of the sequence of topics which the group has explored in successfully arriving at the fourth and last phase of the process. As mentioned earlier in the book, the information processor using the Backtrack Frame must himself consider the context in which the Backtrack is being used. The test condition for context is simply if all the individuals involved have been present during the entire discussion. If so, the Backtrack will cover only those pathways which were explored and which yielded positive results. The dead ends are ignored. However, a full Backtrack is called for if there is at least one individual present who missed some or all of the previous discussion, and who will require that information to carry out their responsibilities—a decision maker nearly always falls into this category. A full Backtrack typically begins with a report of how the issue was first brought to the manager's attention, then a representation of the set of pathways used in the first three segments of the process—defining the difference, pathfinding, and surveying—and terminating with a report of the desired state reached at the termination of the third phase, that is, the set of pathways which lead from the present state of the organization to the desired state with the high quality information gaps identified. By using the full Backtrack, the manager accomplishes two important things: First, he provides the high quality information developed in the earlier phases to the individuals who missed those phases; secondly, he orients the members of the group who have been present during the earlier phases, accessing with them both the high quality information they previously generated, as well as a sense of accomplishment which places them in an optimal posture to complete the process they have so effectively begun. Such a Backtrack will provide the high quality information in a tightly packaged format which the new members will appreciate. Thus, the new as well as the old members of the task force are brought into alignment, and the pre-conditions for a smooth and effective team effort are established. Such an approach avoids making any assumptions regarding the ability the members of the group have either to understand written material (circulated, for example, prior to the meeting) or to recall in detail with accuracy the earlier events which had led to this meeting. All too often, in the authors' experience, the implicit reliance on notes circulated before the meeting to create the kind of alignment required for close teamwork spells disaster. Often the only thing the participants have in common as the meeting gets under way is the set of notes they've brought along with them which they have read superficially, if at all. Reliance on memory usually produced the same low quality situation. The small amount of time invested in the full Backtrack will pay handsome dividends in terms of effectiveness and efficiency in the meeting.

Since the manager in charge of the meeting for this phase will know beforehand both whether there will be new members included who need the information, and exactly what the initial Backtrack information will be, it will be easy for him to prepare a visual representation of the tracks to be presented in the first Frame. Such visual representation provides the outline of an external map which can be used powerfully to assist group members in staying in context and to allow them to know at all points in the ensuing presentation where they are in the overall process. This sense of orientation is essential for an effective and efficient meeting. Since the topic here is representational, the subject of the second book in this series, we only nod at it in passing. The reader might consider some of the visual representations presented in segments two and three of the model as candidates for the construction of appropriate and effective visual aids.

FORMAT FOR EVALUATING

The manager has aligned the group by the use of the full Backtrack Frame which includes, naturally, the Outcome Frame, that is, the Backtrack will include a representation of the characteristics of the desired state which is the payoff. The manager then secures the agreement of the participants that they accept the Frame as an adequate representation within which to work. We recommend at this point that he explicitly specify the sequence of events—the order of things to be accomplished in this meeting. The overall target state for the meeting will typically be presented. This overall outcome is then broken down into a number of explicit intermediate outcomes which structure the meeting. Those managers using the Precision Model are encouraged to consider the following sequence:

1. Description (brief) of the purpose of the meeting—the desired state or Outcome Frame.
2. The Backtrack Frame (includes desired state characteristics)
3. Acceptance of the Frame by participants.
4. Representation of each of the pathways which purport to lead to the desired state.
5. Each time an information gap is encountered during the presentation of each pathway for consideration, the individual who has developed the high quality information be requested to provide it.
6. Once all the pathways have been tracked with the appropriate high quality information gaps filled, the participants are invited to discuss each of the alternative pathways, focusing on the question: *Does this pathway get us to the desired state?* Any alternatives which fail to receive an affirmative answer to the question are dismissed at this point.
7. All the pathways which survived the first question are now each evaluated in turn by the group with reference to the question: *Is this pathway consistent with the long term goals and plans of the organization?* This step insures the overall ecological soundness of the pathways for the organization.

Any alternatives which fail to receive an affirmative answer to the question are dismissed at this point.

8. The group is invited to consider combining the various surviving pathways so as to maximize organizational resources.

9. The decision point—the group selects the alternative(s) by means of some decision-making model and develops an implementation schedule.

We have already commented on the first three steps in this format. The fourth and fifth steps are primarily representational skills—a topic which belongs appropriately to the second phase of high quality information processing—the subject of the second of the books in this series. The Frames and the Pointers will be of use in these steps. The Frames are employed to control the direction of the presentation or discussion of the material in the presentation—particularly the Outcome Frame. Each of the steps in the suggested sequence defined an Outcome Frame for that section of the meeting. For example, during the fourth and fifth steps, discussion of the presentation material relative to the specific pathway under discussion are encouraged and acknowledged. Conversely, any comments, questions, statements concerning material not relevant to the specific pathway under consideration are to be rejected immediately and with courtesy. The Frames thus allow the information processor in charge of the meeting to act in a principled, precise, and powerful manner to maintain control over the direction of the meeting so as to arrive at an excellent outcome efficiently. As stated previously, it is important that out-of-context comments, questions and statements be dismissed with speed and courtesy. Should a member of the task group challenge the dismissal of a comment, question or statement, the information processor should use the Relevancy Challenge defined earlier —that is, courteously invite that person to justify the inclusion of the communication in question by demonstrating its relevance to the Outcome Frame operating at that time. For example, if during the fourth step in the process, where a pathway considering the increasing of sales of item X is under consideration, one of the members of the task group were to point out that it would be easier to cut back production of item X, then the following exchange might occur:

PM: .... that it would be one hell of a lot easier to simply cut back production on item X than go through all these sales gyrations which. . . .

GM: (interrupting) Wait a minute, you're off the point—it may well be that you're right about a production cut back being easier but we are considering this (pointing to the flipchart) possibility right now and I insist that we do that. (Then, pointing to the flipchart, where the production cutback is listed as a separate alternative). That's where your comments about the production cutback possibility will be welcomed.

If the production manager were to insist that his statement was relevant at this point, the GM might simply say:

GM: All right, Joe—how specifically will your point assist us in getting to our agreed upon goal—namely, to evaluate the feasibility of increasing sales of item X?

If the member of the group can convincingly demonstrate that the point he is trying to develop does bear directly on the agreed upon desired state (of evaluating the feasibility of increasing sales on item X), then, of course, the manager withdraws his objection and the point is welcomed and considered as is perfectly appropriate. The Outcome Frame and the Relevancy Challenge of the Precision Model offers its user a systematic and explicit way of deciding the relevancy of any communication within the context. The effect of the systematic use of the Outcome Frame, Procedures and Pointers is to create a welcomed discipline to the thinking and communication which occurs in the business transaction independent of personality. The net gain is tremendous savings in the amount of time and energy required to achieve high quality results, especially in meetings. The authors have noted one further long term gain with the use of the Precision Model is that the members of the business organization where the model is employed rather rapidly come to anticipate the use of the Relevancy Challenge in conjunction with the Outcome Frame, and the number of times it is necessary for the information processor in charge to challenge out of context contributions drops quickly as the individuals begin to respect the Outcome Frame and to apply the Relevancy Challenge to their own behavior.

The sixth and seventh steps in the format are fairly straight forward—the task is: having a full high quality representation of each of the possible alternative pathways which purport to lead to the desired state, a decision is to be made as to whether in fact in the judgement of the group members that pathway does lead to the desired state (step 6). Next the decision is to be made as to whether the pathway which is judged to lead to the desired state does so in such a way as to reinforce or, minimally, be consistent with higher level desired states or organizational goals.

The point of checking for an ecological fit with overall outcomes is best made by example.

During an annual review at a large branch of a wholesale hardware chain, the branch manager learned that there was a portion of the inventory that was low which had a very low profit margin and which constituted the slowest moving portion of the standard inventory. Considering all the facts available to him, he determined to phase that portion of the inventory out simply by not ordering any further stock in those categories. Thus, he reasoned, he could simply sell off the inventory on hand and discontinue those items—the floor space gained could be put to better use. Within a few months after the decision he was informed by his floor manager that the items in question were gone. He instructed her to order additional units of their faster moving, higher profit margin items. Over the following six month period, the branch manager watched with alarm and bewilderment as his gross sales fell off steadily. When the head office demanded an explanation for this unprofitable turn of events, the branch manager had to admit that he was baffled. He had tried advertising, special sales, special packages, and in each case there was an appropriate increase in sales but once the special devices were discontinued, the sales dropped again—he expressed the situation as —"I can get them in and I can sell to them, but I can't get them to come back regularly." The branch manager now requested assistance from the head office. A trouble shooter was sent to him. After a week the troubleshooter was still stumped when, in a meeting, he asked the Difference Question of the floor manager, "What is different in the stock situation between 6 months ago and today?" The answer being, "We got rid of some of that small stuff." Tracking down "that small stuff", he learned of the decision made by the branch manager to discontinue that part of his inventory. The mystery was now solved. The head office had learned years ago that "that small stuff", which was such a slow moving, low margin part of the inventory was one of the items that was an essential part of the inventory. Wholesale customers expected to be able to do their entire buying at a single location. If the wholesaler who they had bought from in the past failed to stock "that small stuff" they would begin to search for a wholesaler who did. Thus, the head office had always insisted as part of the overall marketing strategy that the branches carry "that small stuff". The branch manager had made an excellent decision given the information that he had—a decision which had disastrous consequences.

The point, of course, is that there is sometimes information available at the higher level of a business—in this case a marketing strategy —which decisions at a lower level must take into account or suffer serious negative consequences. In the restricted context of the branch operation, the decision to discontinue a part of the standard inventory appeared to be a sound business maneuver. Seen in the light of the larger context or system, such a decision is highly unecological —hence the need for a well informed and articulate representative of that level of the organization. This representative will be very active during the seventh phase of the meeting—guiding the members of the meeting to an appreciation of some of the fits or misfits of the various alternative pathways with respect to the overall ecology of the organization.

The Pointers will be of great value in the sixth and seventh as well as the eighth step of the Evaluation format to insure that the discussions proceed effectively with high quality information.

The ninth and final step in the format is the decision point itself. It is at this point that all the alternatives individually and in combination have been evaluated both with respect to their ability to lead to the Desired State and with respect to the overall outcomes of the organization. The Precision Model has been used through both to maintain direction and to insure a consistently high quality of information—thus guaranteeing that the input to the decision point is information which is both relevant to context and of a high quality. At this point the members of the meeting come to a decision.

THE DECISION POINT

Since the explicit purpose of this book is to offer a set of procedures which allows the user to develop high quality contextually relevant information, it would be inappropriate for us to propose a decision making model for employment at this step in the format. We note, however, that whatever model for decision making the reader selects for use at this juncture, it will involve the universal information carrying code—language—and as such is subject to the same set of language engineering tools we have established in this book for the other types of transactions which occur in the world of business—the Precision Model. Therefore, no matter which of the various decision making models the reader employs, we encourage you to demand the same high quality information in this activity as we have demonstrated you may come to expect through the use of the Precision Model in other business contexts. Arriving at a decision from a number of potentially effective solutions to implement is a complex process which we explore in the context of the second phase of high quality information processing—the second book in this series. There are, however, several remarks concerning the use of language and information we offer to assist the information processor in this complex activity. First of all, assuming the information processor has developed high quality information as input to the decision point and each of the pathways solutions have already cleared the barriers of *will this alternative get us to the Desired State?* and *is this alternative consistent with organizational goals?* then any disagreements which arise among the decision making group are due to the fact that there is information each of the disagreeing decision makers has in their individual personal internal maps or representations of the possible solutions which is at present not in the shared map or representation of the group. Such disagreements can be efficiently and gracefully resolved to the satisfaction of all if the Difference Question and the Precision Model questioning techniques are sensitively used to elicit from each of the internal individual maps of the parties who disagree precisely the additional information each is using to evaluate the possible pathways solution. Drawing such additional information from the internal maps of the disagreeing parties and using it to enrich the shared representation of the alternatives is typically a rewarding experience in itself and the former disagreements dissolve once the basis of the original difference is made explicit.

In recent years the business community has shown an interest in and, in some cases, a preference for, decision making models which employ *objective criteria.* We take this interest to be evidence that portions of the business community have recognized both the complexity of the decision making activity and the fact that traditionally decision making has been a subjective, intuitive and highly idiosyncratic activity. We ourselves are in full agreement with the movement toward a more thorough and explicit representation of the complex activities of business. Indeed, this book is itself a presentation of an explicit set of language engineering tools which allow the user to develop high quality information to upgrade business performance. However, we wish to caution the reader that in our opinion there is not, nor can there be, any completely *objective* decision making model. Decision making is a uniquely human activity and human beings are, in communication terms, noisy channels. By noisy channels, we refer to the fact that no matter how disciplined the decision maker, there will be highly personal perceptions and weighting in the individual internal maps which occur outside of the awareness of the decision maker which will influence the outcomes. An engineered information channel such as the temperature gauge in the cab of the crane or the indicators on the computer console are clean—almost noiseless in communication terms—and thus there is little or no interference or distortion of the signal—the information such channels are engineered to carry. Such engineered channels are special purpose—designed to carry one and only one class of information. Human beings are general purpose information processing channels. Those of us who work in the world of business are also fathers, wives, mothers, husbands, golf players, sailors, movie goers, art buffs, lovers, fighters and perhaps some of us are even wild horse riders. Our behavior in each of these activities is distinct, and to appreciate and enjoy the full range of activities which are our right as human beings requires that we have a degree of flexibility which is unavailable in any engineered information channel. Thus in each of the *objective* decision making models, a close inspection will reveal an intuitive leap is required. This intuitive leap is a device which is designed to measure the subjective preference of the decision maker and to represent that preference in an objective code—a number, for example. In *The Rational Manager* we find an excellent example of such an intuitive leap.

> Next the manager goes over these WANT objectives and establishes their relative weights, using the scale of 1–10, with the most important WANT receiving the number 10. As he gives each objective more thorough consideration, he changes his preliminary weights until he has achieved a set of numbers representing the relative importance that he places on each objective.

Kepner & Tregoe (p. 197)
The Rational Manager

In the above text the word *weights* is used to describe the process of assigning a numerical value to objectives and alternatives. We must, of course, understand this word as a metaphor as they intend no literal weighing with a physical scale. The process of the assignment of a numerical value is described in metaphoric terms and is itself unexplored—the intuitive leap we previously referred to. All *objective* decision making models have their intuitive leaps—the color wheel which the decision maker adjusts until the portion of color exposed relative to the whole area that could be exposed represents how strongly they prefer the objective or alternative at issue. . . . What is required to lift such intuitive leaps from the realm of the unexplored, unanalyzed and therefore the poorly understood to an explicit model—note we choose the word explicit, not objective—is a set of techniques which as Kepner & Tregoe (p. 230) say *make the invisible visible.* These techniques are treated in our book on representation—the second in this series. Again, with respect to the complex activity of decision making, the Pointers, especially in conjunction with the Difference Question, offer the user the choice of upgrading such intuitive functioning to the level of high quality information. It seems obvious to us that the use of an explicit set of techniques which develop consistently high quality information will always prove to be more effective than such intuitive leaps.

One of the decision making devices which has come into vogue in the last few years is the cost benefit or cost effectiveness analysis. In the authors' experience managers, executives and directors who have an excellent track record as decision makers have a tendency to use this device to justify decisions which they have reached intuitively. The proof of this is the dozens of examples of such excellent decision makers rejecting the finding of the cost effectiveness analysis if it fails to support the decision they have already reached intuitively. Thus, given a conflict between what is concluded by the cost benefit analysis and what their own unexamined or only partially examined sense of what the best course of action is, these decision makers give priority to their experientially based intuitions. The amusing thing is that in most of the cases the authors' are personally acquainted with, the intuitive based decision proved to yield excellent results. Again, the point we wish to make here is that the Precision Model offers an alternative to such situations. Through the sensitive use of the Pointers and the Difference Question, the decision maker can upgrade his intuitions from a vague, low quality status to high quality information which can be explicitly examined. As any of these managers would agree, cost effectiveness studies which are later dismissed are definitely not cost effective.

CASE STUDY I (4th SEGMENT)

In presenting the final portion of the transcript of the interest-inventory situation, we continue the format begun in Surveying by simply identifying the Precision Model pattern being used in the second column along side the transcript to assist the reader in understanding the communication patterns involved.

In the original meeting, during the surveying phase, the original list was significantly altered. Specifically the first, fourth and fifth alternatives were dropped by mutual agreement of the GM and the DM. The revised list of possible solutions now as the two men enter the meeting stands as follows:

1.   Increasing divisional sales on type B motors specifically by an intensive training school for sales reps on the type B motor
2.   Cutting back production on type B motors with the labor force involved being shifted to increased production of type A series motors and SX power units.
3.   Repackaging—creation of the SX power unit B motor combination.

(some minutes into the meeting after preliminary greetings had been exchanged)

GM: Well, Tom, we're here this afternoon, as you know, to make a decision about which of the alternative solutions to your sliding margins problem we will implement.

Outcome Frame
—desired state
for the meeting

I've had the three possibilities listed there on the flip chart (points to a flip chart where the three alternative solutions are listed). . . .

Backtrack Frame —very abbreviated since the DM has been present throughout

I will consider our meeting here today a success when we can decide on one or more of these courses of action and determine how specifically to implement them.

Outcome Frame —identification of evidence that desired state for the meeting has been achieved

The point of deciding on and implementing one or more of these possibilities, as you are well aware, is to get your profit margins which have slid in the last reporting period "back up where they belong", as you so aptly said at our last meeting.

Outcome Frame —desired state for the overall process

Is that a fair enough way of putting it?

requests acceptance of the Frames

DM: Yes, George, fair enough, I'm chompin' at the bit, rarin' to go.

GM: Good! Did you get the information I had sent over to you about the costs of the training school and so on?

filling of information gaps identified in previous meeting

DM: Yes, thank you.

GM: All right, let's take a look at the first of the remaining alternatives. It says increasing divisional sales on type B motors—specifically by an intensive training school for sales reps on the type B motor.

Outcome Frame —next alternative

DM: Yeah, this is my baby. You know I talked to old Larry right after our last meeting and had him review each of his sales reps performance on the newer type Bs. I had him sort the sales reps who did well on the series B motors in the last reporting period into one stack and those who did not do well into another. He brought the two stacks into my office and set them on my desk. I told him that some of the power associated with the head office was beginning to rub off on me— he's always grumbling about my spending too much time in meetings up here—and then without explaining what I was doing I pointed to the stack of reps who had done well and stated baldly that all of those guys had attended that special intensive training school on the B series last year. And then I pointed to the other stack and claimed that these had not attended that school. I really enjoyed watching old Larry's face. He didn't know what the hell was going on, and of course, he knew that I hadn't checked the records on who attended the school. I had him bring in the records on school attendance and match them against my claim. George, it turned out that I was right in every case but three. . . . In addition to baffling old Larry, it really confirmed in my mind the value of that intensive school —I want it, George.

filling of information gaps identified in previous meeting

GM: A little piece of magic for old Larry, eh, Tom. . . . all right, I take it that you have also taken a look at the preliminary cost figures on the school?

DM: Yes, they were higher than I expected, George, but I'm willing to commit those resources because I'm really personally convinced that the school thing will do the job for us.

filling of information gaps identified in previous meeting

GM: OK, Tom, let's get explicit about this alternative. How specifically will the school thing do the job for you?

Action
Blockbuster

DM: Well obviously, after the sales reps have gone through the intensive course, they will sell more B type motors.

GM: More B type motors than what?

Comparator

DM: Well, more than they are presently selling, of course.

GM: How many more will they sell, Tom?

Action
Blockbuster

DM: Well, . . . that's a tough one. It's really hard to predict how much we will gain from the school, George. I just don't know how to quantify it . . . but I'm really convinced myself. Do you have some objection to the school, George?

GM: (chuckling) No, no, Tom, I have no objection to the school. It's obvious to me that you are personally convinced that it will do the job for you. I know that you have looked at the cost figures for the school, and now I'm trying to get you to look specifically at the gain you will achieve by running the school. Let me put it this way. What information do you presently have available that would allow you to make an educated guess about how much you might gain in increased sales from the school?

Evidence
Question

DM: Oh! All right, now I understand. You had me worried there for a moment. Well, . . . uhmmm, one problem is that the older reps—the ones that will be attending the school really perform differently from the younger sales reps and . . .

GM: Whoa, hold on Tom! One problem with what?

Noun
Blockbuster

DM: Oh, sorry, I was thinking out loud—what I meant was one problem with trying to compare the sales reps who haven't been to the school with those that have is that they are really different kinds of performers—so I wouldn't trust the figures I would get by comparing the two groups.

GM: OK, let me make sure I understand. You're trying to come up with an estimate of how much in sales figures you can anticipate gaining from running the school. You considered comparing the performance of the sales reps who have already been through the school and their track record on B type motors with the guys who haven't been through the school and their track record on B type motors.

Backtrack
Frame—limited to
the outcome
presently being
worked on

Have I stated it accurately, Tom?

request for
validation—
acceptance of
Backtrack

DM: Yes, and I don't trust that comparison because all the guys who have been to the school already are young guys who have been with us less than three years and all the guys who haven't been to the school have been around much longer and the two groups really perform differently in lots of other areas.

GM: *All* the guys, Tom?

Universal
Blockbuster

DM: Huh, I don't understand, . . . all the guys? . . . Oh, I get it. There's what's his name . . . Ken. Yes, that would give me something I trust.

The behavior of the two men will by now be quite familiar to the reader. They are employing the same technique that commonly occurs in phase three of the model—specifically, the technique of isolating an information gap and assigning responsibility to a responsible agent to elicit the information required. In this case, they carry on with a consideration of the other alternatives while the information is being developed for them. The two then determine that although it is possible to cut back production of type B motors, they would have to switch back again later and the cost would be prohibitive: An excellent example of the value of checking for the ecological fit. The alternative is attractive when evaluated with respect to the divisional situation and easily passes the test question—*does this pathway get us to the desired state?* However, as soon as the information regarding the long term plans to phase out the older series of motors, replacing them with the newer type B series is available, it is obvious to both of the men that this alternative fails to pass the ecological check question—*is this pathway consistent with the long term goals and plans of the organization?* Thus the alternative is dismissed from further consideration at that point.

GM: Tom, let's take a look at this last alternative?

Outcome Frame
—consider the next alternative

DM: OK, I'm ready. (glancing over at the flip chart, he reads)—repackaging—creation of the SX power unit/B motor combination.

GM: All right, who is going to create this combination package?

Noun Blockbuster

DM: I made the assumption that my division would be responsible for creating the package.

GM: Good, I agree with that. How specifically would your division go about creating this package, Tom?

Action Blockbuster

DM: I have had a series of planning sessions with my people about this and they have come up with some preliminary plans.

GM: Fine! Please fill me in on the particular plans they've come up with.

Noun Blockbuster—note: form is a command equivalent to the strict question *which plans specifically?*

DM: All right! My first take on this runs something like this (moving over to the flip chart in order to write down the salient points of the plan as he briefly presents them). On the production side of the plan, the only wrinkle will be the creation of a heavy duty set of cables to connect the power unit and the B motor. I've started a field search for cable design which . . .

GM: Tom (interrupting), excellent so far—let me make a request of you in your presentation here. If it's possible for you, please list the major components of the plan so I have an overall view and then go back to each component and fill me in one more of the details.

format instructions to establish Outcome Frame

The DM presented his understanding regarding the market information available to date. He detailed his own attempts to secure further information both through staff in the head office and through his own sales reps. The GM expressed his dissatisfaction with the quality of information regarding the market presently available and his satisfaction with the steps Tom had taken to upgrade that information.

DM: The last major piece involves the advertising of the new package—both media and through our sales force. I want a forceful campaign which really points out and emphasizes the advantages of the new package. I believe. . . .

GM: (interrupting) Excuse me, Tom. A question—what advantages of the new package in particular do you want forcefully pointed out and emphasized?

Noun
Blockbuster

DM: (smiling) Yes, an excellent question. . . . and a very short answer—I don't know. . . . however, I have taken steps to discover what advantages the customers will most readily appreciate.

GM: What specific steps have you taken to get this information?

Noun
Blockbuster

DM: I've selected a couple of customers— one who has been with us for some time and a couple of rather new ones. These customers were scheduled to receive both SX power units and type A series motors. I had Larry arrange with them to accept the new package in lieu of the type A and separate SX power unit. My idea is that this field experiment will allow me to get from the customer directly, the advantages that they perceive. Once I have that information I will know how to organize both the advertising campaign and to train our sales reps to present the advantages of the new package. How does it sound to you George?

GM: Tom, I'm impressed. This whole thing started ten days ago with a difficult situation and it is moving rapidly toward a creative new package which I personally believe will prove to be attractive and successful enough that the head office will adopt as a mechanism to accelerate the transition from the old series type A motors to the newer series type B. I believe that you may have done all of us a service with this solution. I presented your unrefined proposal to several of the people

here in the head office since our first meeting and their response was uniformly favorable. I would like your division to have
the responsibility of implementing the
package as a pilot for the rest of the cor-
poration. My sincere compliments!!

At this point in the meeting the information the GM had requested
regarding the effect that the last intensive school training had on the
sales reps performance in selling the newer type B series motors
arrived. Tom had previously received a phone call from his division
indicating that Ken had sold an average of 25% more type B motors
in the six month period immediately following the school experience
than he had in the six month period immediately preceding the
schooling. Further in the last six month period—the period six to
twelve months following the school—Ken's average had dropped but
it was still 20% above his performance in the six months just prior
to the school.

Training Manager (TM)

TM: Here are the figures you requested.

DM: Thank you, wait a second while I take a look.

DM: I got my figures here for the difference in Ken's performance. Let's see how well they fit.

GM: What! This doesn't make any sense. Tom, didn't you say
that Ken's average jumped around 20 to 25%?

DM: Yes, that's the information I got from my personnel
man. Why? What do your figures from the other divisions
show?

GM: They show an average performance increase of only 2 to
3%. Something is wrong somewhere. Jerry (the Training
Manager), are you sure about these figures?

TM: These are the figures you asked me to get.

DM: Well, if these figures are right . . . maybe I'd better re-consider that school. I'm not even sure that it would be cost effective to run that. . . .

GM: (interrupting) Hold on a second Tom. Jerry, you said that these are the figures I asked you to get?

TM: Yes sir, I believe so.

GM: Well before we pull our hair out, let's find out exactly what these figures represent. Jerry, these are figures of what?

TM: These are figures which show the average increase in sales effectiveness on type B motors for two 6 month periods—the six month period just prior to the school and the six month period immediately following the school.

GM: Which school specifically?

TM: The special intensive school on the newer Type B motors conducted in March of last year near Redford.

GM: OK (muttering) . . . the average increase in sales effective-ness on type . . . wait for just a second. WHOSE average increase in sales effectiveness, Jerry?

TM: Why, all the sales reps in all the divisions except Tom's.

GM/DM: (overlapping and interrupting the Training Manager) ALL the sales reps?

TM: All of them except, as I said, those in Tom's division.

GM: So you did, so you did (with a sigh of relief).

At this point with all of the information gaps filled (except for the figures on the gain from the training school), the GM and DM discussed various combinations of the alternatives remaining. Subse-quent to that discussion, the two men reached an agreement on their decision. The final phase included the development of a time schedule and the assignment of responsibilities for the various phases of the alternatives selected. The two men spent some time designing into the time schedule specific ways of checking at that point in the execution of the decision for information which would indicate that the decision was having the desired effect. The GM made the authorizations necessary at the head office level to put the decision into implementation.

This last exchange with the Training Manager demonstrates the value of the Precision Model questioning of figures specifically. Had the GM not had the Precision Model Blockbusting questioning techniques available, the alternative in question would have been represented as not being cost effective, and may have been inappropriately dismissed (note the wavering the DM does when the figures are presented). The GM's response here is most enlightening.

. . This doesn't make any sense . . something's wrong somewhere . . .

Such a response strongly suggests that the GM had already reached an assessment of the pathway in question, and when the figures fail to support that assessment, his response is disbelief. This is, in the authors' experience, not an unusual response for a good decision maker to exhibit in such a case. Typically such an information processor will tirelessly ferret out the discrepancy that he has detected between what he expected based on his experience and the information offered and what the figures show. The Precision Model questioning simply makes that ferreting out process efficient and effective.

There is, however, an even more important point to be taken from this exchange. It is clear from the transcript that the initial communication of the request for information made by the GM and responded to by the training manager was ineffective—that is, the information that the GM requested was not the information that the training manager understood him to have asked for. The message—the instructions to the training manager—intended by the GM was not the message received—the response made by the training manager. This much is obvious. The outcome of this communication is that the GM failed to receive the information he requested, and further the training manager has wasted some amount of time in gathering the wrong information. The consequences could have been more severe—the graver consequences were avoided by the timely use of Precision Model questioning. However, the GM still does not have the information requested and the training manager still will have to now execute the task which the GM had originally given him. There is, at this point no effective way of determining where the communication went awry—nor is there in our opinion much value in such an endeavor unless some effective procedure to avoid further instances of this type of communication would result. As mentioned in the introduction, one of the most powerful operating assumptions— perhaps the single most important characteristic which distinguishes an amateur from a professional communicator—is the rule of thumb:

> The meaning of a communication is the response that communication elicits, independent of the intention of the communicator.

By this rule, the GM would accept responsibility for the miscommunication and seek ways to elicit feedback from those members of the organization who he will typically be issuing instructions to. There are many effective ways to accomplish this. One obvious and fully effective feedback mechanism for a manager who has mastered the Precision Model is to instruct his subordinates in the tasks he wants them to carry out, invite any questions regarding his instructions, secure an agreement that they understand the task instructions, and then Precision Model their understanding of the task instructions so that the manager knows unequivocally that the message he intended is the message received.

Actually, in the authors' opinion, there is an even more efficient choice in this area—that is, simply to train the manager's subordinates in the Precision Model. Thus when the manager in charge issues instructions, the subordinate involved Precision Models the manager regarding the instructions until the manager in charge is convinced that the message he or she intended has been received. The increase in efficiency (reduction of wasted time and effort) and effectiveness (carrying out the instructions appropriately and in a timely manner) under such a system is astonishing.

It might be mentioned in passing that planning tends to involve projections over extended time periods. It is not unusual for a business to develop five and ten year plans to guide them toward long range outcomes. The scope of such plans are enormous, and the issue which frequently arises during or directly after the development of such a plan is one of application and relevancy. That is, granted that the plan is intelligible enough for the members of the business organization involved to come to some general, albeit vague, appreciation of the desired state identified by the plan, the question becomes "how, specifically, does the adopting of this plan effect my behavior here and now and in the days to come?" The specificity guaranteed by the systematic use of the Precision Model will allow a re-chunking of the long term goals into smaller time units and specified actions on the part of each member of the business which results in a unified team effort to achieve that desired state. The optimal plan sets out not only the desired state but a description of the desired state in terms which are relevant for the human beings who will be carrying that plan out—that is, in terms which are specific for the humans involved. For the laborer, it will be cast in terms of the machines and material he works with on a day to day basis. For the sales rep it will be cast in terms of number of customers contacted during a time period or number of units sold. For *each member* of the organization involved, the Precision Model allows a description of how his behavior would be different if he were doing his part in achieving the overall plan. For the planners at the top of the hierarchy, it may be appropriate and useful to think in five year increments. For the worker at the point of production or service, if his energy and cooperation are to be elicited, descriptions about differences in his behavior on an hourly, daily or weekly scale must be developed and offered.

In this last section of the transcript the GM uses a maneuver to which we wish to call the reader's attention:

DM: All right! My first take on this runs something like this (moving over to the flip chart in order to write down the salient point of the plan as he briefly presents them. On the production side. . . .

GM: Tom (interrupting), excellent so far—let me make a request of you in your presentation here. If it's possible for you, please list the major components of the plan so I have an overall view and then go back to each component and fill me in on more of the details.

In this exchange the GM is literally specifying the sequence of information he prefers—he is arranging a format with the DM which suits the particular style he prefers in being offered information. Information offered to a manager in a sequence which matches his preferred processing strategy makes it extremely easy and efficient for the manager to accept such information and to act on it in an effective manner. This is, of course, a crude form of higher level engineering of information channels. More refined engineering requires high quality information about the strategy that the manager typically uses to accept and represent information to himself. The power of such higher level and refined engineering of information flow is properly a topic in the art of representation—a topic treated in the second book in this series. The interested reader will find a general discussion of this subject in Neuro-Linguistic Programming co-authored by John Grinder. The proposal is that the manager instruct the members of the business organization who routinely report to them to present the information in a format which matches the information processing and representational strategies the manager receiving the information will employ in any event.

CASE STUDY II (4th SEGMENT)

We turn now to the final segment of the transcript which began with the sales manager noticing that he was losing approximately 10 sales a month of special units. In attendance at this meeting are three members of the group who have been involved from the beginning, and two men who have not. Thus, consistent with the model, the information processor in charge (the GM) will spend a period of time presenting a full backtrack of the events which have lead up to this meeting. Again, as in the other segments of the overall model since this is a multi-person meeting, the GM will rely heavily on Frames to give direction to the meeting and to control the relevancy of the contributions of the individual member to insure an effective and efficient meeting. As in the previous transcript, we simply annotate the transcript with the names of the specific Precision Model techniques being used.

Attendance: GM, PM, Pers, CEO, CH.Exec.Com

GM: This meeting was called to select an action plan from those which have been developed in order to get us from the present state of losing sales due to inadequate production to a level of production which will meet budgeted sales. We have been unable to hire enough skilled workers since two new plants opened in the area and have therefore initiated a series of meetings to determine how we can change working conditions to attract the people we need.

Outcome Frame —desired state for the meeting

A listing of alternatives was the starting point for our Survey meeting. In that meeting we developed action plans to an acceptable level of precision to know what gaps there were in the pathways. We assigned responsibility for completing the gaps and that information will be presented at this meeting.

Backtrack Frame —rather full since there are two new members to the group

During this meeting, we will bring everyone to the same level of high quality information regarding the alternatives so that we have a complete shared map of the present state, the desired state and the alternative pathways available between them. The shared map will contain all the high quality information necessary for us to arrive at a decision on the basis of the complete map. The purpose of this meeting is to ensure that the shared map is adequately precise for that task and to arrive at a decision and an action plan based on high quality information.

Outcome Frame —specifying steps (structure) for the meeting

We'll proceed by completing the backtrack for each item on the pathways chart, and filling in the gaps. Then we'll consider each pathway to see if it will get us to the desired state. The desired state is to increase production on a regular basis so that we can meet sales requirements and deliver all orders by making changes in working conditions. For all those which meet this requirement, we'll do an ecological check. That is, determine if the plan contradicts or enhances other corporate goals not considered to this point. After this step, we will consider combinations which might work better than the single proposals and put any of them to the same test.

At this stage of the meeting, all information available should be shared by each participant. We will decide whether it is adequate to make a decision on or not. If not, we will provide the precise gaps which need to be filled before we arrive at a decision and adjourn until those gaps are filled according to a schedule which we decide. Otherwise, we will arrive at a decision and prepare an action plan.

Outcome Frame
—specifying steps
(structure) for
the meeting

(At this point, the GM shows a chart of the tree structure which was generated at the Pathfinding meeting. He briefly explains the procedures which they used in developing the structure and traces the development of each pathway.)

Backtrack Frame
—continuation of
former back-
track with use of
shared visual
representation
(flipchart)

(He then moves to a chart developed from the Survey meeting and explains that the starting point for each one of these Survey charts was a specific pathway generated in the Pathways meeting. The chart for the pathway of raising wages looked like the following one.)

RAISING WAGES   How much?
                                 Whose wages?
                                       All
                                 Special skills
Required information
              % required
              cost/mo.
                    Cost/benefit
                          create categories
                          discuss with union representative

(He then recaps the information which was   Outcome Frame
received in response to the basic questions   —next step
considered and relates that information to   outcome,
the specific gaps which needed to be filled. At   consideration of
this point he asks for the information to fill   one of the
the gaps.)   alternatives

GM: First, if any of you have information   Efficiency
which makes the alternative impractical to a   Challenge
degree that removes if from serious consider-   (relative to the
ation, I'd like that information now.   present Outcome
                                                    Frame) for the
                                                    first alternative

Pers: I've recommended a 12% raise. Our   filling in of a
past experience in other departments is that   previously
we don't make an impact until we get to   identified
10%. One of the plants we're competing with   information
pays more and so we have to beat them.   deficit

GM: More than what? And to whom?   Comparator and
                                                       Noun
                                                    Blockbuster

Pers: To all production workers. More
than we are presently paying. Some are making more than our base because they're getting a shift differential.

GM: How much more?   Action
                                                    Blockbuster

Pers: They pay 2% more on an average but they pay 3½% more to experienced assemblers and welders. The ones in the other plant getting shift differential make about 3% more.

GM: OK. What about the cost/benefit figures?

returns discussion to next item in present Outcome Frame

PM: If we gave the raise across the board and got the people we wanted it'd be a net cost of $15,000. If we gave it only to the special skills workers it'd be a net cost of $1,000. or less.

GM: Net of what, specifically?

Noun Blockbuster

PM: Well, accounting did the calculating but the way I figured it was to take the total cost and add the cost of the regular time for the workers we'd need to hire and subtract the cost of overtime that we wouldn't have to work. For those special units, I figured we wouldn't need any overtime which would actually make a small savings except we'd have to pay the special guys on the regular units, too.

GM: OK. That's into the next item. Does anyone have anything they need to know on this item?

request for input to present Outcome Frame

CEO: Yeah. A $15,000 cost is out of the question.

GM: I'd like to hold evaluation until we've got all the information on these items. Joe and Pers, here, have done a lot of research and may have information which we don't share yet. Let's move to the next item.

Relevancy Challenge (relative to present Outcome Frame)

FLEXTIME   What is it?
           Who would be covered?   all production, foreman,
           Special areas   supervisors
           Implementation   assembly, maintenance, emergencies
                                   customer service, foreman

Required information
     (same as in Survey section)

GM: Let's start with the research you did. That will help to get an overall understanding of potential benefits and obstacles.

> Outcome Frame
> —procedure

Pers: I started by reading the literature on it. I couldn't find a single case of anyone who started and then went off the plan. That seemed a pretty good recommendation. There was a lot of talk about increased productivity too. We talked to three companies who were using flextime and they said they liked it and that they had productivity increases. They all reported that employees liked it and that absenteeism was decreased significantly. They also said there were fewer problems with tardiness. The only problem area we uncovered was with foremen and supervisors. They had trouble adjusting to not being there to control the production workers all the time. Most eventually adjusted and a few who couldn't, quit.

> filling in of
> previously
> identified
> information
> deficit

GM: How, specifically, did productivity increase?

> Action
> Blockbuster

Pers: Well, most of them couldn't actually measure it because it was done in clerical and service areas. The ones who did it in production areas, I couldn't get any figures from.

GM: What stopped you?

> Boundary
> Crossing

Pers: One company wouldn't reveal them.
. . . I think they must have been pretty good.
. . .

GM: How, do you know they're pretty
good?

Action
blockbuster

Pers: I don't know it, but they were still
using the system and they said they wouldn't
get rid of it for anything.

GM: And the others?

Recycle
Procedure

Pers: The others said they couldn't measure it but they knew it was up.

GM: What stopped them from measuring
it?

Boundary
Crossing

Pers: They had made other production
method changes at the same time and didn't
know what could be attributed to flextime.
They had increase of 15 and 22 percent in
units per man hour.

GM: OK. Does anybody want more information here before we move into the application gaps?

request for input
to present
Outcome Frame

CEC: Yeah. Pers, what makes you think
we can reduce absenteeism with this plan.

Pers: Well, I didn't say we could. I guess I
don't know whether we would or not. It just
seemed as if we might. The literature reports
a decrease in most cases.

GM: Pers, you said "They all reported that
employees liked it and that absenteeism was
decreased significantly." "Did they *all* have
significant decreases in absenteeism?

Universal
Blockbuster

Pers: Yes.

GM: What, specifically, were the decreases?

Action
blockbuster

Pers: The three I talked to reported 22, 34, and 50%

GM: OK. Anything else? (pause) Let's move on to considering production needs. Joe?

PM: Well, our first meeting produced a lot of excitement. The more I talked to my people about it, the more I liked it. It takes 5 hours to complete the assembly cycle for special units and 3 hours for regular units. The men have been involved in a lot of extra set-ups because it never works out to complete units in a day. I never thought the men would be cooperative in the longer day we'd need to take advantage of this but it turns out that they don't like wasting time with extra set-ups either and they really liked the idea.

(the analysis of production needs continued with the production manager giving an outline of the timing requirements and how they would have to fit in. The availability of set-up men was tentatively fixed by arranging production so that 2 special units and 3 regular units, per line, would be assembled per day. All the scheduling problems anticipated in the Survey meeting were taken care of as well as a few others such as line start-up and security. The precise formulation of information required and how to obtain it, provided a framework which enhanced the possibility of other gaps being discovered in the Survey meeting and a summary of the information. The results of the use of the Precision Model was apparent in the following exchange regarding "Other demands".)

PM: We took care of the gap regarding customer relations by working out a plan with SM that would actually provide more hours

Outcome Frame
—next step
outcome

filling in of
previously
identified
information
deficit

of coverage than we are giving right now. We're both happy with the results and he's drawing up a bit of promotion to go with it. He thinks it'll be an improvement that'll pay. We sorted out the inter-department stuff pretty easily because we don't have much and none of it's on a demand basis. We decided it would be up to us to match with their needs. Then we sat down and said to ourselves, "Who, specifically, are the 'others?' and "What, in particular, are their needs?" We came up with a group that we'd overlooked. Outside suppliers and shipping and delivery would be on different schedules. It was pretty easy to work out ways to meet their needs when we knew who they were.

(They moved onto the specific mechanisms for making it work, such as core time, and there were few questions. The quality of the information which was presented left no doubt that they had done a thorough job and had reached adequate precision for this stage of the meeting. The following exchange was one of the few which took place besides the actual presentation.)

filling in of previously identified information deficit

CEO: With those kind of hours, how can you be sure that foremen and supervisors are there all the time?

PM: We can't and they might not be.

CEO: Some foremen have to be there!

GM: What would happen if they weren't?

Boundary Crossing

CEO: They might not produce. Just goof off. Or there might be trouble on the line that needed a special decision.

PM: We've established an on-call maintenance man and a supervisor for all hours so we don't think we have to worry about trouble or emergencies. As far as goofing off goes, I don't think it'll be a problem because we'll know the state of production when we go home at night and can check it when we arrive in the morning. Also the production planning will be a lot tighter than it's ever been because we'll complete each unit at night and start new ones in the morning.

(The meeting was finished with this alternative at this point. There were no gaps to be filled for the CEO or CEC. The information presented had been so precise that they didn't need any further details or proof of the adequacy of the information gathering process.)

Each alternative was considered in turn using the full Precision Model as appropriate. Profit sharing was simply passed on as a proposal about which the original committee had no authority and their judgement was that it wouldn't be economically feasible to investigate without higher authority. When the concept of a short week with longer days was reviewed the CEC insisted that the plant 'couldn't be closed on a regular business day". The GM quickly determined with the Precision Model that the CEC's concern was with the idle capital that an unused plant represented. The response was that the plant would be operated the same number of hours per week as before. Further, it was discovered that the increase in productivity in those hours would reduce costs and possibly allow for a reduction in the selling price. The result might be a greater demand which would actually increase the total production. This particular investigation revealed some new and valuable information which was applicable to the flextime proposal as well.

Based on the high quality of information presented to them and the method of presentation, the meeting had no trouble agreeing on their selection of flextime as the best alternative to meet their personnel and production needs. They also approved the raise in wages as a back-up plan in case the flextime didn't attract the required people to produce up to planned levels. The raise was to be implemented if the problem hadn't been corrected in 3 months. Specific authorizations and responsibilities were allocated according to the plan presented. The CEO and CEC were impressed with the efficiency and smoothness of the whole process.

BACKTRACK

In this chapter we presented the model in the context of the fourth step of problem solving—Evaluating. A format was offered as a series of Outcome Frames leading from a set of alternatives to the selection stage. The steps are as follows:

1. The overall desired state or Outcome Frame
2. A Backtrack for information and orientation
3. Acceptance of the Frame
4. Representation of each alternative
5. Filling of information gaps with high quality information
6. Consideration of each pathway against "Does this pathway get us to the desired state?"
7. If so, is it consistent with long range objectives—an ecological check
8. Possible combinations of alternatives.
9. The decision point.

The importance of the ecological check was stressed. Too often, particularly in so called 'fire fighting' situations, the fit of an alternative with the rest of an organization and its long range plans is ignored. The result is more 'fire fighting', or worse. The only way off the constant panic alert is to consider the organization as a whole.

The requirements of decision making were discussed and we noted that it is not an objective problem. All systems which claim to be objective have a subjective point hidden within them. We suggest the use of the Precision Model to elicit the differences in personal representations which account for the differences which may arise in a decision making process.

CONCLUSION

It is our purpose in writing this book to provide a model for obtaining information of appropriate quality for business. We are not proposing that this model is a replacement for the effective models for management created by those who have gone before us.

We concur with their lament over the lack of communication skills available to management. We wish to show that effective communication, like any other complex human skill, has structure and is, therefore, learnable. Our model is, rather, an effective technology which can enhance the power of those other models.

Managers live in a real world. They do not, however, operate directly or immediately on that world. They are separated from that world by chains of information which get longer and longer. The managers must operate with maps or representations which they use to guide their behavior. These representations are removed from the real world by engineered channels and by the natural, universal process of human modeling. The final representations are internal.

The most thoroughly studied and best understood of the representational systems is human language. Human language systems are themselves derived representations from a more complete model—the sum total of the experience the particular human has had in his life. Linguistic representations have been described explicitly and a formal model has been developed. The Precision Model relies only upon an explication of the intuitions which every native speaker has of his language and an explicit framework developed from the recognition that management is constantly engaged in the process of seeking outcomes.

PRECISION is a book about the first phase of high quality information processing for business. The second and third phases will be dealt with in forthcoming books. This book has presented a model for verbal information processing which defines precision in management communication and provides the model to get it. The first requirement is that the information be of high quality. The highest quality information is realized when the object or action is immediately observable. The second requirement is that the high quality information be appropriate to the task at hand. That is, it is in context. A Precision statement, therefore, will be one which has the highest quality of information appropriate to the context in which it is used.

The Precision Model has three sets of tools which have different specific functions and operate on different cues. The first set—Frames—establish and maintain the context necessary for precision. They define the boundaries of exploration and respect both the need to know and the need not to know. They create the framework which allows the manager to explicitly identify the appropriate quality of information. One natural outcome of this is that the manager knows where he is in his movement toward the overall goal at all times and is able to orient others to that outcome. There are three Frames, as follows:

—The OUTCOME Frame. By the use of this Frame, the manager establishes the next target state or outcome that is the immediate concern of the transaction. Once established, this Frame provides an explicit standard of relevance and efficiency within which information may be organized.

—The BACKTRACK Frame. This Frame provides a mechanism to review or trace the development of the information maps which is relevant to the outcome established.

—The AS-IF Frame. This Frame provides a technique for creating a context to access information which would otherwise be unavailable because of some present state restriction.

The Frames are powerful tools for eliciting the highest quality information desired and available in an efficient manner. They provide access to relevant material while avoiding the usually painful procedure of sorting through offered information which is not useful in the context. They eliminate the apparent need for dealing with emotion brought to a meeting, or the familiar issue of hidden agendas. The framework provided by this part of the model is a powerful addition to communication technology in its own right.

The second set of tools in the Precision Model, we refer to as

Procedures. These operate on their own set of cues and are specific procedures for maintaining Frames. They assist the information processor to maintain the trajectory established by the Outcome Frame. These Procedures provide efficiency. They allow the manager to make leaps which may prove productive. They do not get to any information which cannot be elicited with the Frames and Pointers alone. They may speed the process if used sensitively. The Procedures we call:

—The EVIDENCE Question. The question, "What will you accept as evidence," can be used to direct attention to a representation of a desired state.

—The DIFFERENCE Question. The question, "What is the difference between (any present state) and (a related desired state)" can help to elicit the difference which is to be eliminated by an action.

—The EFFICIENCY Challenge. The question, "What factors are known which will eliminate this potential course of action from consideration," can prevent time being spent obtaining high quality information about an alternative which isn't feasible.

—The RELEVANCY Challenge. The question, "How does (statement) relate to the outcome agreed on for this meeting," is a challenge to any statement which in the perception of the information processor is not relevant to the outcome. This procedure demands that the information source justify his statement relative to the context.

—The RECYCLE Procedure. Provides a memo of return points. Any part of a statement which is less specified than might be desirable is kept track of and no vital information will be lost when other tracks are followed.

—The MISSING LINK Procedure. The question, "How will that achieve what we want?" is a special adaptation of the Relevancy challenge to develop new branches in the phase known as Pathfinding.

The third set of tools in the Precision Model is a set of direct responses to language cues—Pointers. These are the tools for obtaining high quality information. That is, they demand increasing specificity. We refer to these as follows:

—The NOUN BLOCKBUSTER. A request that a noun or noun phrase be specified further to obtain the part of the representation intended by the information source.

—The ACTION BLOCKBUSTER. A request for more specification about how an action is to be performed, that is, what specifically that action is.

—The UNIVERSAL BLOCKBUSTER. A request that members of a group be differentiated in a useful way, inviting a closer look at a representation.

—The BOUNDARY CROSSING Pointer. A request for the specific conditions or consequences which make an action either necessary or impossible.

—The COMPARATOR Pointer. A request for the standard or object which is being compared to.

The companion workbook for this phase of high quality information processing provides lecturettes, structured experiences, and exercises for trainers. A trainer who has become adapt at the use of the Precision Model can use the materials to facilitate the spread of these valuable skills throughout an organization.

This book has dealt only with the verbal component of communication. The highest quality of information, as we have maintained through this book, is behavioral. In human communication, therefore, the highest quality information is non-verbal. The structure of non-verbal communication, which we will deal with in the second book of this series, is even less studied and generally understood than the structure of verbal communication.

It is the experience of the authors that non-verbal communication does, indeed, have structure and, therefore, is learnable. An increase in verbal communication skills will provide significant rewards whatever the level of non-verbal communication abilities.

The second area of information processing, which is the subject of the next book of this series, is the representation of information. This includes the various ways that we represent experience both internally and externally, and the use we can make of that knowledge. It includes how we represent information non-verbally and how the representations of others can be known without the aid of verbal cues. We also cover other language patterns which relate to these representations in powerful and creative ways. The technology represented in the second book allows major leaps to be made in representing information. The effective use of these techniques require the prior development of verbal communication skills.

The third area of information processing, the translation into action, provides applications of the skills and experience which are developed from the first two areas. These are techniques which take advantage of the patterns which all living things must have. They access wired-in functions in ways useful for obtaining outcomes in any human interaction. These techniques include the tools to teach individuals how to solve problems and develop other internal processes. These processes are no longer invisible. They can be observed and taught. They are explicit and structured processes which can be modeled and learned by any manager.

A final comment on the organization of this book is required. The authors have used the Precision Model tools to write the book along with various other language tools such as the frequent use of metaphor. We have presented the information gathering part of the process in chapters which indicate there are separate and distinct chunks which must be followed in order and separated. We want to assure you that this was merely a presentation convenience and that the order need not be separated in the manner presented nor separated so precisely. The only requirement is that an information processor know exactly where he is in the process at all times. If the chunks presented are not followed in the same manner, the Precision Model can still be called upon whenever necessary to establish position in the process and proceed from that point.

The framework of problem solving was chosen as a convenient and useful vehicle for presentation which would find common ground with the experience of all managers. Whether you are the manager of a unit of a company with only a few employees, general manager of a division or of your own company, CEO of a large organization, or a member of a Board of Directors, you will have the experience of some form of problem solving and the frustrations which have been part of that process. The model we have presented will smooth that process for you, removing much of its uncertainty and inefficiency. It will permit you to accomplish your goals with a feeling of confidence and satisfaction, knowing that you have got the most from your people in a creative yet comfortable way.

A major portion of management communications involves problem solving. When they are not solving immediate problems of varying sizes, most managers are solving future problems—referred to as planning when formally recognized. The model you have just read is more useful than in that context alone. Limited to that area, it would increase your capabilities of a manager. Applied to any situation where information needs to be elicited or a specific outcome from communication is desired, it will make your powers stand out from managers without this technology and from your own past performance.

Using the Precision Model, you will notice that all meetings you hold, for whatever purpose, will run more efficiently and be more satisfying to everyone involved. Whether the meeting is large or only two people, the combination of establishing Frames and asking the right questions will be appreciated by those affected, whether they notice the precise difference or not.

We indicated throughout the book that planning is directly suited to the format presented. Planning has all the same steps and goals as problem solving. The basic difference is the orientation to the future and, often, a more comfortable time constraint. We want each reader to get the full benefit of the more generalized model, however, and realize that the Frames, Procedures and Pointers constitute a powerful technology which can be applied to many areas. The application will require only that the present and desired state be known. The Outcome Frame will then allow you to move smoothly to your goal.

Resource allocation, conflict management and matrix management are variations on a theme: Variations which require a high degree of communication and meeting skills. Many managers founder in this situation or environment. An explicit desired state, which is agreed to at the start of a meeting, is required. "We are working toward a common goal; the best solution to the problem of allocating company resources. Specifically, the allocation of engineering resources to the three projects we have in process now." is such an example. From the beginning, specific intermediate steps or procedures may be specified and appropriate questions used to elicit a shared representation of the situation from which an allocation can be agreed upon. Conflict, which is often assumed to be part of this situation, can be treated as an information deficit and the relevant information elicited.

Performance appraisal is another major area where the model can be usefully applied. Many plans which require these formal appraisal sessions, such as Management by Objectives, are unsuccessful due to the inability of managers to carry out the sensitive meetings required. We recommend with such a system that the purpose and structure of the meeting be stated on a form provided the manager and subordinate. Further, the manager can state the outcome and get agreement at the start of the meeting. An agreed outcome and framework will enable the Outcome Frame to be used comfortably and successfully and move the meeting smoothly to a satisfactory conclusion. The pointers will insure that information which is required for a comprehensive appraisal can be easily elicited.

Any interviewing situation can, of course, use the Precision Model effectively. The Pointers will provide the tools to elicit whatever information is desired in the most efficient and comfortable manner. Establishing Frames will enhance the power of any interviewer.

Negotiation, too, can benefit from the model. The Pointers can assist in gathering information about each position and in prodding review of inflexible positions. The most powerful tool in this area, however, is the Outcome Frame. By establishing an agreed upon outcome for the negotiation, some desired state which both parties want, a basis for agreement will be established. Once this is done, both sides will be on a trajectory to a common goal which can be speeded by appropriate questioning. The authors recognize the unique problems involved and have a specialized model for negotiation. We note, however, that the addition of the Outcome Frame alone to the technique of most negotiators would increase their power and their ultimate success.

Business is *the* human outcome oriented activity. We have created a model, a communication technology, which recognizes that feature and explicitly makes outcomes a central focus. Each Procedure, each specific Pointer, can be related back to the outcome. The easiest access to the information required and the elimination of conflict in that process is provided. The Precision Model will elicit information in the most efficient manner possible—efficiency measured by resources used to get the outcome desired.

We invite you to become familiar with the model presented. Make it part of your repetoire of management skills. Notice, as this happens, how many areas of your day to day operations benefit from the generalization of the model you have learned. May you be delighted at the increase in your personal power and influence as you get results which had eluded you before.